WE ARE THE AGGIES

Number Seven: The Centennial Series of the

Association of Former Students

WE ARE THE AGGIES
The Texas A&M University Association of Former Students

By JOHN A. ADAMS, JR., '73

Foreword by RICHARD ("BUCK") WEIRUS '42

 TEXAS A&M UNIVERSITY PRESS, College Station and London

Copyright © 1979 by the Association of Former Students of Texas A&M University
All rights reserved

Library of Congress Cataloging in Publication Data

Adams, John A   1951-
  We are the Aggies.

  (The Centennial series of the Association of Former Students ; no. 7)
  Includes index.
  1. Texas. A&M University, College Station. I. Title. II. Series: Texas. A&M University, College Station. Association of Former Students. The centennial series of the Association of Former Students; Texas A&M University ; no. 7.
  LD5309.A84   378.764'242   78-21782
  ISBN 0-89096-062-3 (cloth)
  ISBN 1-58544-088-4 (pbk.)

Unless otherwise indicated, all photographs were supplied from the Texas A&M University Archives, the files of the Association of Former Students of Texas A&M University, and the author's collection.

Manufactured in the United States of America
First Paperback Edition

Dedicated to the invincible
Aggie Spirit
through which has been nurtured an uncompromising
loyalty and love
for
Texas A&M.

Contents

Foreword	ix
Acknowledgments	xi
1. Ex-Cadets Unite	3
2. The Alumni Association	15
3. Round Pegs and Square Holes	29
4. Alpha Phi Fraternity	39
5. Football, Former Students... and Trouble	51
6. Train Ride to Valley Junction	67
7. Farmers Fight	87
8. Warring for the World and for A&M	101
9. Hullabaloo, Caneck! Caneck!	117
10. Vintage Years	135
11. The Military Legacy	149
12. Unselfish Devotion	163
13. A Partnership in Higher Education	183
Appendixes	207
Comments on Sources	226
Index	227

Foreword

Governor Richard Coke set the foundation of the Aggie Spirit when he said in his address opening the Agricultural and Mechanical College of Texas, on October 4, 1876, "In time these halls will become classic, and the strong men of Texas . . . will after we have been gathered to our fathers, meet in these halls and with grateful hearts . . . chant the praises of their *alma mater.*"

Nearly fifty years later, a great Aggie, Marion Church '05, president of the Association of Former Students in 1923–1924, chanted those praises in these words: "A man's loves have been defined under three heads—for his home, his country, and his God, but I would add another category, distinct from those, yet holding a hallowed place in the heart of every man so fortunate—and that is love for his college." And so it has been for over these past one hundred years; all those who are fortunate enough to have attended Texas A&M are never quite the same again, because they will always chant the praises of their alma mater. They love this school in many different ways. It is a spirit that is easy to see but impossible to describe or explain to anyone else. As in Colonel Dunn's song, "The Spirit of Aggieland": "But there's a spirit can ne'er be told . . . ," just *felt*—in a swelling of the throat, tears in the eyes, rapid pulse, and goose pimples on the flesh, when thoughts return to Aggieland.

And so it was when a young graduate student, John Adams '73, came to see me, asking permission to write the history of the Association of Former Students as his master's degree thesis in history. I told John I didn't believe it could be done, as such a project is filled with the dangers of omission and so shouldn't be attempted. Also, I did not think the records were complete enough and that factual data and photographs simply were not available. But, more than that, I felt the history of this association would be the same as the history of the Aggie Spirit and therefore something that could not be defined.

I have seen the Aggie Spirit in people from all walks of life, and feel it very deeply myself, but the Aggie Spirit involves a multitude of people over a long span of time, wars, peace, depression, and good times. Since the first day of school in October, 1876, interaction has taken place between the people who have worked, taught, and studied here. Something happens to them in a deep, spiritual way, and they are never quite the same again. When in later years they meet someone from College Station, there is an immediate bond of friendship, a feeling of shared experiences, a common bond that defies description.

My deepest fear about a book telling the story of the association is that thousands of loyal, dedicated, hardworking Aggies will not be named or recognized. Such an organization as ours is not created and nurtured by only the few people mentioned in this book; rather, this association is in action anytime two Aggies meet, anywhere in the world—at an athletic contest, on an airplane, at an A&M club meeting, at an Aggie Muster, at a class reunion, at Silver Taps, when putting on their Aggie rings, at yell practice, on the intramural or drill field, or in the classrooms, laboratories, apartments, parties in public or private places, and churches.

John Adams has captured the Aggie Spirit in a unique way as he has related the basic theme of this association—that is, the former students' love for the school and for each other. You will note that in the early days former students helped each other obtain employment. Most A&M clubs were founded for that purpose. Later, they stepped in and helped the students and administration solve their differences. But, of most significance were the former students' efforts to help worthy students with financial assistance.

The Association of Former Students has always been ready to help the university with its timely needs—even to the extent of determining those needs—such as the Century Study and the Blueprint for Progress. Through the years, former students have served on the Board of Directors, on the Council, as class agents, as high school representatives, and on a host of committees, traveling great distances at their own expense and only too pleased to serve. This quality shared by Aggies of the past hundred years certainly meets the "love" that Marion Church '05 emphasized.

"How fortunate to have had a loyal, dedicated staff through the years!" declared 1956–1957 Association President Louis R. Bloodworth '32. After a number of faculty or staff members performed secretarial duties for the Board part-time, E. E. McQuillen '20 became the first full-time executive secretary in 1927, with J. B. ("Dick") Hervey '42 to follow in 1947. Nearly forty years of unselfish service by those two great Aggies through the Great Depression and World War II gave the Association of Former Students a foundation and a continuity not found at most universities. It was a miraculous feat to keep Aggies in touch throughout the world during WWII. Perhaps the Aggie Musters each April 21 during those trying years made the significant difference in Aggie traditions and impact on the association.

I believe John Adams '73 relates the Aggie Spirit as coming to people from a feeling of gratitude or debt to Texas A&M for teaching knowledge and skills while giving those students an experience out of which they will become dedicated, concerned members of society. One thing is for sure: they will be better people because they learned to *care*—because they are Texas Aggies.

Congratulations, John! You have done the impossible.

Richard ("Buck") Weirus '42
Executive Director

Acknowledgments

I am deeply indebted to numerous people at Texas A&M University and throughout Texas for their assistance and encouragement in the preparation of this book, which began as my thesis for the master's degree in history. I especially thank Dr. Allen C. Ashcraft '51 and Dr. Henry C. Dethloff for their guidance, professional expertise, and continual encourment. I received invaluable, unwavering encouragement from Richard ("Buck") Weirus '42, Director of the Association of Former Students, and his entire staff. Charles R. Schultz, Archivist, Texas A&M University, and David L. Chapman '67, Associate Archivist, were extremely cooperative in every way possible in the location of invaluable material for this study.

Without exception the many Aggies interviewed were generous with their time and unstinting in their efforts to provide information and documentation. Everett E. McQuillen '20, Lonnie B. Locke '22, Buck Weirus, and J. B. ("Dick") Hervey '42 gave many hours of their time to help clarify the complicated series of events throughout the association's evolution. I also thank Gail S. Hogan, who assisted greatly in the early preparation of the manuscript, and Jerry C. Cooper '63, who helped me immensely in the collection of the illustrations. I am greatly appreciative for the moral support, love, and encouragement my parents have given me through the years. Their guidance and wisdom has been instrumental in giving my life both drive and purpose.

Finally, and most importantly, my thanks goes to my son, John III, and to my wife, Lucia, who has been patient and understanding when she did not have to be and strong and resourceful when she did.

John Adams '73

WE ARE THE AGGIES

The bleak, open prairie provided a grim setting for Texas A&M's early students. Cadet life during the early years revolved around (*left to right*) Gathright Hall (classrooms and dining hall), one-story dorms, and Old Main (classrooms and administrative offices).

1. *Ex-Cadets Unite*

Being a Texas Aggie is a lifelong experience. For many it begins at birth with a Howdy bib that says "Howdy, I'm a little Texas Aggie." Families speak of generations of Texas Aggies. Children are indoctrinated with Aggie football, lore, and traditions and sport Aggie T-shirts long before they reach the A&M campus. Once enrolled in Texas A&M University, whether for a semester or for four years or more, membership in that "one great fraternity" is automatic and virtually irrevocable.

The Texas A&M University Association of Former Students is an international fraternity of men and women who have one thing in common—they are Texas Aggies who have retained a remarkable bond of loyalty, support, and love for each other and for the school they attended. The Association of Former Students is the fifth dimension in the development of Texas A&M University as a unique educational institution. It fosters a special attitude toward life. It is the structure that makes the education and the life of a Texas Aggie a continuing experience.

The Association of Former Students provides the organizational framework that has for a hundred years fostered and channeled the special Aggie spirit into a productive human resource. It is a not-too-silent partner in promoting the efforts of Texas' first public institution of higher learning to maintain excellence in teaching, research, and public service. The association has been an effective instrument in aiding the student in his search for knowledge and in supporting the former student's incentive and opportunities to lead a useful and productive life in a democratic society.

An old Aggie wrote many years ago that at Texas A&M, "the poor man's son and the rich man's son stand precisely on the same footing. . . . Each student is judged by what he is and does. . . ." By the 1890's, A&M's President Lawrence Sullivan Ross, the already legendary "boy captain" of Texas Indian wars, Confederate cavalry brigadier, and former governor, could boast of the success of A&M graduates as engineers, architects, farmers, ranchers, military officers, and educators. "Not one has ever proved a gambler, drunkard, or idler in the great hive of industry," he said. In the 1970's, President Jack K. Williams noted that "Texas A&M has established a national reputation for student quality, job opportunities for graduates, alumni support and volume and quality of research programs." As one Aggie "joke" has it, "What do you call an Aggie five years after he has taken his first job?" The answer is "boss"!

"Aggies are doers, not booers," then United States Vice-President Gerald R. Ford told an assembly of Texas A&M students in 1973. *Doing* is one of the great Aggie traditions. Aggies not only want to "Do it all this fall" on the gridiron, as bumper stickers proclaim, but they want to do it now, and, as other bumper stickers say, "Aggies do it best!" Whatever *it* is, Aggies have been doing it for a hundred years, and they are intensely involved in doing it everywhere in the world. Along the frozen tundras of the North Slope of Alaska, in the deserts of Arabia, on the ranches of Nicaragua, or in the forests of Africa you are far more likely to find an Aggie than a Dr. Livingstone.

"If you ever visit the Khairathabad Mosque in Hyderabad, India," writes *Houston Post* columnist Lynn Ashby, "you may hear the soft chant of a mysterious prayer from the Himalayas: 'Hullabaloo, kaneck, kaneck,' because an Aggie, Mohammed Haq lives there." Ashby also noted that another Aggie, Dr. Jacobus D. Bothma, is professor of wildlife management at the University of Pretoria in South Africa. Among others, Emmanuel B. Kuanyin is in the Peoples Assembly in Khartoum, Sudan; Dr. Winston Suarez-Arauz is a veterinarian in Bene, Bolivia; and Dr. Orland Olcese is president of the Agrarian University in Lima, Peru. There are Aggies in the administration of Harvard as well as those of universities in India, Saudi Arabia, and Bangladesh. On almost any page of the *Centennial Directory of Former Students of Texas A&M University* one will find among the eighty thousand listings Aggies from such diverse spots in North America as Norcross, Georgia; Manitoba, Canada; Lexington, Kentucky; San Diego, California; and Three Rivers, Texas.

No Aggie astronaut as yet has walked on the moon, but to be sure, it was an Aggie who put the astronauts there. Gerald Griffin (class of '56) was flight director on the first eleven Apollo missions. He was director, too, of the Apollo Twelve flight that landed Alan Bean (a University of Texas graduate) and Charles Conrad on the moon. Griffen had the astronauts roused from their slumber one morning to the tune of the Aggie War Hymn as a special reminder to Alan Bean that while a "T-sippin'" University of Texas graduate might be about to walk on the moon, he was there by the grace of Texas A&M University. Bean was later made an honorary Texas Aggie.

"Next to the Alamo in San Antonio," wrote Nicholas Chriss of the *Los Angeles Times*, "the Texas institution that is talked about and bragged about—in addition to being joked about—perhaps more than any other is the Texas Aggie." Because Texas Aggies are not like the rest of the world (thank goodness), the "Aggie joke" has become a part of the folklore of Texas A&M. People talk about Aggies because they are different, and Aggies are proud of it. Aggies tend to be "a little bit square." As one recruiter for a large corporation put it, the Aggie is usually level-headed and sober, has good grades, and believes in hard work. Texas A&M has a military tradition with a great record of service and loyalty. It commissions annually more officers than any school except the national military academies. It has the largest agricultural enrollment in the nation and has produced more engineers than agriculturists. It stresses a common-sense education but embraces the dimensions of a highly sophisticated research program that numbers it among the top twenty universities in the nation in funded research. Its programs in the liberal arts and education combine to provide a diversified and rich university complexion. Texas A&M is a university that strives to teach Aggies how to make a living and to be useful and productive members of society, and it is a university that cares how Aggies live. That caring has been institutionalized in the Association of Former Students.

"A man's loves have been defined under three heads—for his home, his country, and his God, but I would add another category, distinct from those, yet holding a hallowed place in the heart of every man so fortunate—and that is love for his college," said Marion Somerville Church '05, a renowned Texan, lawyer, and former student at Texas A&M. The purpose and mission of the multifaceted former student organization of Texas A&M is

Gerald Griffin '56, NASA flight director during the Apollo 12 mission, was the first to pipe the Aggie War Hymn to the moon.

simple: to promote the interests and welfare of Texas A&M and its students and to perpetuate ties of affection and loyalty formed during college days. The inception of what is now the Association of Former Students of Texas A&M University may be attributed to members of the first class of Texas A&M, who began their college training when the Agricultural and Mechanical College of Texas, the state's first public institution of higher learning, opened its doors in October, 1876.

Texas A&M began classes during an exciting year in the history of Texas and the nation. Ulysses S. Grant was in his last year as president. His term marred by scandal and upheaval, Grant apologized to Congress for the shortcomings of his administration "based on inexperience"—although he had been in office more than seven years. In early 1876 a novice inventor named Alexander Graham Bell had patented the telephone. The little-known sport of baseball had made a hit during the spring, and later, on June 23, 1876, General George Armstrong Custer had had a disastrous encounter with the Indians at the

The Spirit of '76

Thomas Sanford Gathright, first president of Texas A&M (1876–1879).

Governor Richard Coke of Texas was most optimistic about A&M's potential during its opening ceremonies on October 4, 1876.

Little Big Horn. On July 4 the nation had celebrated its centennial, and Richard Coke, a close personal friend of Lawrence Sullivan Ross and an avid supporter of public higher education in Texas, had been reelected governor of the state. By early October, 1876, there had been eighteen reported Indian raids in East Texas. On Monday, October 2, 1876, Texas A&M officially began the enrollment of its first students.

Governor Richard Coke, accompanied by A&M's first president, Thomas Sanford Gathright, addressed a meager gathering of local Bryan, Texas, residents, well-wishers, faculty, and students on Wednesday, October 4, 1876, during inaugural ceremonies held on campus. Texas' first choice for head of the new college had been Jefferson Davis, former president of the Confederacy, but when Davis declined and recommended Gathright, who then held the position of superintendent of education in Mississippi, Gathright was unanimously selected for the position. The initial registration of only 6 students greatly disappointed Gathright and his faculty. However, as time passed, enrollment rose. Spirits and morale improved when 48 students were registered by the end of the first school term. A total of 106 Aggies, or "Farmers," as they were soon called, were in attendance on June 25, 1877, at closing exercises.

Built on an open, mesquite-covered prairie hospitable only to the natural wildlife and vegetation of the area, the new campus provided a grim setting for students and faculty. William Andrew Trenckmann '78 recalled that in late 1876 the new campus was "in a still somewhat pioneer time, large herds of deer frequently ran across our drill field and for a time a Mexican lion would prowl about our student home seeking prey." The common hardships of higher education during those days encouraged a sense of unity and comradeship among those associated with the A&M College.

Early requests for information about admission to the college were handled directly by the president's office:

Jan. 9th 1877

Mr. Jos. Richardson
Dear Sir

Your favor of the 5th inst. came to hand yesterday evening and our president being absent, in attendance on the meeting of the Directory in Austin, it becomes my duty to reply. I will answer your inquiries seriatim.

1st   To enter our lowest class a boy should be fourteen years of age, should read well in 5th reader, should have gone through Fractions in Arithmetic and should have some knowledge of Eng. Gram & Geography and should write legibly.

2nd   The State is entitled to send one hundred and one state students, three from each senatorial district, one from each congressional district, and two from the state at large appointed by the U.S. Senators from this state. The congressional appointees are appointed by the congressmen of the respective districts.

3rd   Total expenses of a student from this time to the close in June next, including board, washing, lodging, fuel, lights, tuition, books and two suits of clothing will be one hundred and ninety dollars. The rooms are neatly and comfortably furnished and hence the cheapness of our college, being just half what it costs to maintain a boy at another similar school. The expenses of a state student for the time above mentioned, will be $33.33 less. or $156.67. This is the first College opened by the state of Texas, has ample means to ensure to it permanency & success and on these grounds especially appeals to Texans for support. The salaries of professors are paid out of the U.S. fund, and does not cost the people of the state one dime.

Very Respectfully. W. A. Banks, Prest. pro. tem.

P.S.
Our Steward's Hall is the best equipped establishment of the kind I have ever seen, and our Steward has shown himself capable [of] not only fighting men but feeding them. His fare is as good as at any hotel in the state. If you think the information in this letter would be of interest to your people, you are at liberty to publish it.

Very Respectfully
W. A. Banks
Prest. pro. tem.

Please send me a copy, if you print.

(The steward or dining hall manager referred to in the postscript is General Hamilton P. Bee, who served in the Confederate Army during the Civil War. His tenure as steward lasted only through the 1877–1878 school year.)

The first few years passed slowly. Inadequate housing, student discipline problems, differences among the teaching staff, and funding problems plagued the school. Enrollment increased during the 1877–1878 session to 331 yet fell during the next two school sessions from 248 in 1878–1879 to 144 in 1879–1880. Qualifications for admission were not rigorous in those days. Students had to be at least fourteen years old, male, of good moral character, and able to enter upon the prescribed studies. All students were required to serve in the Corps of Cadets, wear uniforms, and follow military discipline as directed by the commandant of cadets.

Left, Gathright Hall during the 1880's served as the site of the earliest Alumni Association annual meetings. *Right*, A&M President John Garland James (1878–1883) helped to organize the young school and instill *esprit de corps* within the student body.

Conflicts soon developed among the faculty about management of the corps and about the question of what an agricultural and mechanical college should be. During the summer of 1879 an argument erupted among the members of a faculty selection committee determining cadet promotions for the school year 1879–1880. "Anti-Gathright" professors blocked the usually automatic approval of John C. Crisp '80 as the cadet senior captain, or cadet corps commander, as the position is known today. Governor Oran M. Roberts and the Board of Directors conducted an investigation into the unrest in mid-November, 1879. After a review of the Crisp case and interviews with each of the six professors, the directors decided to fire the entire faculty except for an adjunct professor, Louis L. McInnis, and including President Gathright effective December 1, 1879. The ejection of the faculty resulted in a change of academic philosophy under the new administration of John Garland James.

The college turned from the classical pursuits to a curriculum based entirely on agriculture and engineering. Colonel James, formerly superintendent of the Texas Military Institute in Austin, Texas, was urged to bring with him any of his faculty he felt would aid in assisting the college back to a "positive" course.

The Association of Ex-Cadets

Although he was chief administrator for only three years, President James, a graduate of the Virginia Military Institute, strengthened the military training program and helped encourage among the student body the *esprit de corps* that became the source of the modern Aggie Spirit. That certain spirit which gave rise to the formal organization of Texas A&M's parent alumni association developed among the students of the first four classes. By 1880 the first four sessions at A&M had been attended by a total of 729 students, most of whom had completed only a year or two of study before dropping out to take jobs. The cost of a college education—two hundred dollars per year, which included room, board, tuition, and uniforms—was simply too great to be borne by most A&M students for a sustained four-year period. Students who completed three years of study received a departmental "certificate." Four years of study were required for a degree in scientific agriculture (S.A.), civil and mining engineering (C.E.), or language and literature (A.B.). Texas A&M awarded its first degrees, both in civil engineering, to William Harrison Brown and Louis John Kopke at commencement exercises on June 23, 1880.

The previous year, on June 26, 1879, at Bachelor's Hall in Houston, former cadets living in Houston hosted a reception for A&M cadets. At the Houston meeting students agreed to hold a gathering of former cadets at the college to coincide with the 1880 commencement. The objective of this first meeting on campus was to establish an organization to keep a record of all former cadets who had matriculated in the A&M College of Texas, "thus promoting and maintaining fellowship." The following former cadets were present (the first date indicates the year of enrollment and the second indicates the year of departure from A&M):

        William Markham Sleeper '76 ('79), Waco
        William Andrew Trenckmann '76 ('78), Wilheim
        Pinckney Lovick Downs '77 ('79), Waco
        Edward Everett Fitzhugh '78 ('80), Waco
        Edward Benjamin Cushing '77 ('80), Houston
        George Washington Hardy '76 ('79), Millican
        David Ellington Alexander '77 (no listing), Marshall
        William T. Small '78 ('82), Fort Worth
        Robert Carleton Chatham '77 (no listing), Navasota
        William Harrison Brown '78 ('82), Navasota
        Thomas A. Fuller '77 ('81), Paris

These cadets organized the Association of Ex-Cadets, and resolved that at every commencement of the college as many as possible would meet. The A&M Board of Directors agreed to set aside a day at each commencement for the general meeting and public exercises to consist of "an oration and an essay by ex-cadets, and an address by a distinguished gentleman."

A printed letter was mailed to all former cadets from Cedar Bayou, Harris County, Texas, on July 1, 1880, by the newly elected chief secretary of the association, Edward B. Cushing '80. The letter requested all interested former cadets to respond by taking part in the second meeting of the association to be held during commencement exercises in June, 1881. Cushing urged all former cadets to send information concerning their whereabouts and activities since leaving the college in hopes of "keeping afresh the feelings of fraternal regard which existed among us while we were under the kindly care of our alma mater." All those "who had left the college in good standing" were awarded membership upon payment of the initiation fee of twenty-five cents and annual dues of twenty-five cents in coins or postage stamps.

Perhaps anticipating the modern *Directory of Former Students*, Cushing requested the following information for use in compiling a listing of all former cadets: "When and Where born? Parents name? If foreign, when did you immigrate to Texas? When did you

During the earliest days the faculty eagerly encouraged the development of the Alumni Association. The members of the 1883 staff were headed by Professor of Chemistry Hardaway H. Dinwiddie. *Left to right, top row:* Lieutenant John S. Mallory, commandant; William L. Bringhurst, professor of physics; James R. Cole, professor of English; and John D. Read, M.D., surgeon. *Middle row:* Rudolph Wipprecht, professor of languages; Dinwiddie; and William P. Hardeman, agent of the Board of Directors. *Bottom row:* Roger H. Whitlock, professor of mechanics; Robert F. Smith, assistant professor of mathematics; Louis L. McInnis, professor of mathematics; and George W. Curtis, professor of agriculture and horticulture.

matriculate? Did you graduate; if so, when and in what department? When did you leave college? State briefly items of interest, and what has been your occupation since leaving the college; and if married, when and to whom? Also state if there has been any deaths among ex-cadets in your vicinity." As a final note, Cushing added this last comment: "In this movement it is, we believe, to your interest to cooperate."

William M. Sleeper '79, of Waco, was elected the first president of the Association of Ex-Cadets. Sleeper entered the college in January, 1877, and while at Texas A&M he was captain of Company C. After receiving a three-year certificate, he returned to Waco to practice law. The office of first vice-president was filled by W. A. Trenckmann '78 from Wilheim. Trenckmann entered the college in the fall of 1876 but was unable to finish his requirements for the first session because he dropped a math course. He contracted measles in early 1877 and was sent home by the college doctor. Nevertheless, he returned to the college for additional study, finishing his requirements for a certificate in literature. Pinkney Lorick Downs '79 was named second vice-president. After receiving a certificate

Pioneering members of A&M's first class gathered in reunion on the steps of the YMCA Building in June, 1921. *Front row, left to right:* W. J. Bryan '79, Abilene; Charles Rogan '79, Austin; P. L. Downs '79, Temple; W. M. Sleeper '79, Waco; and L. J. Kopke '79, Beaumont. *Second row:* F. W. Fort '79, Waco; P. H. Levy '79, Navasota; J. B. Dubb '79, Benchley; Reverend Malcom Buck '79, Sterling City; R. D. Bowen '79, Paris; and J. S. Steward, Houston. Pictured alone in the rear center is Sam Wilson, assistant to Bernard Sbisa in the Mess Hall. Wilson and Sbisa were the only two staff members on campus in 1921 that were also at A&M during 1879.

in agriculture, Downs worked in Waco and was later a board member of the Texas Agricultural Experiment Station. Plans for the next annual meeting included the selection of Thomas A. Fuller '81 as essayist and William Harrison Brown '80 as orator. The main address for the 1881 meeting was to be given by Texas Congressman Roger Q. Mills.

In June, 1881, Frank A. Reichardt '79, chairman of the Committee of Arrangements, sent out reminders and invitations to all who had replied to E. B. Cushing's request for data on former cadets. The second annual meeting of the association was scheduled for College Station on Wednesday, June 22, 1881. Reichardt's 3" × 5" invitation was also a notice or token to serve as a "certificate to procure the usual rates on the Railroads." The only access to the college was by foot, horse, or the Houston and Texas Central Railroad, which ran from Galveston through Houston, Hempstead, and Bryan to its northernmost terminal at Corsicana. Reichardt wrote to Louis L. McInnis, A&M's professor of mathematics, requesting him to make arrangements for accommodations for the Honorable J. C. Walker of Galveston, who was to deliver the main address instead of R. Q. Mills. The Association of Ex-Cadets managed to hold annual meetings at every commencement through 1883.

An early cadet unit accompanied by its sponsor in the late 1880's.

Cadet artillery drill in front of Old Main during the early 1880's.

By the mid-1880's some sidewalks had been built and trees planted. In this view cadets assemble for their daily inspection.

At the last meeting of the Association of Ex-Cadets a statement of objectives provided a legacy that was to become one of the most inspiring rituals or Aggie traditions: "Being composed of the Alumni of the College, many of whom annually pass from its halls into the bivouac of life, it is but meet that we should form and ever preserve an organization for uniting us fraternally, and always at necessity's call, extend a helping hand to an old comrade. In reunion we meet and live over again our College days, the victories and defeats won and lost upon drill ground and in classroom. Let every Alumni answer at roll call."

The reference in the last sentence to the "roll call" is significant. The return of the former cadets to the college during June for commencement exercises provided an opportunity to muster as a body and reflect on the "good ole' days" while students. It was also a time to recognize and honor those among their ranks who were no longer living. In later years, when the Association of Ex-Cadets had ceased to be, the tradition of the roll call was preserved. Minutes of the Alumni Association, formed in 1888, note that the roll call was read at the end of each meeting to honor those members who had died during the past year. The use of the roll call of fallen comrades was to be continued throughout the years, and it became an integral part of the Aggie Muster Ceremony held on April 21 of each year.

The muster tradition, as did the A&M College, the Association of Former Students, and the indomitable Aggie Spirit, grew from those few seeds scattered on the rugged soil of the Brazos prairies back in 1876. The experiences during their student days, although rough and trying, were to be a hallmark and stepping-off point for all interaction between Aggie former students and their alma mater. There were times when nothing grew well and other times when the growing was better. The Ex-Cadets Association soon wilted on the vine, but with spring came a new bud.

The Origins of the Muster Tradition

Cover of an early program of the Association of Ex-Cadets, which gathered on campus yearly during graduation week in June.

2. The Alumni Association

The Ex-Cadets Association became inactive after 1883 as hard times beset the college. With the opening of the University of Texas in Austin in that year, legislative funding for the "branch" in College Station withered. Epidemics of measles and dysentery and numerous cases of pneumonia struck the students and faculty. Seven deaths occurred during the winter. One professor died of what the college physician described as dysentery. The college adopted a three-year curriculum in agriculture or engineering which required shop or field work in keeping with the vocational emphasis and which led to a certificate instead of a degree. Student enrollment, which for a short time exceeded 500 in 1879–1880, dropped to 108 by the spring of 1883. The *Galveston Daily News* wrote that the A&M College should be closed and its buildings converted into a lunatic asylum. Professors and students departed, and President James left without waiting for the Board of Directors to accept his resignation. Remarkably, hard times seemed to generate an even deeper commitment and love for the school among former students. This commitment precipitated the "battle of the universities" as Texas Aggies fought during the 1880's for better funding and for the very existence of the A&M College. This struggle also produced a new and more vigorous former students' association.

When the University of Texas opened, the A&M College came under severe attack in the state press. Austin papers, sensing that the A&M College was draining state funds from the university, argued that the college was poorly located and badly administered and was "an agricultural and mechanical elephant in the hands of the state." University adherents proposed closing down the A&M College and transferring its "branches" to the university in Austin. On the A&M campus, faculty squabbles, inadequate facilities, and small budgets contributed to frequent faculty turnovers.

The bottom was reached during the 1883–1884 school year, but almost imperceptibly the college turned the corner with the beginning of the fall term in 1884. That year Lieutenant John S. Mallory, the commandant of cadets, organized the 133 enrolled students into Companies A, B, and C. New students already received the appellation "fish," which signified a raw, slightly odious, and lowly creature which was swimming in waters over its head. The regimen of corps life, the relative isolation of the college, and the interdependence within this small pioneering community dedicated to the great purposes of a higher education created the bonds of brotherhood and loyalty that inspired first the organization of the Ex-Cadets Association and then, in 1888, the Alumni Association.

Discontented with the inactivity of the Association of Ex-Cadets, Frederick E. Giesecke '86 and Walter Wipprecht '84 in June, 1886, led a group of recent A&M graduates and students in the formation of a new organization to supersede the defunct associa-

Left, Walter Wipprecht '84, shown here as a senior, provided outstanding leadership and foresight during the Alumni Association's early days. He served both as secretary and president of the association. *Right,* Frederick E. Giesecke '86 was an early faculty member and innovative alumni leader.

The Ross Volunteers at drill during the 1890's.

tion. Giesecke was a senior cadet at the time. During commencement week he drafted a proposed constitution for the new alumni association with the help of the following committee:

Alumni Association Organized

T. D. Rowell '85	J. N. Davis '85
J. W. Carson '86	J. M. Carson '86
A. L. Sherley '85	E. W. Spann '85
M. D. Tilson '86	C. L. Burghard '89
I. A. Cottingham '88	J. M. Wesson '83
W. F. Woodward	J. B. McQueen '84
Walter Wipprecht '84	

All of the above men were either students at A&M, professors, or residents of the local Bryan area.

In the interim between June, 1886, and commencement in 1887, the first constitution of the "Alumni Association of the A&M College of Texas" was reviewed and edited. It was printed for distribution in June, 1888, by Pilot Book and Job Print of Bryan, Texas. In the foreword of the document the sixteen members of the constitution committee, all graduates of A&M, expressed the purpose of the group to be "an Association for the promotion of friendship, and the advancement of popularity that our college has enjoyed so extensively."

Giesecke, from Brenham, was elected the first secretary of the Alumni Association. (After graduation he became an assistant professor in the Mechanical Engineering Department from 1886 to 1888, and at age nineteen he was made head of the Drawing Department.) An executive committee, consisting of the president and the secretary, was to "look after the interest of the Association, and transact all business of the Association when not in session." Sessions or regular meetings were to be held at the college during commencement exercises. An initiation fee of one dollar was required by all new members, and thereafter the dues were one dollar annually.

This first consitution was clear and concise, but one section of it ultimately crippled the effectiveness of the organization. Section 2 of Article 1 stated, "Any graduate of the A. and M. College shall be entitled to become a member, provided no three members shall vote against his petition." This limitation of membership to graduates only constituted a drastic change in membership requirements from those of the Association of Ex-Cadets, which enrolled any former student. Organizers of the Alumni Association believed that graduates were best able and most willing to support the college. This assumption in time proved to be not only false but also detrimental to the college and to the growth of the organization.

Many years later, in 1951, Giesecke stated in a letter to Dr. David B. Cofer, archivist of the college, that "it was a mistake to limit the membership of the Association to graduates." After the turn of the century Giesecke and Walter Wipprecht, among others, worked diligently to have the constitution revised or amended to include all former students.

The A&M College also experienced a substantial reorganization in 1888. Louis L. McInnis, that lone survivor of the 1879 faculty firing, became chairman of the faculty, a position created by the Board of Directors in 1883 when the board eliminated the position of president. McInnis assumed the job in January, 1888, following the death of Hardaway

Hardaway Hunt Dinwiddie, president of Texas A&M, 1883–1888.

Louis L. McInnis, president of Texas A&M, 1888–1890.

The Agricultural Experiment Station

Hunt Dinwiddie. McInnis also assumed the pleasant responsibility of organizing the Texas Agricultural Experiment Station, created by the Hatch Act of 1887 and approved by the Twentieth Texas Legislature. The experiment station, operated under the auspices of the A&M College, provided opportunities that went far beyond its central purpose of facilitating scientific research and experimentation in agriculture. It provided fifteen thousand dollars of new money for the operation of the college, an amount that increased by one-third the college's annual operating budget. Thus, the station relieved the sorely pressed finances of the college and provided an opportunity for expanding the faculty and class offerings.

McInnis established eleven academic departments in the college: mathematics, English and history, agriculture, mechanical engineering, civil engineering and physics, horticulture and botany, chemistry and mineralogy, veterinary science, drawing, languages, and military science and tactics. Frank Arthur Gulley joined the faculty as director of the Agricultural Experiment Station. Mark Francis, who would achieve distinction as the "father of the Texas cattle industry," came as associate professor of veterinary science, and Henry Hill Harrington, eventually to become president of the college, joined as professor of chemistry and mineralogy. The faculty was expanded from eight to eighteen between 1885 and 1888. Many of the faculty members drew part or all of their salary from Hatch Act funds. Moreover, legislative appropriations allowed for the construction of two

John Carson (*left*) and James Carson (*right*), the famous twins of the class of 1886. John Carson served as president of the Alumni Association in 1889–1890.

new dormitories (Pfeuffer and Austin halls), Assembly Hall, a new chapel, and two new residences for faculty, who, in those days, were housed on the campus.

By 1888, then, the college seemingly had moved from a dire situation of famine to a happier time of feast. The more jubilant atmosphere may have been conducive to the organization in that year of the Scott Guards, a crack cadet drill team soon to be renamed the Ross Volunteers. In 1888 the college graduated sixteen students, seven of whom received degrees in agriculture and nine in engineering. The dark decade of the 1880's closed on a note of bright anticipation for the college and the Alumni Association.

The Alumni Association provided, as did for a brief time the Association of Ex-Cadets, desperately needed public support for the floundering college, and it boosted the morale of students in the school during the dark decade of the 1880's. Now, in 1889 and 1890, faculty and former students sensed the advent of brighter days for the college. The Alumni Association celebrated its annual meeting on June 7, 1889, in the college chapel. A. L. Sherley '85 presided over the meeting, which featured speeches by Professor McInnis and John D. Fearhake '89, representing the cadets. The Nineteenth Infantry Band from San Antonio provided music and entertainment for visiting alumni. The business session was held that same afternoon at three o'clock in the chapel, and the graduating class of 1889 was elected *en masse* as members of the association. John W. Carson '86 and Walter

The 1890's: A Watershed in A&M's History

Members of the first Texas A&M football team in 1894.

20 WE ARE THE AGGIES

The Texas Aggie Band during the mid-1890's.

Wipprecht were elected president and secretary/treasurer, respectively, of the 1889–1900 Alumni Association. The first issue of the *College Journal*, published in November, 1889, and sponsored and published by the students' Austin Literary Society, stated that it would be a "hearty pleasure" to extend through its columns "greetings" to all alumni of the college. The *Journal* recognized that "The success of the Alumni of any institution is the best and truest indication of its usefulness and prosperity—no other standard of measurement is so accurate. If the graduates of a college are unsuccessful, unworthy of positions of honor and distinction, to just that extent is that college a failure."

Walter Wipprecht was elected president of the Alumni Association for the 1890–1891 term. Having served as secretary/treasurer, he was eager to be involved with the activities of the college and the association, and his efforts centered around making as many former cadets as possible aware of the association's existence and its anticipated role in the development of the college. Wipprecht had received his certificate from A&M in 1884, had become an instructor in the Departments of Chemistry and Physics, and in early 1887 had returned to his father's German homeland to study advanced chemistry at the University of Jena in Saxony. In late 1888, short of funds and homesick for Texas and his alma mater, he had returned to A&M to teach chemistry and to conduct the first chemistry research for the Agricultural Experiment Station. Wipprecht's term as president of the Alumni Association launched one of the most exciting and productive decades of the Aggie experience.

The 1890's marked a watershed in the development of the A&M College and the

Alumni Association. Intercollegiate athletics—and most especially football—appeared on campus. And no longer would Aggies have the reputation of being "unwashed, unlettered, and unlearned." Electric lights were installed so that budding scholars could "burn the midnight oil." Deep water wells were drilled. Aggies could bathe without having to borrow a professor's wooden tub or take a dip in the farm pond. Alpha Phi Fraternity became the third organization of A&M former students to exist within a decade. It was organized to admit former students without degrees, who far outnumbered those with degrees, especially since no degrees had been awarded anyway between 1883 and 1887 when the college had adopted a three-year curriculum. The *College Journal*, the first student publication, soon yielded to the *Battalion*, which remains today as an outstanding daily newspaper. Also in the 1890's alumni organized the first placement bureau, and its work goes on today. The class agent became an integral part of the alumni organization. The Aggie Band made its debut, Aggies marched off to their first great war, and, more important, Lawrence Sullivan Ross came to A&M.

Lawrence Sullivan Ross

The selection of Governor Ross as president of the A&M College on July 1, 1890, reinvigorated flagging interest in the Alumni Association and awakened statewide public interest in and support for the college. Governor Ross was selected for the presidency of A&M while he was still serving in the statehouse in Austin. He had a distinguished and almost legendary career as an Indian fighter, Confederate Cavalry brigadier, and statesman. He was the "boy captain" who at the age of sixteen had led Texas Rangers against the Comanches and at eighteen had defeated Chief Peta Nocona in hand-to-hand combat and had rescued Cynthia Ann Parker from the Comanches. His cavalry exploits behind Union lines during the Civil War were ventures of unbelievable courage and daring.

Governor Ross's appointment as president meant that A&M's pioneering state of development, the sheer struggle for survival, had ended. Ross's strong character, military background, public stature, and legendary image, and to no little extent his ability to channel larger legislative funding to the college, marked the end of more than a decade of uncertainty. Although there might later be threats to close down what early critics of the college called the "cancer on the Brazos," Ross's appointment meant that A&M had come of age. The college began to receive public acceptance and recognition as a useful experiment in higher public education. It was widely said throughout Texas that parents "sent their sons not to A&M, but to Governor Ross."

The College Journal, Battalion, *and* Texas Aggie

Prosperity, growing enrollments, and a new commitment to scientific agriculture, engineering, and military training developed during Ross's tenure as president between 1891 and January, 1898. A new spirit and purpose swept the student body at A&M and slowly infected the former students. F. E. Giesecke, in a form letter sent to all alumni in October, 1892, encouraged renewed participation in the Alumni Association. His letter informed the alumni that the executive committee of the association had decided at its last regular meeting in June, 1892, to "subscribe to the *College Journal* for those members who had paid their annual assessments up to and including that of 1891–1892." The dues at this period remained one dollar, as prescribed in the Alumni Association Constitution of 1888. Each issue of the *College Journal* contained various articles of a literary nature composed by the students and faculty. It published "Alumni news as can be obtained" to keep students and former students alike informed of the activities of the alumni. New subscriptions gave the publication badly needed operating revenue, and the association gained a

Lawrence Sullivan Ross in 1863 in the uniform of a brigadier general, CSA.

President Lawrence Sullivan Ross (1891–1898) with the members of the 1892 faculty. *Left to right, seated:* F. E. Giesecke '86, Roger H. Whitlock, James C. Nagle, Charles W. Hutson, Ross, R. H. Price, T. C. Bittle, Charles Puryear, and J. H. Connell. *Standing:* Mark Francis, Henry H. Harrington, and Captain B. C. Morse.

Cadets in dress uniform before Old Main, late 1890's.

The 1898 football team included (*left to right*) R. B. Cousins (end), "Babe" Astin (tackle), and George Dowell (quarterback), shown here with the Assembly Hall in the background.

Left, The class agent concept was instituted in the early 1890's in order to help maintain class unity. Here, Agent Philip Bohlmann '76 addresses his class during the annual spring banquet sponsored by the Association of Former Students. *Right*, Buell C. Pittuck '94 served twice as president of the Alumni Association — 1895–1896 and 1904–1905.

means by which to publish announcements of its events and miscellaneous information. In 1893 the *Battalion*, a news tabloid instead of a literary magazine, replaced the *College Journal* as the official student publication.

The *College Journal* and the *Battalion* allowed the alumni contributing editor to print many items of information in each monthly publication. Such entries as changes of address, honors and promotions, foreign travel, club activities, and military service, to name a few, were included in the alumni section. Alumni editors, usually the elected secretaries of the association, often gave unsolicited bits of information for the benefit and general knowledge of the reader. One such helpful entry concerned the art of growing hair: "To make hair grow, and to prevent its being gray: Bay rum, 1 qt.; table salt, half a teacup; castor oil, one drachm; tincture of cantharides, one drachm. This tonic is very stimulative and not oily enough to be disagreeable."

The *College Journal* and the early *Battalion* were the forerunners of today's comprehensive monthly publication sponsored by the Association of Former Students—*The Texas Aggie*. *The Texas Aggie* is much like the *Journal* of the early 1890's in that it is a monthly magazine printed to provide news concerning the former students of the school in an effort to keep interest in the university alive. *The Texas Aggie* is edited and financed solely by the Association of Former Students.

E. W. Hutchinson '89 presided over the eighth Alumni Association meeting held on June 6, 1893. After a lengthy report, Treasurer F. E. Giesecke concluded his presentation on alumni affairs with the statement that as of June 5, 1893, the association had a total balance of $80.70 on hand. In his remarks he stated that there had been some difficulty in

The campus by late 1900 began to take on a new look as streets were established and trees grew.

the collection of dues. He made no mention of the fact that the nation was then in the throes of the most severe depression it had ever experienced. The financial problems of the association were discussed by the collective gathering, but no solution was found. Except for the dismal financial report, the annual meeting was uneventful.

The executive committee met after the regular meeting to discuss possible means of persuading the alumni to become more actively involved with the association. This involvement was to include the regular payment of dues by all alumni in order for the association to have funds with which to operate. Association dues in the past had been used primarily, if not exclusively, for postage stamps. In an effort to involve more former students in the activities of the association, the executive committee decided that each class would have a class agent, whose responsibility would be "to correspond with the members of that class to try to induce them to return to the college for commencement." The introduction of the class agent, coupled with editorials and personal notes in the *Journal* and the *Battalion*, helped promote a personal link between former students and the associa-

Class Agents

The Alumni Association 27

tion. The use of the class agent as a point of contact for his classmates was to develop into one of the strongest attributes of the association's organization. Although only partially used in the late 1890's and early 1900's, class agents have since been very important to the association.

The First Football Game

Many former cadets and alumni took an increasingly active interest in the affairs and well-being of the Corps of Cadets. During Thanksgiving of 1894 many former students returned to the campus to attend the grand ball. Faculty, cadets, dates, and alumni enjoyed the evening. During their visit the alumni stayed with the various cadet units in the dorms and attended reveille and breakfast with the cadets in the mess hall. The day was made especially memorable by the advent of football on the A&M campus. Buell C. Pittuck '94 commented that "the event of the day was the football game, witnessed by more than 500 people." That event pitted the "Farmers" of A&M against Ball High School of Galveston. The opening contest of the 1894 season was a victorious effort for the Farmers, who won 14 to 6. Pittuck said of the cadets, "When a good play was made the boys would make the air resound with yells and screeches and such hideous sounds as only College boys can make." The former cadets tremendously enjoyed the campus activities and the football game, and in future years many alumni activities would be planned around the Aggie football season.

In the December, 1894, Christmas edition of the *Battalion*, A. M. Ferguson, editor of the alumni section, commented on the high morale of the alumni and the Corps of Cadets. Ferguson wrote of the corps, "No doubt all ye old graduates will be glad to know of the excellent moral tone that pervades the corps at the present time. Discipline was never better. The boys have organized and equipped a band of 16 pieces, and it adds not a little to the military feature of the college."

By late 1894 the Alumni Association was well established. But alumni reunions held during commencement exercises attracted only a small number of graduates, even with the addition of the individual "class agent" for each class. Although membership in the Alumni Association was limited to graduates of the college, many nongraduates returned to the college for commencement and supported the college statewide. Because they were excluded from the Alumni Association, these nongraduate former cadets would soon foster an organization of their own which was more spirited and energetic in the support of A&M than was the Alumni Association.

3. Round Pegs and Square Holes

Over all, the last years of the 1890's were productive ones for both the college and the Alumni Association. The college had never been more stable and prosperous; funds needed for construction and maintenance of new housing facilities, classrooms, and a new mess hall were appropriated by the legislature. A deep-well water supply was developed by the college, and bathing facilities with running water were in use for the first time. Governor Sul Ross, as president of the college, instilled in the students and faculty a sense of purpose and direction. The December, 1894, issue of the *Battalion* said of Ross, "He is a grand man and doing a grand work—a work that will live when the College walls have crumbled, and growing with the growth of the state, will bless generations yet to be."

Four events stand out in the affairs of the Alumni Association in the last five years of the nineteenth century. First, the association adopted a constitutional change in June, 1896, to replace the charter document of 1888. Second, the birth of the beneficial Alumni Bureau would help graduates obtain jobs. This bureau is known today as the Texas A&M Career Planning and Placement Center. Third, to obtain a more direct control over the policies and management of A&M, the Alumni Association urged the governor to appoint at least one of their members to the Board of Directors. Finally, and most important, a rival former student association emerged which offered innovative ideas and leadership and resulted in the development of a stronger, broader-based, and more effective association of Aggies.

The Constitution of 1896

Although there was general agreement that the association's constitution of 1888 was a good instrument, many urged that it be updated. Between June, 1894, and June, 1896, J. H. Forman '87, B. C. Pittuck '94, Wipprecht, Giesecke, and others pushed for a revised document "to take the place of the old one, which had long proved unsatisfactory and inadequate to the needs of the Association as it existed only in tradition." An additional factor that persuaded the alumni to react was the fact that the amendment to the constitution of 1888 had been destroyed by fire a few years earlier, and no copies survived. At the eleventh meeting of the Alumni Association on June 8, 1896, in the Austin Society Hall, the matter of the revised constitution was presented for adoption. A committee presented, with the approval of the executive committee, their proposed changes to the 1888 draft. The revised constitution was basically unchanged from the 1888 document. The name of the organization remained the Alumni Association of the A&M College of Texas, and its purpose was to "bind the alumni as far as practicable into unity of influence." Membership continued to be limited to graduates, although steps were provided to admit nongraduate former students on a special basis, and the initiation fee dues remained at one dollar. During the meeting the constitution of 1896 was adopted without debate, and the secretary

Cadets in a woodworking shop during the mid-1890's.

was advised to have five hundred copies printed, one to be mailed to each member in good standing.

The major change in this new constitution, in keeping with the implementation of the "class agent" concept in 1893, was a provision allowing the election of second vice-presidents, to be selected as follows: "One vice president to be elected from the classes number from '78 to '84 inclusive, and one from each succeeding group of five classes provided that when the last group shall number three classes it shall thereafter be entitled to a second vice president."

The membership requirements were revised slightly to allow "any former student who shall have attended regular classes for at least two years at this college" to make application to the Executive Committee. The Executive Committee then would "ascertain if the applicant is eligible for election to membership." This attempt to bring more former students into contact with association activities was severely hampered by a clause imposed by graduate members of the Executive Committee: "All ex-students so elected shall be entitled to every privilege of this Association *except* the right to hold office" (italics added). Changes were relatively few despite many proposals demanding a complete overhaul of the organization. The changes that were implemented in the new constitution of 1896 had but one intent—to bring more former cadets into the mainstream of college and alumni endeavors.

Cognizant that bonds of friendship and good fellowship could not alone maintain loyalty and support for the Alumni Association, the organization sought to make itself useful in other ways to its members and especially to prospective members—the future graduates of the A&M College. A particularly effective device which provided distinct bene-

30 WE ARE THE AGGIES

Three cadets in the tailored uniform of the late 1890's.

Alumni Bureau

fits for A&M students was the creation of the Alumni Bureau, which functioned as a job placement agency. Alex W. Ferguson '94 proposed to the alumni at the annual business meeting in June, 1896: "In order that the interest of this college and its Alumni may be advanced, an Alumni Bureau should be established for the purpose of aiding graduates in securing positions and jobs in teaching, agriculture and business." The bureau, he suggested, should be directed by a special elected secretary for the term of one year. This first secretary, Ferguson stated, would be in charge of organizing the bureau on such a basis "as in his judgment will best advance the interest for which it is proposed." With the unanimous approval of the Alumni Bureau by the association, F. E. Giesecke, already an avid supporter of the college and the association, was selected to fill the position of Alumni Bureau secretary. His selection assured the initial success of that agency. Giesecke was respected not only by the students and alumni but also by businessmen and educators statewide.

The Alumni Bureau, in addition to its chief function of placing graduates in jobs, became an active lobby in support of the A&M College before the Texas State Legislature. The primary issue for which the bureau lobbied was the repeal of the act requiring all A&M College graduates to take an examination for a teacher's certificate. Unlike Texas A&M graduates, persons holding diplomas from the University of Texas and private institutions of higher learning throughout the state were not required to take an examination. The bureau was encouraged by the collective association to appeal to the legislature to repeal this "obvious oversight." A change in this law would expedite the placement of graduates into teaching positions, and many graduates would be eligible to fill teaching positions as temporary jobs while waiting for positions in the business world to become available. The Alumni Bureau was unable to win a repeal of the requirement, but in time the high school teacher certification program did expand its regulations to include a requirement that all graduates of a Texas college, university, or private institution of higher learning be certified, thus giving A&M students equal opportunities for teacher placement.

Giesecke worked diligently to notify all former students of the new placement service. His most productive contacts were with A&M clubs statewide. Many club officers and members were active in the business community and agriculture and provided the bureau with notices of new jobs. A&M clubs in Houston, Austin, San Antonio, and Dallas had the most success in helping find jobs for former students and recent graduates. Soon the *Alumni Quarterly*, sponsored by the college administration and not the Alumni Association, embraced the idea of job placement. A former student needed only to contact the alumni secretary in the president's office: "If you are out of a position, or want a better one, write the College Alumni Secretary, giving your qualifications and what salary you would expect. We would like to make this office of service to you in securing employment."

When the *Alumni Quarterly* ceased publication, *The Texas Aggie* incorporated a strong job placement service. Ike Ashburn, who became executive secretary of the association in December, 1923, wrote, "Do you want a technically trained man for a job? Are you in search of a position? If so write The Association and let us help you to locate your man or locate yourself." Ashburn, popular with both students and former students, stressed the role of the association as one of service to all Aggies. His theme during the 1920's for the association was, "We are here to serve you."

Today's modern placement office and employer information library is much advanced over the efforts of the Alumni Bureau of the early 1900's.

With service in mind, he began a new bi-weekly placement column entitled "Round Pegs and Square Holes." Success of this endeavor depended primarily on the response of former students in all walks of life. Ashburn, in his column, encouraged placement assistance with this brief editorial:

If you want a good technically trained man for a position in your organization call on the Association of Former Students.

If you want to make a change in your work, file your application with a statement of your record and training with the Association.

Last week we placed two former students in good positions.

Now we have on file the applications of several good men in engineering, athletics, and agriculture, and vocational education.

We will investigate the merits of each man before recommending him and will try our best to give you a serviceable suggestion.

Do Not Be a Round Peg in a Square Hole.

Do Not Keep a Round Peg in a Square Hole.

If you hear of an opening notify us and we will help to fill it. By so doing you will render a service to some ex-student and at the same time to some employer.

Ashburn's efforts created a considerable response. Monthly job calls were posted for referral. The variety of vocations solicited covered every field of endeavor worldwide:

We want a cotton breeder for a Lockhart firm.

Round Pegs and Square Holes 33

British Central Africa wants a tobacco expert at salary of 800 pounds per year and expenses to and from Nyasaland.

Needed: Plant Pathologist for work in Honduras.

Want vocational teachers in agriculture.

Have position for young Aggie engineer with paving experience. Salary $175 per month in growing city. Quick action.

Until the mid-1930's, the association was the sole support of the placement service. Everett E. McQuillen '20, who succeeded Ashburn as executive secretary, hoped eventually to transfer the placement services into the hands of the college administration. Finally, in 1939, Wendell R. Horseley, on the staff of Texas A&M, assumed the duties of placement coordinator. In addition to these duties he helped needy students find on-campus jobs.

Horseley, who served as placement director until 1967, continued to expand the placement services of the agency. After being housed in four different locations in the Systems Administration Building and then Goodwin Hall, the University Placement Office finally found a home in the YMCA Building. With the completion of the Rudder Tower portion of the Memorial Student Center, the placement offices were moved to their present location in late 1973 under the direction of Louis Van Pelt '62.

In 1969 the teacher placement function of the office was transferred to the newly created College of Education, which coordinated teacher placement until 1974, when these duties were transferred back to the University Placement Office. The move enabled educators, counselors, and administrators to consolidate all the placement and job counseling in one office and more adequately assist all graduates. In the spring of 1975 today's placement office, the Career Planning and Placement Center, was created.

Another dimension to the career services made available to the A&M student has been Cooperative Education. In 1963, Dean J. G. ("Mickey") McGuire of the College of Engineering made available co-op jobs for engineering students with major corporations statewide. In the fall of 1977, as many as 10 percent of the students in engineering (about seven hundred Aggies) were on co-op jobs in alternating semesters. As a result of this rapidly expanding interest, a new university-wide program in Cooperative Education began, under the direction of J. Malon Southerland '65, in conjunction with the Placement Center. Now co-op jobs are available to almost every A&M student through six colleges of the university: engineering, agriculture, liberal arts, architecture, science, and veterinary medicine (biomedical science).

Although placement is no longer a direct function of the Association of Former Students, the Placement Center continues to place numerous graduates and alumni in a multitude of jobs and teaching positions worldwide. Moreover, the pioneering work of the Alumni Association through its Alumni Bureau created an atmosphere of care and concern for the welfare of the student, encouraged the development of the Association of Former Students along the lines of a service organization, rather than a fraternal society alone, and resulted in a larger, more active, and vital alumni group.

Concurrent with its decision to provide placement services for Aggies, the Alumni Association petitioned the governor to appoint at least one alumnus of the college to the

The campus at the turn of the century. *Left to right:* campus dorms, Gathright Hall, Old Main, Ross Hall, Foster Hall, and the Old Chapel or Assembly Hall.

Board of Directors of A&M. The June, 1896, issue of the *Battalion* ecstatically supported the association's request: "Having been a student of the college, an Alumnus is more intimately acquainted with its purposes and needs than anyone else, and having reached the full vigor and maturity of manhood, will espouse the cause with that energy and fearlessness which can only be inspired by love for his alma mater." Andrew L. Banks '79, an A&M professor and vocal alumnus, led the vanguard of former cadets in seeking alumni representation on the board at the June, 1896, association meeting. Banks said that even if he stood alone as a "committee of one," he would push for a full airing of the matter. The alumni formally adopted a resolution to be forwarded to the governor requesting the appointment of an Aggie to A&M's governing board. In an eloquent address, association President Phineas S. Tilson reminded members that A&M had just completed its twentieth annual session and that there were many prominent and educated graduates among the state citizenry who could adequately represent the alumni and the college. He noted that older educational institutions across the nation had "at least one" representative of the college or university alumni on their board.

Edward W. Hutchinson '89 of Houston was selected as the member of the association whose name would be forwarded to the governor as a "competent and suitable man for the position with the request that he be appointed to the first vacancy that may occur." While a cadet, Hutchinson was the senior captain of the corps in 1888 and 1889. After graduation he worked for the college as a bookkeeper and held key positions in both the Alumni Association and the Alpha Phi Fraternity. He was a successful businessman and worked closely with the board on various occasions. P. L. Downs '79, Tilson, and President Ross were appointed to a committee to draft a letter to Governor Charles A. Culberson encouraging him to recognize Hutchinson as the official board designee of the Alumni Association.

Governor Culberson, not coincidentally, was already on campus. He was honored guest at a grand banquet held in the mess hall. Professor William B. Philpott, toastmaster,

The Board of Directors

Dining with Bernard Sbisa

sat at the head table with Governor Culberson on his left and former governor Ross on his right. Prominent local politicians and the Board of Directors were in attendance. After remarks by Andrew J. Rose, president of the Board of Directors, and by P. L. Downs for the Alumni Association, Governor Culberson addressed the gathering. The governor spoke of the need for well-established, effective institutions of higher learning in Texas. No mention was made concerning board appointments or the financial needs of the college. For those gathered who were disappointed in his speech, he closed with a reassuring word: "In my present position my conduct may have been criticized, but when you take into consideration that I represent not one institution alone, but all of them and all the people, I think you will see that I endeavored to act for the best, and that all things will work together hereafter for the upbuilding of this splendid institution."

The banquet meal, prepared by college steward Bernard Sbisa, the Austrian-born New Orleans chef who prepared hearty and tasty meals for Aggies for more than fifty years, is worth noting:

Olives	Caviar on Toast	Mangoes
	Pickles	
	Ecrevise a la Horley	
	Julienne Potatoes	
	Spring Chicken au Champignons	
	Cheese Straw	
	Ferris Dove Ham	
	Imported Smoked Tongue	
	Chicken Mayonnaise	
	Vienna Rolls	
Three Pyramid—		Coconut Macaroons
Lady Fingers		Wafers
Assorted Cakes—		
Egg Kisses	White and Gold Cake	
Neapolitan Cream		Brick Ice Cream
Combination Jelly		Whipped Cream
	Salted Almonds	
	Ice Tea and Coffee	
White Wine		Champagne

Campaign for a Board Member

Later in the year, Downs, Cushing, and J. D. Fearhake '89 went to Austin to lobby for the addition of Hutchinson to the Texas A&M Board of Directors. They spent considerable time in an unproductive effort to convince Governor Culberson to recognize and support their chosen representative. Then, in November, 1896, much to the surprise of the association delegation in Austin, not one but two positions on the board became vacant. Upon hearing this news, more members of the association went to Austin to help lobby for at least one of these two appointments. Governor Culberson, although a friend of the college and frequent visitor to the campus, remained silent on his intended action. Many thought the appointments would be delayed until late January of the new year, when other key positions were usually filled.

Happily, this was not to be the case. Before his departure for the Christmas holidays on December 23, 1896, Governor Culberson ended the suspense by announcing that

Left, W. B. Philpott served as toastmaster and campus coordinator for many Alumni Association events. *Right,* Mr. and Mrs. Bernard Sbisa in front of the dining hall about 1900.

Early A&M football game on December 2, 1899, against LSU.

Round Pegs and Square Holes 37

Captain Frank A. Reichardt '79 was appointed to the 1897–1898 Texas A&M Board of Directors. Reichardt, a Houstonian born on November 5, 1860, was popular with both the cadets and the faculty. While at A&M he had been commander of Company A, and upon graduation he entered private business. The Alumni Association was elated over the appointment even though their selected representative, Hutchinson, had not been chosen.

Despite its achievements, the Alumni Association was by definition an exclusive organization which failed to incorporate most Aggies into its membership. Whereas more than three thousand Aggies had attended A&M for varying periods of time before 1900, fewer than two hundred had received degrees. Being an Aggie, however, was not a thing of "degree." Those who left the college without a diploma, as most did, took with them a unique love and appreciation for the institution they had attended. Higher education in nineteenth-century Texas was a rare and special privilege, if not a luxury, that few could afford, and then often only for intermittent periods. But the A&M experience, even a short one, seemed to be doing something special for young Texans. It enabled them to obtain jobs as engineers, educators, agricultural teachers, and scientists. It was converting unlettered, unwashed, and undisciplined young Texas boys into educated, confident, disciplined, and purposeful young men. And those young men knew it and appreciated the opportunities which even an abbreviated A&M education offered. They were no longer round pegs in square holes. Thanks to the A&M experience, Aggies could assume positions of leadership in the world of business, engineering, agriculture, and the military. "Not one," President Ross could boast in 1896, "has ever proved a gambler, a drunkard, or idler in the great hive of industry."

4. Alpha Phi Fraternity

Edward B. Cushing, who served as secretary of the original Ex-Cadets Association back in 1880, in 1896 organized a group of Texas A&M cadets and former cadets from Houston into a so-called fraternity so that all who had "worn the gray" might be forever acquainted. The new organization, known as the Alpha Phi Fraternity, was formed with the hope of bringing together the former students who were excluded from membership in the Alumni Association because they had never received a degree from Texas A&M. Over the previous twenty years only 150 degrees had been awarded, while more than three thousand former students had attended the A&M College for differing periods of time. Cushing believed that many nongraduate former cadets could be of great help to A&M College since "the old students of this college are now taking place in the front rank of the professional and commercial circles of the state and figuring prominently in its politics. . . ."

The Houston organizers quickly moved to expand Alpha Phi into a national fraternity for the former students of the A&M College. At the June, 1896, commencement the organizers of the new Alpha Phi Fraternity gathered for their first annual meeting. Members elected Cushing their first commander, or president, and appointed a committee to draft a constitution. Former cadets were informed, through editorials in the *Battalion*, that membership would be both rewarding and helpful in keeping track of old college friends. A fraternity book was to be given to each former cadet upon receipt of his application for membership; it contained a list of members with current addresses and items of interest so that each former cadet could be informed of the whereabouts of his classmates. The Alpha Phi fraternity book set yet another precedent for the *Directory of Former Students*. Echoing the sentiments that led to the establishment of the Alumni Bureau, the fraternity also pledged itself to aid its members by "rendering assistance . . . in securing employment." In the September, 1896, issue of the *Battalion*, an Alpha Phi editorial signed by "Number One" encouraged all former cadets to send in their applications and informed all prospective members that a constitutional committee was "working hard and their efforts will no doubt result in a set of laws that will be unexceptionable." This anonymous writer closed with a question to arouse interest: "How does 'Alpha Phi Hall' strike you? See next issue of *Battalion*."

Former students of the college now had two associations representing them: one for graduates only—a proscription that markedly limited the potential size—and one for graduates and nongraduates. Both professed the same objectives, adopted similar programs, and met during the June commencement week at the college. At first glance they appeared to be rival instead of complementary organizations. In the January, 1897, special Alpha Phi edition of the *Battalion*, Andrew L. Banks pointed out that very few alumni had returned to campus in support of the Alumni Association and the college. He also noted

Andrew L. Banks, a mathematics teacher, along with E. B. Cushing was a strong leader in the formation of Alpha Phi Fraternity.

that relatively few graduate former cadets were even members of the Alumni Association, and he indicated that the association did not include any representation of the on-campus student body, nor did it heed the suggestions of the nongraduate former cadets. Nevertheless, he encouraged all not to let these criticisms "deter" them, since Alpha Phi intended to "work in perfect harmony with the Association." The tone of his remarks, however, suggested little prospect for harmony or cooperation between the two former student organizations.

Alpha Phi Programs

Even more embarrassing to the Alumni Association was the fact that Alpha Phi organizers proved to be a tremendously energetic lot. Moreover, in the 1890's Greek letter fraternities, which included secret meetings and initiations, were much in vogue; also, Alpha Phi had a military cast to its internal structure, and in 1896 as the talk of war with Spain over Cuba grew more excited, the already strong appeal of the martial spirit added to the attractiveness of Alpha Phi. If these factors were not enough, the young fraternity of A&M men developed several programs and organizational features so successful that they have remained an intrinsic part of the modern Association of Former Students. A directory of former students, a job placement service, the inception of the idea for a former students' building or meeting place on campus, and, most important, the development of local chapters of former student clubs and broad-based membership qualifications were all

40 WE ARE THE AGGIES

inspired by Alpha Phi. The Alpha Phi Fraternity became a major catalyst in the development of the modern Association of Former Students.

The Austin and Calliopean Literary Societies of the college allowed Alpha Phi to have exclusive use of the January, 1897, issue of the *Battalion*. This issue carried a complete copy of the newly written Alpha Phi constitution and bylaws. Two thousand copies were published and distributed in an effort to inform as many former cadets as possible about the new organization. On the last page was an information sheet and application blank for membership in the fraternity. Alpha Phi left the former student little choice but to join the fraternity or be an ignominious character: "The man who has no love for his Alma Mater, and who has no desire to renew the association of student days, must be classed as an abnormal creature—unless he was a disreputable character and left in bad odor."

It was expected that a Greek letter organization would be more prestigious than the Alumni Association, which was viewed by many as inactive and outdated. Membership in Alpha Phi was open to every former cadet who had completed at least one term at college. Initiation into the fraternity required two steps. The first step, or "degree," was conferred at the time a former cadet made application and took a pledge to support the organization. The second "degree" was earned by participation in an annual reunion on campus. This second degree consisted of various ceremonies of initiation and an acceptance into the main body of the fraternity. It was rumored in mid-1897 that "some of the old boys were feeding a fine goat on the side" to be ridden as part of the initiation ceremony. The goat never made an appearance, so far as is known, but the comment to prospective members was "ride a goat and be an Alpha Phi."

Distinguished members among the former cadets received the honorary title of "veteran." This distinction was to go to those who had "attained prominence through their own efforts." There could be no more than twenty-five such "veterans" at any one time, and a former cadet could not be chosen as one for at least five years after joining Alpha Phi. All nominations for veteran status were to be made at the annual June meeting, and no more than five could be elected at any one meeting. In some respects designation of "veterans" set a precedent for the inception in 1962 of A&M's Distinguished Alumni Award program, which recognizes the achievements and services to society of outstanding Aggies.

Alpha Phi's military orientation appealed to former students, whose college life revolved around the Corps of Cadets. The daily life of the student of the A&MC in the 1890's followed an intensive military regimen. The cadet's day began at 6:00 A.M. when the roll of the drum, and after 1893, the sound of the bugle, announced reveille. Cadets assembled for roll call, returned to their rooms to dress, put their rooms in order for the day, formed up again at breakfast call, and marched to chow. The meal was concluded by a call to attention; cadets filed out of the mess hall, formed ranks, got their orders for the day, and marched to class. Guard duty was posted for twenty-four hours a day. At the end of the class day, military drills and exercise were held on the drill field. Cadets ended the day with a "study call" at 7:30, tattoo at 9:45, and taps at 10:00. The A&M College, opined one critic, was a "military peacockery"—but whatever it was, college life created an unusual bond of love and loyalty among Aggies.

College Life

It was fitting then that Alpha Phi organize along military lines. Officers included the commander, the vice-commander, the officer of the day, the adjutant, and the quartermaster. A color bearer, sergeant, corporal of the guard, and "commissary and sentinel" comprised the secondary positions concerned mainly with record keeping for the fraternity. The executive committee, called the Campus Council, included the commander, vice-commander, and adjutant. The council could dismiss the commander or any officer with cause, could suspend the bylaws if necessary, and was empowered to spend up to 75 percent of the annual dues in the interests of the fraternity. There was also a special committee on the "organization of secret ceremonies." Business meetings and initiation ceremonies were secret, and the "password" was inviolable. The constitution stipulated that the annual meeting could be held during commencement week in June of each year. Knowing that their meetings and activities might conflict with the activities of the Alumni Association, the constitution pledged the fraternity to work in harmony with the Alumni Association "if it advanced their mutual interest."

Besides publishing a directory of all former cadets, the "Fraternity Book," Alpha Phi Fraternity made a genuine effort to place as many unemployed former cadets in jobs as possible. Its job placement activities operated parallel to the activities and goals of the Alumni Bureau. In addition to a well-organized fraternity, a directory, and a job placement service, Alpha Phi proposed that a "suitable building" be constructed to help coordinate and house the activities of the cadets and former students of the Alpha Phi Fraternity. As a practical matter, visitors to the A&M campus desperately needed housing facilities. In those days there was no hotel, motel, or other kind of accommodations—indeed, there was no incorporated community of College Station, and would not be until the eve of World War II. Bryan, in the 1890's, was a long, hard, dusty ride on horseback from the campus. Visitors had to stay in the homes of faculty or bunk in the cadet dorms. Alpha Phi's interest in a visitor center stimulated a similar plan by the Alumni Association. In 1901, J. H. Freeman '88 proposed that three alumni be named to solicit funds to support the building of an Alumni Center. The Alumni liked the idea and named Freeman, A. L. Banks, and H. P. Jordan to a committee to investigate the possibility of securing funds and a building site on the main campus. The following year, Banks reported that $544.00 had been pledged for construction costs, but that is as far as either the Alpha Phi or the Alumni Association prospect ever went. The dream of an Alumni Center took seventy years to become reality.

Local Alpha Phi Chapters

Alpha Phi's greatest contribution to the building of a strong, cohesive former students' association developed from its efforts to organize former students into local clubs. Plans called for an "organization with state and local chapters to be organized for social reunions and the like throughout the state wherever three or more ex-cadets reside." The local chapters, designated by a number in the order of their chronological organization, selected a distinguishing name.

Former cadets at the college organized the first local Alpha Phi chapter or club in 1897, following three years of informal activities by local former students. It was designated and named in honor of the founder of the fraternity: "Edward B. Cushing Chapter No. 1, APF." The college chapter, during its first week, numbered 46 members and was expected to reach more than 150 members within a month. Colonal T. Hadley Franklin '80, a Houstonian and close personal friend of Cushing, was the first president of this chapter. A chapter was organized in Bryan and called the "Thomas H. Gathright Chapter of Bryan." Captain John Q. Tabor '79, president of the chapter, said the local organization

The Ross Volunteers in 1901.

The 1898 football team was captained by Hal Mosley '98, shown holding the ball.

was named "for the grand, good, noble and sympathetic first president of the college." This was one of the few chapters that did not carry a designation number.

San Antonio organized a chapter in late 1897 which proved to be the most active and vigorous of the Alpha Phi local chapters. Professor Buell C. Pittuck, sponsor of the San Antonio group known as the "Sul Ross Chapter No. 2, APF," noted: "We named this chapter L. S. Ross not because he was one of the most distinguished of the governors of this state, nor yet because he was a gallant soldier, but because he has done more for the young men of Texas than any other man in her broad domain, and it will be the purpose of this chapter to maintain the honor of the name."

The full impact of the local chapters is difficult to trace. A few items distinguish the Alpha Phi chapters as special, innovative clubs. The Alpha Phi groups were the first to organize continuous local A&M clubs, they were the first collectively to encourage an A&M organization encompassing all former students, and they established a statewide network which for the first time favorably publicized the college and worked through local legislators to build legislative support for improved funding. Andrew L. Banks, alumni editor of the March, 1897, *Battalion*, informed the alumni that "the ex-students of the University of Texas had been called on through the press to take some active part in shaping legislation for the benefit of their Alma Mater. So it behooves our Alpha Phi men to bestir themselves and get chapters well organized throughout the state." This word of warning led to the formation of numerous chapters in late 1897, which it may be surmised paid substantial dividends by large increases in state funding for the A&M College over the next decade. By the turn of the century local Alpha Phi chapters had become the foundation for today's structure of Texas A&M Clubs, located all over the United States and in many parts of the world, which give so much of their time and effort in support of what Cushing called "good ole' A&M."

Ross's Death— 1898

Just three days after the turn of 1898 a tragedy befell the A&M College: Lawrence Sullivan Ross died at the age of fifty-nine. The heroic Indian fighter, Confederate general, Texas statesman, and A&M College president had been a central figure in Texas history. His contribution to Texas A&M during a most difficult time in the college's evolution was immeasurable. He commanded the support and cooperation of legislators, faculty, students, and former students. He realized early in his administration that the former students of Texas A&M could do more to insure the college's continued growth and expansion than any other single force. He believed in Texas A&M and its students. For that reason he was able to place the college on a sound academic and financial footing by the turn of the century. Seven months before Ross's unforeseen death, the *Galveston Daily News* said of this great Texan: "Under President Ross the college has grown in the knowledge and esteem of the people of Texas until it holds a place second to no institution in the state." The deep appreciation of and love for Ross held by every Aggie was expressed in the words of Charles C. Todd '97. Todd, valedictorian of the class of '97, later became commandant of the Corps of Cadets, president of the Brazos County A&M Club, and a successful lawyer. In his address at memorial services for Governor Ross on January 16, 1898, Todd said:

I bear tribute to the life of General Ross not as a soldier or as a statesman, that is left for his companions in war and state, but to his perseverance, kindness, and encouragement to us while students of this institution. To the Alumni of this college he needs no monument of marble, for his

The funeral bier of President Ross in early January, 1898. Former Texas Governors (*left to right*) Charles A. Culberson, Oran M. Roberts, John Ireland, and Joseph D. Sayers flank the casket.

image will ever remain fresh within our memories. His was the hand of encouragement extended to us when the dark shadows of failure threatened to envelope us, and despair would fain have taken the place of hope. In him we knew the master firm in requirements, yet ever ready to give praise to duty well performed, and encouragement to those worthy of it. As such we loved him, and as such we mourn for his loss second only to the loss of a father.

Seven years ago he found this college struggling for existence, since then, through his exertions mainly, it has risen to its present grandeur and usefulness. During that time he learned to love the institution, to love the students, as he was revered by them. During his presidency he gave them advice such as if followed would make them all men among men.

The Alumni Association and the Alpha Phi Fraternity both took part in memorial ceremonies honoring President Ross. The idea of a lasting memorial was discussed in late

Alumni of Texas A&M were involved from the beginning in the Spanish American War. Among A&M war veterans of Teddy Roosevelt's "splendid little war" were (*left to right*) Thomas Scurry, Captain George W. McCormick '91 (Alumni Association president, 1899–1900), and Lieutenant Milby Porter '91.

The Spanish-American War

January and early February, 1898. Original plans called for a marble statue to be erected in his honor on campus. Approval for the project, along with the needed funds, delayed the unveiling of a lasting tribute for more than twenty years.

In June the Alumni Association passed a special resolution commending the "prompt and enthusiastic" response of the alumni and faculty to "the call for men to bear arms in the defense of our country" in the Spanish-American War. The Alumni Association urged that outstanding A&M men be given direct commissions and "high places of responsibility in the Volunteer Guard" being assembled for the invasion of Cuba. Captain E. J. Smith, recently elected commander of Alpha Phi, was singled out by the Alumni Association to be highly recommended for service in the army. This was presumably not intended to be a move to undermine Alpha Phi, but was a vote of confidence in Smith; Smith, however, never joined the army.

San Antonio International Fair— November, 1899

The Sul Ross (San Antonio) Chapter No. 2 of the Alpha Phi Fraternity, under the joint leadership of Alex M. Ferguson '94, Charles E. Burgoon '95, and William B. Philpott, had become an unusually vigorous A&M club. It was always well represented at the annual campus meetings and supported many local activities among Aggies living in the San Antonio area. The club helped organize the San Antonio International Fair scheduled to open in November. The San Antonio former cadets persuaded city officials to name Saturday, November 4, 1899, "A&M College Day at the San Antonio International Fair."

Victory parade in the streets of Havana, Cuba, January 1, 1900.

This day was to be the climax of a week of festive parades, parties, poultry contests, livestock shows, flower shows, band concerts, and horse races.

The main attraction for visitors and former students would be the appearance en masse of the Corps Battalion from the A&M College. The Corps of Cadets had achieved distinction throughout the state during the college's first twenty-five years by appearances at parades and fairs. In 1878 the Cadet Corps had made its first "corps trip" to Houston to take part in the San Jacinto celebration and annual Houston parade. In the years that followed this first appearance, numerous trips were made by the corps to Houston to take part in Texas Independence Day activities. The trips to the San Jacinto battlefield were widely publicized throughout southern Texas. The corps took part in sham battles outfitted with weapons and artillery, enjoyed a luncheon on the grounds, and usually paraded the streets of Houston. The *Battalion* made this comment concerning the April, 1897, Houston corps trip: "The grand street parade came next and as the battalion, in column of companies, passed some prominent part of the city, it was always a signal for an outburst of applause from the crowds that had gathered on sidewalks, house tops, and every conceivable position to get a glimpse of the gallant boys in gray, and especially, were the

Alpha Phi Fraternity 47

Cadets form up in front of Old Main for a march to the Brazos River about 1900.

fair ladies of Houston and visiting towns loud in their praise of the gentlemanly and soldierly bearing of the A. and M. cadets."

Cadets made excited preparations for the trip to the San Antonio Fair. A special train departed A&M early Friday afternoon, November 3, with its "jolly passengers" and was delayed for two hours on the outskirts of Austin as a result of a freight train accident. Once the tracks were cleared, the train proceeded to New Braunfels, where the passengers were provided with a barbecue meal by local supporters of A&M. The travelers reboarded the train for the final leg of the trip, arriving in San Antonio at 9:00 P.M. The cadets were housed in the city armories, and the faculty was accommodated in the "elegant apartments" of the Hotel Menger. On Saturday morning the Cadet Battalion formed on Alamo Plaza and, led by the A&M Cadet Band, marched through the streets of San Antonio to the fairgrounds for the opening ceremonies of "A&M College Day at the Fair."

Varsity vs. College

After a morning of flower shows, poultry displays, horse races, and a "baby show," the fairgoers moved to the infield of the race track for the scheduled 1 P.M. football game between "the College boys and the varsity eleven." The University of Texas team arrived nearly two hours late, and by kickoff time, at 3:15 P.M., the crowd had grown in excess of five thousand. The *Battalion* believed the crowd to be the largest ever to witness a football game in Texas. It probably was. Hundreds of former students from A&M were among the crowd to watch what promised to be an exciting gridiron contest.

48 WE ARE THE AGGIES

The 1902 "Champions of the South." This team, coached by J. E. Platt (*top row, center*), was the first A&M team to beat the University of Texas. The score was 11 to 0.

The "Varsity eleven" on two previous occasions had easily outscored the "College eleven." A&M College coach W. A. Murray and team captain Hal Moseley had prepped the team with the latest tactics of football. The "Farmers," as students from A&M were called, had completed their 1898 season by defeating Tulane 22–0, LSU 52–0 and Baylor 33–0.

The A&M College Day game proved to be a toughly fought contest, centered mainly at midfield. After numerous punt exchanges, a Varsity player broke away late in the second quarter for a 45-yard touchdown run. Until this touchdown, the Farmers had held the Varsity to relatively few yards. The *Battalion* reported of the A&M offensive ability: "Using the famous 'guards back' style of play, they started down the field in a not-to-be-denied way. Play after play of these formidable ground gainers was uncorked and the ball went merrily down the field, bringing joy to the hearts that thumped wildly beneath those natty gray uniforms and breeding heart disease to the followers of the 'Varsity, over whom a deep, dark cloud with mournful trimmings and ebony linings was slowly settling."

Despite A&M's alleged prowess, the first half ended with the score 6–0 in Varsity's favor. Following a ten-minute intermission, Varsity began second half action by kicking off to A&M. After a few minutes of heated play at midfield, where both teams exchanged possession by punts, Varsity gained control of the ball and began to drive into A&M territory. But the Farmers held, forcing Varsity to attempt a field goal on the third down. (Before 1906 only three downs were allowed in each series of play.) The ball went wild, struck

Alpha Phi Fraternity

on the five yard line, and bounded toward midfield, where it was downed by a Texas player. Once downed by Texas, the umpire awarded the ball to the Varsity only yards from the goal line. But the Farmers protested bitterly, arguing that the ball had never been touched by an A&M player. Violent dispute broke out on the playing field when the umpire insisted that possession of the ball went to Texas. The Farmers felt the decision was gravely unfair. Team captain Hal Moseley picked up the game ball and led his team off the field to the train station and home to College Station without completing the game, and the referee awarded Varsity the victory. An Austin *Daily Statesman* sportswriter was surprisingly charitable toward A&M in his account of the game: "the game as a whole demonstrated the fact that the A&M College is to be the great future rival of the University for football honors." The following year, in 1900, A&M and Texas began playing their annual Thanksgiving Day ball game, beginning a rivalry that continues.

Alumni Association and Alpha Phi Unite

While the San Antonio Fair may have initiated a continuing gridiron rivalry between A&M and Texas, it was especially significant because it helped bring an end to the rivalry between Alpha Phi and the Alumni Association. Excited by the success of the joint efforts of all former students at the San Antonio Fair, and encouraged by an aura of comradeship and good feeling, W. B. Philpott, recently elected grand commander of Alpha Phi, Edward B. Cushing, Alex S. Ferguson, president of the San Antonio chapter of Alpha Phi, and others urged the two bodies to merge. No record exists of the actual disbanding of Alpha Phi. The Alpha Phi membership, along with their reunion programs, local chapters, and fund-raising efforts, were totally absorbed into the Alumni Association in 1900. While no constitutional revision was made to alter association membership requirements, all former Alpha Phi members, irrespective of their graduate or nongraduate status, were welcomed into the Alumni Association.

5. Football, Former Students... and Trouble

Despite enthusiasm generated in 1899, from 1900 to 1908 the Alumni Association continued to be handicapped by poor membership turnout and a lack of operating funds. The merger of the Alumni Association and the Alpha Phi Fraternity failed to be as inspiring as had been anticipated. Attempts to organize an official Alumni Association publication, to be known as the *Alumni Quarterly*, also failed. Efforts to attract alumni and former students to the annual meetings at the college were unproductive. Texas A&M clubs replaced the statewide Alpha Phi chapters, but the clubs grew slowly because of poor participation. Continued alienation of nongraduate former cadets by many alumni caused bad feelings. Although these circumstances and disorders were discouraging, a small nucleus of faithful alumni and former students worked diligently to reverse these trends and solve the problems.

Approximately 378 degrees had been awarded during A&M's first twenty-four years of operation, and of this number, an estimated 225 graduates were active in association activities. Some 3,000 former students were limited to token membership as a result of the Alumni Association constitution of 1896. This factionalism required mending before association revenues and participation could increase. The efforts of Alpha Phi during 1897–1899 seemed fruitless in light of the continued ostracizing of former students without degrees. Interestingly, it was an athletic event that had produced the union of former students' organizations, and it was sports, prominently football, that rejuvenated the bond of former students to the college.

Football Questioned by Faculty

At the close of the 1901 football season, the faculty and some college administrators began to complain that too much emphasis was being placed on sports, mainly football. The 1901 football season ended seven years of collegiate competition, during which the A&M teams compiled a 15-13-2 record. Until 1897, students or faculty had served as volunteer coaches for athletic activities. In 1897, students hired C. W. Taylor to serve as coach. When the Board of Directors, in 1901, hired George S. Whitney at a salary of one thousand dollars as physical director to take charge of the gymnasium and natatorium and to "direct the athletic sports of every character among the students," faculty members began to believe that sports had gone too far. The A&M faculty passed a rule prohibiting A&M football teams from meeting other Texas educational institutions in competitive football. The alumni, to put it mildly, were outraged.

Alumni Defend Athletics

The Alumni Association gave its unequivocal support for intercollegiate sports, stating that "athletics is conducive to health and development of young manhood resulting in the best interest of the college." Under pressure from the alumni, the Board of Directors "encouraged" the faculty to rescind its action and asked faculty members to support all sports programs. The faculty reluctantly complied but continued to complain.

The 1901 football team. Note the intertwined "AMC," which was the logo of Texas A&M during this period.

The 1902 A&M football team in Houston scoring to beat the University of Texas. Until the formation of the Southwest Conference in 1914, the two schools played at a neutral site, either Houston, San Antonio, or Dallas.

Alumni thought the support of athletics so important that they appointed a committee chaired by Harry P. Jordan '95 to encourage the faculty to permit the future advancement of all A&M sports programs. In late 1902 the administration created the General Athletic Association, a student-faculty committee supervising all athletics. The name was changed to the Athletic Council in 1906, and this body was responsible for game scheduling, ticket sales, athletic business, and other items relating to the sports programs at the college. In the fall of 1902, as if in response to the encouragement of the administration and the Alumni Association, the Farmers of A&M defeated the Varsity eleven of the University of Texas for the first time, 11–0. The 7–0–2 record of Coach James Edward Platt resulted in the team's being named champions of the South. By 1903, with the assistance and support of the alumni, athletics was given a permanent, if not prominent, place in development.

The students and former students became increasingly interested in the advancement of college sports. This enthusiasm had the effect of drawing more and more alumni back to the campus during football season and creating more interest in their alma mater. Slowly, events and social functions were being conducted on campus during home football weekends. These early activities were a prelude to active class reunion programs.

Accommodations for visitors at Texas A&M football games became increasingly insufficient. Notices were printed in the Bryan papers encouraging residents to warn their relatives and friends of this inconvenience. Visitors were also encouraged to "bring your own lunch," since dining facilities were few. Campus facilities were equally taxed during commencement periods, causing the administration to announce that "admission was restricted in the mess hall exclusively to those guests from a distance." Cadets often gave up their rooms to accommodate guests. Travel between the campus and Bryan also continued to be difficult. To relieve this problem, trains were scheduled to run from Bryan to the campus on both railroad tracks every hour and "therefore no special inconvenience will result." The problems with visitor housing and transportation continued for years.

An Alumni Center

In 1902 the Alumni Association asked the college Board of Directors for permission to use part of Gathright Hall as a home for the alumni. The alumni said they would be willing to supply funds and labor to decorate the accommodations. The idea of using space in an existing campus building was seen as a more feasible action than the collection of funds for the construction of an "Alumni Hall," but by mid-1903 no action had been taken, and no space had been made available in Gathright. Efforts to obtain campus space also failed in 1904 and resulted in the appointment of another committee in 1905 to "secure funds for building an Associational Hall." There is no record of the 1905 committee taking any action, but in 1906 a group of professors on campus constructed a private hotel called the Shirley which provided some relief. A gasoline-powered interurban trolley between the campus and Bryan began operation in 1910 and further eased the problem of inadequate guest accommodations at the college. Throughout the years from 1900 to 1910 attendance by alumni at A&M football games increased rapidly as the Aggies began to field championship teams.

Football may have had something to do with one of the most critical confrontations in A&M's history between the president of the college and the students and alumni. A number of situations, including a prohibited trip by the Corps of Cadets to a football game in

The Shirley Hotel, erected in 1906. Before construction of the YMCA, the Shirley served as the headquarters of many on-campus alumni activities.

The Great Trouble

Dallas between Texas A&M and the University of Texas in 1907, aroused the students and former students as nothing had done before or since.

Henry Hill Harrington assumed duties as president on September 8, 1905, after the departure of David Franklin Houston, who resigned to assume the presidency of the University of Texas. Although warmly welcomed by the students, Harrington experienced great difficulty in solving campus problems created by overcrowded conditions due to a housing shortage. During the 1907–1908 school term more than one hundred cadets were housed in thirty-six tents near the present location of the YMCA Building. Student leadership within each class of the Corps of Cadets directed student hostility against Harrington because of harsh conditions.

Harrington further antagonized students when on April Fool's Day, 1906, a number of cadets cut chapel. When the cadets were put in the guardhouse by the commandant, Harrington ordered them released and incurred cadet hostility for interfering in corps discipline. A few months later Harrington reprimanded the sophomore class for hazing the freshmen. Harrington also expressed public disapproval of a *Battalion* editorial criticizing his administration and praising his predecessor, D. F. Houston. The 1906–1907 school year ended seventeen days early because of a typhoid epidemic, but through the summer and until the opening of the 1907–1908 school year the student discontent continued. The cadets returned in the fall of 1907 to find that their hero and supporter, Corps Commandant Captain Herbert H. Sargent, had been transferred. This left the corps without a reliable, trusted outlet and audience for student complaints.

"The Twins" — Mary and Sophie Hutson, (left), both class of '03. The Hutsons were the daughters of history professor Dr. Charles W. Hutson (right), and each earned a degree in civil engineering.

As if the departure of their trusted commandant was not enough, within a week after classes resumed for the fall, Harrington tried to prevent the students from making their annual corps trip to Dallas for the "big game" with Texas. Already entrenched in the tradition of the corps trips, the corps had requested the president's approval for travel en masse to Dallas on October 12. Harrington vetoed this trip without explanation. Infuriated, the corps chartered its own train and traveled to Dallas against the wishes of the president.

Carl P. Brannin '09 of Dallas described another possible cause of tension during the fall of 1907. Harrington and Nathan Powell, adjunct professor of language and campus chaplain, were involved in arguments over personal matters. "Stud Horse" Powell, as the popular chaplain was known to the cadets, had made a habit of renting his chestnut stallion Fernando with its English riding saddle to any paying cadet. Cadets were known to use this means of transportation for a quick trip to Bryan or into the neighboring countryside without permission from the president. Because of this enterprise, Powell was fired in August but was allowed to remain on campus until December 1, 1907, while he appealed. After his dismissal became final in early December, he wrote letters of protest to the state legislature, the Board of Directors of Texas A&M, and the governor of Texas, Thomas M. Campbell.

Tension between Harrington and the student body reached the breaking point during the Christmas holidays in 1907. The young grandchild of popular history professor Dr. Charles W. Hutson, visiting from New York, was believed to have contracted whooping

Football, Former Students . . . and Trouble 55

cough, a dreaded disease which had historically taken its toll among young children. The college physician, Dr. Joe Gilbert, examined the child and requested the Hutsons to quarantine the sick youth until he recovered from his illness. President Harrington, upon hearing of the illness, ordered Dr. Gilbert to quarantine the entire family. He went so far as not to allow servants and guests to enter or leave the Hutson house. This edict, which Dr. Gilbert felt was unnecessary, altered the Hutsons' daily routine, disrupted their Christmas holidays, and hampered Dr. Hutson's teaching obligations. Harrington's overreaction was a result of his fear, most likely more his wife's than his own, that their only surviving, frail child might contract the illness. The Harringtons had lost their firstborn to a previous whooping cough epidemic earlier in 1907. Differences broadened when Harrington demanded that the Hutsons be confined to quarters or leave campus. This treatment made cadets and faculty equally unhappy with Harrington. In addition to the fact that Hutson was a popular professor, his son, Miles, was a member of the corps, and an attack upon the Hutson family was viewed as an attack on the Corps of Cadets.

Following the Christmas recess, the Board of Directors held their first spring term meeting on campus on February 6, 1908. During this board session a committee representing the senior class of '08 requested that it be given time to present complaints concerning President Harrington. Cadets had accumulated a list of charges as evidence of Harrington's mismanagement. The cadets felt that the key charge which might precipitate an investigation by the Board of Directors was Harrington's failure to return fees to students when school had been suspended several weeks early in the previous year "as a result of the typhoid epidemic." The board denied the seniors an audience and answered criticisms of Harrington with two resolutions: (1) any future complaints must be submitted in writing to the president of the board, and (2) the board publicly exonerated Harrington of any wrongdoings and pledged to support him. The board then adjourned its session on Friday evening, February 7, 1908.

The Strike of 1908

On the same Friday evening the senior class met on three different occasions, well into the early hours of Saturday morning, and decided to launch a strike. The new commandant, Captain Andrew ("Bull") Moses, and football coach L. L. Larson addressed the senior class urging them to work out their animosities and not walk out. A secret midnight vote among seniors resulted in a majority pledge to attend drill and uphold the college regulations but not to attend class. At 8:05 Saturday morning when the bugle sounded for classes, no one showed up; thus the AMC strike of 1908 was on.

On Tuesday, February 11, a few cadets did return to classes as a result of a board-faculty joint resolution to suspend those not attending classes. On Wednesday the seniors presented to the board their formal charges and at 3:30 P.M. marched to the armory in Old Main to check in their gear and weapons. By February 13 only 100 of a total of 625 cadets remained on campus.

Alumni React to the Strike

The strike was well into its first week when the Alumni Association and A&M clubs statewide, aroused by the disturbance, began steps to mediate and resolve the confrontation. On February 18 the Dallas A&M Club met to discuss the problem and consider a course of action. After a review of the facts, which included interviews with cadets in the local area, they resolved that action should at once be taken "to secure a meeting of the Alumni Association at the earliest possible date." A committee of three, composed of A. Semones Adams '95, William Hamlyn Furneaux '09, and Howard Woodal '05, was

Left, Joe Utay '08, as a result of "The Trouble," departed Texas A&M along with other class members in early February, 1908, never to return as a student. Utay later finished law school at Cumberland University in Tennessee and for seventy years was active in support of Texas A&M and the Southwest Athletic Conference. *Right,* Commandant of Cadets Captain Andrew ("Bull") Moses about 1908.

assigned to carry out the task. Upon the completion of the Dallas club meeting, they began at once to contact various A&M clubs statewide by "long distance telephone."

All the A&M clubs contacted approved the Dallas club's proposition that action be taken at once. In accordance with this verbal approval, the Dallas committee of three issued a call in writing for a meeting of "all A. and M. Clubs of Texas in the city of Houston, Saturday morning, February 22nd" in order to review the serious situation which existed at the college. In addition to the requested meeting, they encouraged a session of the Executive Committee of the Alumni Association on the same date to help the students and college "shoulder their troubles." Under the signatures of Adams, Furneaux, and Woodal, the communique ended: "We desire to appeal to your love for the institution, and to you as a citizen of this state, to preserve the institution for the education of our Texas boys, and your presence at this meeting is most earnestly requested."

After Houston was selected as the site for the special meeting, James Cravens '82, president of the Harris County A&M Club, began at once to make arrangements for the visiting delegates:

To the Members of the Harris County Agricultural and Mechanical Club:

Gentlemen: Upon request of the Agricultural and Mechanical Clubs of Palestine, Dallas and Temple, we have invited the delegates from the various clubs of the State of Texas to assemble in

Alva Mitchell '94 helped coordinate the Alumni Association's efforts on campus to end the "Strike of '08." Mitchell was secretary of the association from 1906 until 1914.

H. H. Harrington, president of Texas A&M, 1905–1908.

Houston at the Rice Hotel on Saturday morning at 10 o'clock, February 22, 1908, for the purpose of discussing matters affecting the interests of the College.

We have secured the rooms of the Houston Business League for the meeting at 10 o'clock, and you are especially urged to be at the Rice Hotel as early as possible on Saturday morning to assist in entertaining the delegates.

Yours very truly,
JAMES CRAVENS, President

W. J. Walden, '00 Secretary

As plans were being formulated for the Houston meeting, the Executive Committee of the Alumni Association met in special session on February 20 in Bryan. The committee was composed of association President Francis Marion Law of Bryan, Buell Colbern Pittuck '94 of Dallas, and Alva Mitchell '94 of College Station. All had been busy individually during the week trying to encourage students to return to classes. Many other faculty and alumni were also involved in an effort to return cadets to class.

Mitchell, in addition to being secretary-treasurer of the Alumni Association, was an instructor in architectural engineering and drawing at the college. Although his relationship with Harrington had been strained as a result of his efforts to convene the Farmers' Congress on campus, to which Harrington objected, he continued to work for the students' return to classes. The Farmers' Congress, held annually between 1905 and 1916, had channeled considerable public support to Texas A&M. The Alumni Association, in turn, supported the congress's activities as long as the programs were in the best interests of the college.

After a careful review of the events on campus and the action taken by A&M clubs statewide, the Executive Committee "unanimously endorsed the action of President Law in his efforts to persuade the students to resume their work at the college." This action, along with resolutions adopted by the Board of Directors, resulted in a few more cadets returning to the campus. Oddly enough, more seniors than any other class members remained on the campus. With graduation only months away, some were reluctant to lose four years of study and work. While the seniors were cautious in their action, the juniors remained in rebellion and out of class. The juniors pledged to boycott and remain out of class until Harrington was removed from office. Law and others felt if this pledge was revoked, freshmen and sophomores would, along with the protesting juniors, return to class. Law, on February 21, met with the forty-four juniors "represented in person and by telegram" to discuss retraction of their pledge. He promised them that a complete investigation of the administration would be carried out by the association. After two hours of debate, thirty-five of the forty-four juniors voted to allow Law and the association to handle the investigation.

Cadets Return—and Some Do Not

They were additionally promised that their "reinstatement" would follow without punishment or harassment. Since those in favor were a majority of the sixty-five-man junior class, it was hoped that tensions would ease. Similar meetings were planned but never held with the freshman and sophomore classes. Paul A. Casey '08, editor of the *Battalion* and associate editor of the *Longhorn*, said, "Since each of these classes had pledged to stand by the juniors, the individuals of these classes considered the action of the junior class as binding on them also." By late Friday, February 21, 1908, 233 cadets were back on campus. When interviewed by the local Bryan paper, Captain Moses believed that the corps would be back to its normal strength by the following Monday. Law and the Executive Committee departed for the special Houston meeting early Saturday morning confident that they had turned the tide.

At 10 A.M. on Saturday, February 22, seventy delegates or "old A. and M. men" from throughout Texas gathered to review the situation. Of this gathering Paul Casey wrote:

Houston Meeting— February, 1908

The call for the meeting of the old students of the College at Houston February 22nd, was attended by seventy delegates from all parts of the State where there are any considerable number of old A. and M. men. The intense interest possessed these former college men, some of whom have grown gray in the business and professional world, but whose devotion and loyalty to their alma mater is yet so strong a cord that it can pull them away from busy office and counting room to spend a day in considering the things that seem to them to threaten the best interests of the old College.

This special meeting was called to order by John Q. Tabor '81, chairman of the special session of the association. Casey states that the mood of the meeting was largely anti-Harrington. After introductory remarks by Mayor Dave Rice of Houston, E. J. Smith '88 rose, moving that Harrington's resignation be demanded at once. Smith's motion was met with roaring applause and shouts.

However, heated debate followed, which resulted in Smith's retracting his motion in favor of one which authorized the association to conduct a "complete investigation of the

Football, Former Students . . . and Trouble 59

whole trouble" and submit its findings to the Board of Directors for their action. A committee composed of James Cravens, chairman; Frank A. Reichardt of Houston; E. J. Smith '88 of Denison; H. L. Wright '86 of Palestine; and Charles C. Todd '97 of San Antonio were selected to represent the Alumni Association in the investigation.

The investigators were encouraged to review all the student complaints before submitting their report. The alumni felt that it was not in the best interest of the college for the students to go before the Board of Directors. F. M. Law commented of the association's involvement, "The A&M boys would be rattled to a frazzle if not aided by the alumni when bringing their grievances before the college board."

The association also promised the cadets that if they would return and resume classes, "the alumni and ex-students, would undertake to have an open, full and fair investigation, to the end that the truth of the situation might be known and the necessary relief obtained." Two public resolutions were adopted at the close of the meeting. The first asked for the investigation, and the second reaffirmed the desire for the cadets to return to classes. A third confidential resolution was sent to the Board of Directors outlining the above two resolutions and again calling for a complete investigation. This measure was used to further impress upon the board the alumni's concern over the state of affairs at the college.

Investigation Denied

The Board of Directors met at College Station on February 24 to review the requests of the alumni and former students. The request for an investigation was denied, and the board repeated their support of Harrington as president of the college. Pleased with the Houston meeting and dissatisfied with the board's continued protection of Harrington, the senior class turned over all matters concerning the investigation to the alumni and pledged to make no more public statements which might harm their case against the president. By March 10, four hundred cadets had returned to campus, and forty-one of the sixty-five juniors were back in uniform.

While classes slowly returned to normal, the alumni remained persistent in their efforts to encourage an investigation. They met with the board on March 20 to review its inaction. As the committee reminded the board in June, "At an informal meeting held with you gentlemen on the occasion of the laying of the corner stone of Goodwin Hall, in March of this year, you agreed to resume and consider on Monday morning, June 8, 1908, at College Station, such charges or complaints respecting the management of the college, its affairs and faculty, as we, the committee, saw proper to present." The association urged the board to take action before additional problems arose.

During March and April hostilities seemed to cool; however, in May a special junior class edition of the *Battalion* accused Harrington of making false public statements that the college was back to normal. No mention was made concerning the previous problems on campus. The board aggravated this situation when it ordered those responsible for the editorial punished. Seven juniors were suspended, causing the remainder of the student body to protest. The protest might have been more vigorous had it not occurred during final exam week. With this incident added to the long list of grievances, the stage was set for a showdown between the board and the alumni during commencement week in mid-June.

The twenty-second annual meeting of the Alumni Association convened in the Veterinary Lecture Room at 9 A.M. on June 8, 1908. Tension and excitement filled the air.

After reading the minutes of the 1907 annual meeting, the chair recognized E. J. Smith and C. C. Todd. As representatives of the select committee named in Houston, they presented the charges to be filed with the board against Harrington.

Former Students, Unite!

The meeting, similar to others held during the previous days and weeks, was well attended. The past split between the alumni and the former students was closing rapidly. The following passage records the effort to organize all former students into a strongly united body for the support of the college and students: "A motion prevailed to invite all ex-students of the college to sit in the meeting." This trend toward united action was present at all the special meetings of the "old A. and M. men" during the early part of 1908 as they collectively weathered the campus trouble. The student strike, as severe an incident as it was, ended some thirty years of open rejection by the alumni of the nongraduate former cadets and former students.

Financial problems, also a stumbling block for years, were solved when $1,015 was collected to offset the expenses of the association in its investigation. The Houston A&M Club gathered $385 from its members attending the session. The Dallas, Brazos County, San Antonio, Beaumont, Bell County, Colorado County, and Palestine clubs followed suit by donating a combined total of $395. A donation of $50 from the New York City "ex-students of A. and M.," along with numerous individual gifts, placed the association in the best financial position it had known for over twenty years. The penniless years of the 1890's and early 1900's were over. The sentiments of the alumni can best be seen in their 1908 commencement yell:

> A-lum, Alumni, Alumnus,
> Patrons, A. & M. fuss, fuss, fuss,
> Cravens, Todd, and Law! Law! Law!
> Anti Harry, Anti Harry, Rah! Rah! Rah!

C. C. Todd was selected to present the charges against Harrington to the board. Although the list of charges is lengthy, it is only fitting to present it here.

Alumni Charges against the President

1. Harrington was charged as being a man of "high temper, domineering disposition . . . and quarrelsome to the faculty and cadets."

2. The president was charged with engaging in fist fights with both faculty and cadets.

3. The president was said to have made a "murderous assault with a shotgun upon a student" without cause, "using profane, abusive and vulgar language."

4. The association charged that as a result of his actions he was "not in touch with the students."

5. The president was said to have "alienated the faculty." For this reason many had resigned, and the discipline of cadets had dwindled as a result.

6. He was charged with mismanagement of the college, giving more concern to his own affairs than to those of the college.

7. He had willfully withheld maintenance funds due to "patrons of the school at the close of the session of 1907."

8. Further, the association charged that he misused student deposits which were to be refunded to parents if no "property was damaged or destroyed."

9. It was stated that he was drawing more than one salary, "not as president but as

a head of a number of departments connected with the college." This they asserted was, "wrong in principle, if not in law . . . and tended to commercialize the great position he occupies."

10. He was charged by the association with "purchasing a large supply of intoxicating liquor, evidently with college funds." His actions were deemed to be "a detriment to good morals, and a bad example to the student body."

11. He was accused of "wanting in executive ability, and in power to control the student body" because of (a) the strike of January–February, 1908; (b) the fact that he had been hung twice in effigy "on the college grounds"; and (c) the low credibility he held with the student body.

12. He was accused of having hampered freedom of the press, "by favoring and urging the indefinite suspension of the editorial staff of the *Battalion*" when they published a denial to an interview he had with an Austin newspaper.

13. Finally, the association summarized the previous twelve charges by saying that he had "lost the respect of the student body."

In closing, Todd advised the board that the association was prepared to "furnish full and convincing proof of these matters." He urged the Board of Directors to investigate at their earliest convenience, if for no other reason than to satisfy the alumni and parents concerned with the well-being of the college. Todd further stated that he and the association would be willing to aid the board in an effort to "arrive at the truth." The morning session ended with a motion that the report and charges be submitted to the board. With this accomplished, the meeting stood in recess until 2:30 P.M.

The alumni present at the afternoon session waited eagerly for the board's reply as it met across campus to consider the charges. While the alumni waited, reports were heard from seven Texas A&M clubs—Dallas, Palestine, Houston, Beaumont, San Antonio, Colorado County, and Brazos County. The reports were presented by members of these clubs and contained information concerning their organization and activities. The strike had had a definite impact on the organization of these clubs. As a result of the trouble, former cadets had gathered in many parts of the state to lend support in solving the 1908 problems. Many club members worked at their own expense with the association to investigate Harrington. During the late afternoon, after conducting routine business, steps were taken by the association members to amend the constitution of 1896 to include all former students in the association's activities.

A committee composed of B. C. Pittuck, Cushing, J. Webb Howell '94, H. C. Kyle '96, and William L. Dazey '94 proposed the following amendment, which proved to be a giant step toward a unified Alumni Association, welcoming all former students: "Any ex-student who shall have attended regular classes for at least one year at this College and who left the college in good standing may make application for and be eligible to membership in the Alumni Association, enjoying all privileges except the right to hold office in the Association." Thus, perhaps because of football, but especially because of the "Great Strike," former students of the A&M College were united into one cohesive association.

The Board Investigates

Tension was high during the evening meal as cadets, alumni, former students, and parents discussed the eventful day. The Alumni Association reconvened to review an updated report from Cravens on the board's activities. He reported that the board was still taking the association's resolutions under advisement. With no answer at hand, the associ-

Cadets with bedrolls and rations preparing for a hike to the Brazos about 1903.

ation's meeting was adjourned until 10 A.M., Tuesday, June 9. Private debate over Harrington's misdeeds and his mismanagement of the college continued into the late hours of the night.

At 10 A.M. on June 9 the long-awaited news was received, and the Board of Directors made the following announcement in reply to the Alumni Association's charges: "An investigation of the charges and conditions as set out in the resolutions presented by the Association would begin at 2 P.M., Tuesday, June 9th." Even though Harrington was unpopular, the board felt that he had held the school together during trying times with good leadership. The investigation and hearing began on June 10 and ran until June 22. Attorney Hatton W. Sumners of Dallas, representing the association, presented many witnesses and documents. Many former students and alumni felt that item 13, charging that the president had "lost the respect of the student body" had been admitted by Harrington. Sumners communicated with Cravens in Houston summarizing the details of the hearings. On each of the thirteen charges lengthy evidence was presented by Sumners to support the position of the students and association. Over 850 typewritten pages were recorded. In his letter to Cravens, Sumners indicated that the last charge, that the president had "lost the respect of the student body," was the most important.

After ten days of hearings, the board recessed to consider the evidence. To the amaze-

Cadets during the early 1900's.

Cadets in 1908 engaged in target practice. The uniform during this period was patterned after that of Teddy Roosevelt's Rough Riders.

ment of all, Harrington was once again supported by the Board of Directors and found innocent of all thirteen charges.

It is fortunate that the cadets were away during the summer break, or additional trouble and friction probably would have followed this decision. Friction did occur among the faculty and staff. On June 22, 1908, the same day the verdict concerning Harrington was announced, five employees resigned. Among these was Charles Hutson, professor of history and economics. Turmoil and confusion reigned on the campus.

Then, without any advance warning, Harrington yielded on August 7, 1908, and submitted his resignation to the Board of Directors. The resignation was accepted without question. The news of Harrington's action pleased students and alumni alike. At last, months of ill feelings and tension were finally at an end.

Harrington Resigns

F. M. Law and James Cravens, along with the many A&M clubs and individual former students, helped provide a means for the speedy disposition of this potentially damaging circumstance. It is regrettable that the differences between Harrington and the student body could not have been settled and that a breech of faith between both parties prevented the solution. The speedy actions of the Alumni Association, without a doubt, helped to solve the campus difficulties. Its members mediated a workable solution with the students, encouraging them to return en masse to class. With the students' return to classes, the association pledged to mediate and investigate the trouble. The association's actions, if nothing else, prevented a possible investigation by an outside committee, namely, the Texas legislature, which probably would not have been as open-minded as the Board of Directors and the Alumni Association. Only a few years before the trouble, discussions had been entertained in the Texas legislature to curtail the future of the A&M College and possibly close it if necessary. The arguments stated that because of its remote location and costly operating budget the college was not a practical endeavor for Texas taxpayers.

The rallying of the alumni and former students to the support of the college without a doubt helped bring about two of the most important steps toward a better-organized association. The first was the unification of both alumni and former students statewide in the name of the association to support the college. The interest exhibited by the former students in their alma mater, in addition to individual efforts and personal contributions, was unprecedented. Second, the A&M clubs, through which this interest and concern were channeled, became a formative and valuable part of the association's future. Moreover, the relationship of the Alumni Association to the college administration had changed imperceptibly. Not only did the association now play a supportive role in the affairs of the college, but when it came to football and the tenure of presidents, the influence of the alumni could be decisive as well as supportive.

Robert Teague Milner, president of Texas A&M, 1908–1913.

6. *Train Ride to Valley Junction*

Colonel Robert Teague Milner became president of the college on August 7, 1908. Alumni were delighted with Milner's selection. He previously served as state commissioner of agriculture, and in 1905 Governor Samuel W. T. Lanham had appointed him to the Texas A&M Board of Directors. His experience as an administrator, intimate knowledge of the affairs of the college, interest in agricultural studies, and high regard for the Corps of Cadets made him an excellent choice for the position at a critical time in A&M's development.

The confusion of 1908, and the mistrust students and some alumni held for the administration, seemed to evaporate. Moreover, the publicity given the college during the Great Strike had surprising results. Having now heard of the college, its location, and its interesting programs, new students flocked to enroll. The corps, which numbered 600 in 1908, jumped to 825 cadets by November, 1909. Increased enrollments caused expansion of the original organization of the four company-size units into two battalions, each consisting of four companies. Membership in the Alumni Association also rose. The association continued to accept all cadets who had finished one year of college. In 1911 a new alumni constitution officially expanded membership to include all graduates and former students. Thus, the adversities of 1908 seemed to generate great expectations instead of disillusionment.

YMCA Alumni Project

Now that its nettlesome membership controversy was resolved, the Alumni Association entered a new era. Old ideas, such as the construction of an alumni hall, became new realities. Having searched unsuccessfully for ways and means of building their own hall on campus or acquiring existing college space, the alumni in 1910 decided to approach the problem from a fresh perspective. Edward B. Cushing, a member of the executive committee, along with James Cravens of the Houston A&M Club and Alva Mitchell, an A&M professor and secretary of the Alumni Association, presented a plan to build a hall which would jointly serve students and alumni without being idle part of the year. The result of their efforts was the creation by the association of a joint community, student, faculty, and alumni drive to raise money to erect a YMCA-Alumni Memorial Building.

At the 1910 annual meeting Cushing reported that the corps had raised "among themselves" about ten thousand dollars, the faculty about five thousand dollars, and the people of Bryan about seven thousand dollars. Cushing secured a pledge from the Board of Directors "that they will raise 10% of the amount necessary to construct the building." In the excitement of the 1910 meeting, Frederick E. Giesecke moved that the dues be raised from one dollar to five dollars to increase the treasury. "After considerable discussion" this attempt to increase the association's dues met defeat. The funds for the new YMCA would have to become available without the dues increase.

The YMCA Building under construction in 1913 viewed from the top of the rotunda of the Academic Building.

68   WE ARE THE AGGIES

The Association of Former Students held their annual meetings from the 1920's through the late 1940's in the "Y."

Cushing and others busied themselves during late 1910, lobbying in the state legislature for additional funding to improve the dorms and buildings of the college. Since 1900 the Alumni Association had played an active role in lobbying for funding before the state legislature. Although increases in state funding for the A&M College may have been coincidental, A&M budgets did increase substantially over the decade, and a safe presumption is that the efforts of the Alumni Association were at least in part responsble for the improvement. Meanwhile, the fund drive for the YMCA project continued, but donations became increasingly more difficult to obtain. Fortunately, the association, in cooperation with the college, succeeded in obtaining a large construction grant from John D. Rockefeller.

The cornerstone for the YMCA Building was laid on June 10, 1912. Frederick E. Giesecke, college architect, supervised construction. Dedication ceremonies for the Y, which housed a barber shop, bowling alleys, locker room, showers, and swimming pool, were conducted on February 15, 1915. The association first met in the Y on June 7, 1915, but the Y never became the alumni facility that it was intended to become. Once construction was complete, the alumni realized that it would be an injustice to occupy space sorely needed by the college and its students. The building was given over to the college and

Train Ride to Valley Junction 69

The trolley constructed in 1910 provided a "rapid transit" link between the college and nearby Bryan.

The Trolley

the YMCA for their supervision. Once again, the association was without a permanent home, but the benefits of the structure to the college and students were immeasurable. The building is still the administrative home for many of the university's services.

Another dream which the Alumni Association helped to awaken was that of former President David F. Houston, who wanted to establish regular commuter rail service between the college and Bryan. This service, he believed, would relieve the critical housing shortage on the campus and make temporary facilities, as on football weekends, available for visitors. The Board of Directors and alumni representatives prevailed upon private investors from Shreveport, Louisiana, to construct a gasoline interurban line to run from the North Gate of the college, along what are now College and Cavitt avenues, to Bryan. Construction began in 1909 and was completed in 1910.

The *Bryan Eagle* announced the inauguration of trolley service on May 28, 1910: "The people's long dream—rapid transit between Bryan and College, is at last about to be realized and it is enough to cause them to rejoice." Once installed, service by the gasoline-driven trolley was erratic, but it was a great improvement over walking. In 1915 the system was electrified and ran more smoothly. Mrs. Ida Wipprecht Kernodle, daughter of Walter Wipprecht, remembers riding the trolley as a child; the round trip cost twenty-five cents. The country over the five-mile stretch between the college and Bryan was barren except for two abandoned stone houses. In remembering her many trips to the college with her father, Mrs. Kernodle said, "The trolley never had enough electricity when loaded. The cadets would drop off when it reached a crest in the land, help push it up the small rise, then jump back on." Many old Aggies remember the experience. The trolley, though, marked A&M's emergence into the modern age. By 1912, F. E. Giesecke was even parking an automobile on the A&M campus, but the road to Bryan remained a haz-

F. E. Giesecke provided much of the leadership of the association during the 1920's. His active role resulted in the creation of the Association of Former Students and the financial support of alumni for many on-campus construction projects.

Farmers vs. Longhorns

ardous one until the 1920's, when the automobile age brought an end to A&M's trolley.

Perhaps the highlight of the 1910 school year was A&M's victory over the Longhorns of the University of Texas (14–8) in Houston. A specially called session of the Alumni Association followed the afternoon game. In addition to a victory celebration, the meeting was called to "consider important questions affecting needed legislation for the college." When President-elect Kamp McGinnis '00 of Terrell lost his voice from "loud and vigorous cheering over the victory," Andrew C. Love '99 stepped to the podium to calm the boisterous Aggies. A lively debate then ensued over proposals to revise the Texas Constitution as it affected the funding of Texas A&M and the University of Texas. The question then before the Texas legislature was whether or not Texas A&M should remain a branch of the university as provided in the Constitution of 1876. As a branch, Texas A&M was entitled to share in revenues derived from university lands which had been set aside by the Republic of Texas and subsequent state legislatures as an endowment for the university. Since 1883, when the University of Texas opened its doors, A&M had received only token funding from the university endowment, which was administered by the Board of Regents of the University of Texas. Throughout the 1880's and 1890's the university and the college battled over the allocation of funds. Finally, after the turn of the century, supporters of the two institutions began to search for a permanent settlement of the dispute. It must be remembered that before 1926, revenues from the university fund were counted in the thousands of dollars instead of the millions of dollars, for oil had not yet been discovered. Nonetheless, in those days every dollar of funding was terribly important to Texas' money-starved and growing public institutions.

Separating A&M from the University

Edward B. Cushing told the alumni that "A&M has never received its fair share of the said University funds," and therefore it should be separated from the university by the introduction of a new amendment to the Texas Constitution which would also divide the land endowment proportionately between the two institutions. The separate and independent existence of the college, Cushing states, was justified since "the field of action, plan of operation and purpose of the A&M College are essentially and materially different from those of the University." In concluding his remarks, Cushing encouraged the association collectively to bring the matter before the governor, the Texas legislature, and the citizens of the state.

Association President Kamp McGinnis '00 named a committee with plenary powers to lobby for Texas A&M in Austin. In addition to serving as lobbyists, the members of this committee were "empowered to call upon members of the Association and friends of the college for assistance" in an effort to keep them informed of the association's position on such important matters. Over the next decade the question of separation preoccupied the attention of the administration and the Alumni Association. Perhaps it was appropriate that the college association operated from a firmer constitutional base during these trying times.

The Constitution of 1911

As recommended by an alumni study group in 1910, a new constitution, written by Phineas S. Tilson and Edward B. Cushing, was prepared for the consideration of the association. On June 2, 1911, alumni approved each article separately and then accepted the entire document by voice vote. The name, the Alumni Association of the A&M College of Texas; the objective and purpose, "to perpetuate and strengthen lines of affection and esteem formed in college days . . . for the improvement of the A&M College"; the dues,

Tent life in 1908, as cadets await Saturday morning inspection.

one dollar; and the by-laws remained the same as those embodied in the Alumni Association Constitution of 1896.

The major changes in the constitution occurred in membership requirements and in the election of officers. The new constitution stated that any former student of "The A&M College of Texas who shall have attended the regular classes *for at least one session*" (italics mine) would be eligible for the full rights of association membership. New members in this category were to be nominated before each annual meeting. The constitution of 1911 read, "All electives for membership shall be on nomination and *viva voce* unless a ballot be called for by any member present, and then six negative ballots shall be sufficient to reject." This provision for rejection of a former student has never been used.

Except for minor changes in the wording, the membership requirement has remained basically the same since 1911. The constitution of 1911 also included a membership clause for those who received only a postgraduate degree and provision for honorary membership to "any person who has rendered conspicuous service to the Association, or to the A&M College of Texas, or to the advancement of education in Texas." The 1896 constitution had limited membership to bona fide graduates only, while the 1911 constitution was written to encompass all former students. Thus, the basic composition of the modern Association of Former Students came to be after thirty years of trial and tribulation.

The officers of the reorganized association now included a president, three vice-presidents, and a secretary and treasurer, the change being in the number of vice-presidents.

Membership Requirements Changed

Train Ride to Valley Junction 73

Left, The original Aggie ring designed in the late 1880's featured an intertwined "AMC" surrounded by four small diamonds. *Right*, In 1894 a ring committee was formed to design what has evolved into today's Aggie Ring.

By the old constitution, one vice-president was to be elected from the classes "numbering from 1878 to 1884 inclusive" and one for each succeeding five-year period, that is, 1885–1889, 1890–1894, and so on. By 1910 there were six vice-presidents representing graduates from the first thirty-two years of the college, 1878–1910. The elimination of numerous vice-presidents resulted in greater importance being attached to the office of class agent. The class agent enabled Aggies to retain an identification with their class while coordinating class activities with those of the association. And A&M clubs allowed Aggies of whatever class year to relate to each other and to their college on a geographical basis. By 1911 the working structure of that one great Aggie fraternity had been created.

The Aggie Ring

The Aggie Ring became the official emblem of fraternal bond by Alumni action in 1911. The association approved a measure declaring the class ring designed in 1894 to be the "signet ring of the Alumni Association." The Aggie Ring today is the product of years of evolution, born out of tradition and love for the institution.

The desire for a symbol to represent a student's days at A&M was first expressed in early 1889. The end result of the wish was a unique but now forgotten ring. The design selected had the letters "AMC," surrounded by four small diamonds, intertwined across its face. It was cast in solid gold. Only two of these rings exist today. The distinctive design was used only for the class of '89 and was never cast again. Five years passed before the forerunner of the present ring was born. Under the direction of Edward C. Jonas '94, commander of Company C and business manager of the *Battalion*, suggestions for the design of a class ring were solicited. From these suggestions Jonas drew up the preliminary design. Approval by the thirty-two-member class soon followed. Ten dollars was collected from every senior in order to contract a New York firm to cast the gold rings. Two weeks before the June commencement, the first consignment of rings arrived.

All were delighted with the ring's design and appearance. But an inquisitive senior and a chemistry professor, P. S. Tilson '89, ran a test in the chemistry lab to determine the gold content of the ring. To their surprise, they found it had been weighted and plugged with lead. A close look at the other rings in the first shipment revealed the same impurities. With commencement only two weeks away, reordering the entire shipment was impos-

 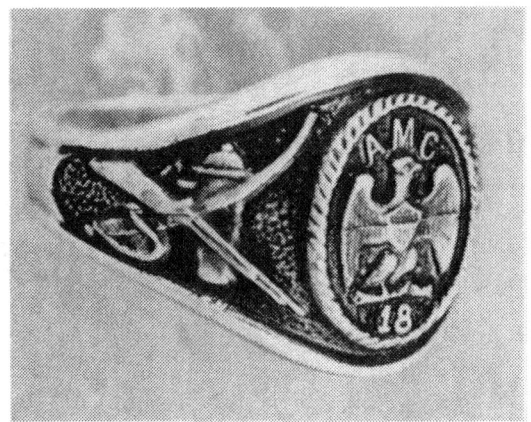

Left, By the turn of the century the cannon was added to one side of the ring and the Lone Star of the State of Texas to the other. *Right,* The letters "AMC" over the eagle later gave way to a crest encircling the eagle, and the words "Texas A&M College" were changed to "Texas A&M University" in 1963.

sible. So each senior was forced to reorder his own ring. Most members of the class of '94 had their new rings by 1897. After considering many possible ring designs, the class of '95 selected the same ring their predecessors wore. And the ring remained unchanged until 1899, when a committee headed by Josh B. Sterns and R. J. Porter met to discuss design changes and then contracting of a new company to cast the ring.

"After much friendly argument," Sterns recalls, "we rearranged the designs and selected a combination composed of the seal of Texas on one side, a cannon and two crossed muskets on the other side. On the top oval we placed a spread eagle with A.M.C. around the top rim and a space for 1899 below." During the discussion much concern was expressed by E. L. Martin to have the classes of 1900, 1901, and 1902 adopt the same design in order to "perpetuate the design as the class ring for the succeeding years." The Linz Brothers Jewelry Company of Dallas offered to quote the junior, sophomore, and fish classes lower prices if they would meet and vote to approve Martin's idea. With the possibility of the price per ring being raised to $10.50, all classes concurred.

The ring remained unchanged during the next thirty years. Year after year each class agreed on the 1894 design for their class ring with only minor changes—a saber and a rifle instead of two rifles, the cannon pointing right instead of left, or the eagle facing right instead of left. In 1933 College President T. O. Walton appointed an official senior ring committee to oversee the handling of the rings and any design modification that seemed agreeable with the students. The consensus was that unless controls were exercised, the ring and its heritage would prove meaningless. Before 1933, many companies manufactured the ring, and practically anyone could obtain a "bootleg" copy. A five-year contract was awarded to Star Engraving Company of Houston in November, 1933, to begin making Aggie rings with the class of '35. In 1934 the state and national flags were added as background to the crossed rifle and saber. The words "A&M College of Texas—1876" were also added around the crest. In 1939 the registrar's office began distributing the ring in order to exercise tighter controls on those who were permitted to purchase it. The year 1943 saw the ring enlarged and the seal raised. When Texas A&M College became Texas A&M University in 1963, the ring underwent a corresponding change.

The Aggie Ring remains a common bond among all former students who have been a part of Texas A&M.

An estimated seventy-five thousand students and former students today proudly wear the symbol of Aggie heritage and tradition. Fierce loyalty has caused many to protect and honor its meaning. There are stories of rings being found on battlefields in Europe, Korea, and Vietnam. One member of the class of '45 lost his ring while on a fishing trip near Corpus Christi in 1952. A year later it was found between two dead Communist soldiers in Korea by another Aggie, class of '50.

Of course there are also stories that tell of the lighter side of Aggie rings. In 1967 the six-million-dollar cyclotron was completed at Texas A&M and operation begun. One Aggie decided to inaugurate the new atom smasher and perhaps gain a valuable keepsake by exposing his ring to the alpha particle beam. Instead of getting a mildly radioactive memento, he got a ring with half the crest melted by the 65-million-electron-volt beam. The ring had to be kept in a lead strongbox.

Wherever Aggies go, the ring serves as a binding link with other former students. It provides ready identification with the good old days and the comradeship acquired while at Texas A&M. Each item on the Aggie Ring carries with it a corresponding symbolism, as described in *The Texas Aggie* of October, 1969:

The Shield on the top of the ring symbolizes protection of the good reputation of the Alma Mater. The 13 stripes in the shield refer to the 13 original states and symbolize the intense patriotism of graduates and undergraduates of A&M. The five stars in the shield refer to phases of development of the student; mind or intellect, body, spiritual attainment, emotional poise, and integrity of character. The eagle is symbolic of agility and power, and ability to reach great heights as ambitions.

One side of the ring symbolizes the seal of the State of Texas authorized by the constitution in 1845. The five-pointed star is encircled with a wreath of olive or laurel leaves symbolizing achievement and a desire for peace and live-oak leaves symbolizing the strength to fight. They are joined at the bottom by a circled ribbon to show the necessity of joining these two traits to accomplish one's ambitions to serve.

The other side with its ancient cannon, saber, and rifle symbolizes that the men of Texas fought for their land and are determined to defend their homeland. The saber stands for valor and confidence. The rifle and cannon are symbols of preparedness and defense. The crossed flags of the United States and Texas recognize the dual allegiance to nation and state.

In 1963 Josh B. Sterns '99 presented a collection of Aggie rings to the association. *Left to right:* Association Executive Director Buck Weirus '42, Josh Sterns '99, and A&M Archivist Ernest Langford '13.

After the happy experience of the November, 1910, football game against Texas, alumni activities increasingly came to be scheduled in conjunction with the gridiron season. In 1911 plans were made for two such fall game reunions. Hal Moseley '99, of Dallas, headed a committee to encourage the Board of Directors to allow the corps to attend the state fair and game against Dallas University in Dallas. The board approved, and the corps trip was a memorable occasion, the Aggies winning 24-0. E. J. Kyle also headed a committee to arrange the program for the 1911 game with Baylor. The Aggies defeated Baylor 22-0, and Charlie Moran's boys racked up a 6-1 season, losing only to Texas 0-6. The season's events proved to be resounding successes, setting a precedent for future years and preserving the interplay between athletics and alumni support for the college. The year had been a good year for the Aggies. The class of 1911 was the largest to date, ninety-eight seniors receiving their degrees. The presentation of diplomas was made by W. A. Trenckmann '78, a member of the first class to graduate from the college. Trenckmann's son Robert '97 was the first son of a former student to graduate from the college. But the

Football and the Former Students

This plaque was dedicated to football coach Charlie Moran at the Thanksgiving Day game in 1949. Moran's six seasons, 1909–1914, at A&M produced a record of 38 wins, 8 losses, and 4 ties.

In the early hours of May 27, 1912, Old Main was destroyed by fire.

warm glow of a happy year closed with the fierce heat of a disastrous fire on the A&M campus.

During the fall of 1911 and spring of 1912, twin tragedies struck the college. At 5 A.M. on November 11, 1911, a cold, rainy morning, the Mess Hall was destroyed by a fire thought to have been started in the vicinity of the kitchen. Despite the efforts of the cadets, the fire gutted the building in minutes. Undaunted by this disaster, Bernard Sbisa prepared breakfast in a makeshift kitchen for nearly eleven hundred cadets by 9 A.M. It was said that this was the only time in thirty-seven years Sbisa was late with a meal! The Mess Hall had been erected in 1897 at a cost of two thousand dollars.

A temporary mess hall was soon built by the cadets, but fire consumed the temporary kitchen attached to the building. This loss resulted in the premature termination of fall classes early in December. An additional cause for closing the college in early December was a meningitis scare in which one cadet was thought to have been infected. Fearful of this crippling disease, some seventy-five cadets had already departed school for home before the official closing.

It was hoped that the spring would be kinder to the college, but tragedy struck again. On May 27, 1912, four weeks after ground was broken for the new YMCA Building, Old Main burned. Cadets and Bryan firemen fought the flames feverishly but unsuccessfully in the early morning hours. Old Main, the first and oldest building on campus, had been both dorm and classroom for every A&M cadet since 1876. It had been the center of all campus activity. Ernest Langford recalls that, "For years on end the commandant's office

Mess Hall Burns

Old Main Burns

Attempts to raze the gutted remains of Old Main with cannons were unsuccessful. Cadets later pulled down the walls with ropes.

was on the first floor—and for an equal number of years freshmen were sent to that office to get a 'bucket of reveille,' a 'box of taps,' or a 'reveille wrench.'"

The fire took a tremendous toll in property. In addition to the Office of the Commandant, Old Main housed the Fiscal Department; the Exchange Store; the Supervisor of Grounds; the Athletic Department; the College Post Office; the Student Publications Office, including the *Longhorn*, the *Battalion*, and the *Student Farmer*; the Publicity Department; numerous classrooms; and the armory. Nearly all aspects of student life outside of dorm rooms and the mess hall, which had already burned, were gone. Various goods from the exchange store, some athletic equipment, and part of the college records from the president's office on the second floor were saved. The rest was a total loss. The rooms in which the archives and records of former students were kept were also destroyed.

Had it not been for the foresight of Cushing and Alva Mitchell, who had compiled a list of all former students for the association, there might now be no complete record of student enrollment before 1912. Of this list the local paper commented, "It will prove to be a valuable record of names of those who were here but will not have their academic records."

As if to add to the confusion, commencement was less than two weeks away. As former students and parents began arriving on campus in early June for the spring commencement and Alumni Association activities, they were shocked and dismayed by the blackened ruins of Old Main. Aggies were heartened, however, by progress in construction on the Y and the obvious signs of a growing student enrollment. After 1906 surging

80 WE ARE THE AGGIES

student enrollments resulted in "temporary" tent housing that seemed to become all too permanent.

President Milner's address to the 1912 gathering of former students stressed the necessity of separating the A&M College from the University of Texas. In response to his remarks it was reported that the legislative committee appointed in November, 1910, accomplished virtually nothing during the last session of the Texas legislature. Milner's comments on the funding problem helped to reinforce the alumni's feelings that action needed to be taken. Because of the loss of the mess hall and Old Main, additional funding was imperative.

In the midst of fiery discussion by the alumni on the separation of Texas' two major schools, Asa J. Neff '03 interrupted the proceedings with the information that Governor Oscar Branch Colquitt was on the way to the college to make "an official visit." Neff reminded the gathering that the governor could not arrive until early Tuesday morning unless he were met at Valley Junction, west of Hearne, by a train or auto to speed his trip. Fully aware of the governor's role in helping the college gain funding (if not out of respect for his position), the alumni decided to charter a train for the final leg of his trip. An alumni committee speedily chartered from the I. and G.N. Railroad a special train large enough to transport the entire former student gathering to Valley Junction as a "reception committee to escort the Governor to the College."

Governor Colquitt to Visit A&M

Asa Neff, James B. Crockett '08, and Charles O. Evans '99 made thorough arrangements. While Love finished last-minute business items, Neff prepared to have the meeting move to the train station on the west side of the campus. The commandant was contacted and asked to have the entire cadet corps at the college railhead to meet the governor's special train upon its Monday evening return. In last-minute action the class of 1912 was elected to Association membership, and an additional committee was created to screen and consider all actions "committing the association to any policy" or position on matters concerning the Alumni Association as a whole. E. B. Cushing was selected to head this select committee, which had an important purpose. Knowing that funding for new buildings and the question of the separation of the schools would be brought to the attention of the governor, the group was to head off any unauthorized discussion with the governor by overzealous alumni and friends of A&M. The association then elected new officers for the coming year and boarded the train for Valley Junction.

Once on board, former students reconvened for the duration of the twenty-one-mile trip. Alumni phrased their request for "prompt and liberal action of his Excellency, Governor Colquitt, in determining to issue State Deficiency Warrants in any amounts that may be necessary to replace the building lost by fire." Another resolution praised the Honorable Walton Peteet, president of the board, and board members for "able services" in the "solution of the college problems." Although no record of the return trip from Valley Junction to the college exists, it is almost certain that funding and the separation from the University of Texas were the main topics of discussion with the governor. The charter cost the association forty-seven dollars for the round trip. The governor received a hearty welcome from the corps and residents of the college. On Tuesday the governor presented ninety-six diplomas to the class of 1912. In his commencement address he gave his approval for a $200,000 warrant or bond for the reconstruction of the Main Building and a new mess hall. The applause was deafening.

The "Welcome Train"

After the commencement ceremonies, the former students and honored guests, including Governor Colquitt, President Milner, Mr. Peteet, and J. R. Austin, state senator from the Brazos Valley, attended a grand banquet prepared by Bernard Sbisa in the "big mess hall," the very same one hastily built by the cadets in November, 1911. Although the hall was drafty and cramped, all enjoyed the evening. Cushing served as toastmaster: "In the midst of all the hard luck and all the trouble the Alumni Association was to be congratulated that this is the first time in eight years that they had the pleasure of the chief executive. The old adage that a friend in need is a friend indeed is so very true." The governor reassured the association that money would be forthcoming. He told them, "We have the funds, the only difficulty is the materials." In closing his remarks he urged the college administrators, with former student support and planning, "to put up a main building to last 50 years." It has lasted more than 60.

The Academic Building

Construction on the new main building or Academic Building, as it was known, started in late 1912. It was completed in 1914 at a cost of $225,000. The Alumni Association had provided vital leverage to obtain the necessary emergency funds to resolve one of A&M's most serious crises, a crisis that soon paled in significance as the very existence of the college itself came under legislative attack.

A Move to Close the College

In the early spring of 1913, the Texas legislature opened debate on funding for higher education. One product of the debate was a proposed constitutional amendment to add academic programs in agriculture and engineering to the curricula of the University of Texas. Texas Aggies responded that the establishment of "another Agricultural and Mechanical College at Austin . . . would simply attempt to duplicate under less favorable conditions the work now being done at the A&M College at College Station." This calculated attempt to undermine the college infuriated the former students, administration officials, and friends of the college. Moreover, hundreds of thousands of dollars were just beginning to be invested in the construction of new buildings and the upgrading of the school's educational programs.

Debate on the subject of separation or consolidation and on division of the Permanent Endowment Fund had begun in earnest in 1908 and 1909 at meetings between the Board of Directors of Texas A&M and the Board of Regents of the University of Texas. At a joint session in 1909, these two executive bodies attempted to formulate general guidelines for the division of the university fund, thereby insuring the continued existence of each institution. Board members agreed that the two institutions would remain separate but share equally in the Pemanent Endowment Fund.

In January, 1911, another joint meeting was held at the Driskill Hotel in Austin. This time a constitutional amendment was proposed to separate the institutions and provide equal funding. Unfortunately the amendment failed to pass in the House of Representatives. Undaunted, the two boards again met, this time in Fort Worth during the 1913 Christmas holidays, to reaffirm their desire to constitutionally separate the university and the A&M College, with each institution to receive its fair share of the endowment fund. The minutes of the Texas A&M Board of Directors noted that separation was the official policy of the college and that Texas A&M agreed to "receive 40% of the permanent university fund."

In early 1913 the legislature again considered the recommendations of the two executive boards. As arguments over the amendment grew, A&M's opponents began a movement to close Texas A&M completely. The intention was to consolidate all state educational training in one central location—Austin—under auspices of the University of Texas. Consolidation, it was believed, would eliminate competitive educational programs and duplicate funding for libraries, laboratories, new buildings, and dorms at two separate locations. It would also mean the end of the A&M College.

Upon being notified of the proposed legislation, Moseley met with the Alumni Association's executive committee in Dallas on April 15, 1913. The provisions of the senate resolution calling for consolidation of the university and Texas A&M were reviewed by the committee. Kamp McGinnis suggested that twenty-five of the most prominent former students be named by Moseley to a committee to "act with the Executive Committee to represent the Association in all matters pertaining to the welfare of the college." The committee of twenty-five former students was formed because the Executive Committee believed that a general meeting could not be well attended at such short notice. This select committee was scheduled to meet at the college on May 6, 1913. The committee included

Aggies Fight for A&M

W. H. Amsler '89
E. H. Astin '99
T. J. Beasley
M. S. Church '05
James R. Cravens '82
E. B. Cushing '80
P. L. Downs, Sr. '79
T. W. Griffiths '00
J. W. Howell '94
E. W. Hutchinson '89
L. J. Kopke '80
J. A. Kyle '90

F. M. Law '95
R. E. Pennington '85
Charles Rogan '79
E. J. Smith '88
P. S. Tilson '89
C. C. Todd '01
W. A. Trenckmann '78
A. Wangomann '90
Joe Utay '08
R. C. Watkins '96
Walter Wipprecht '89

The group met with the Alumni Executive Committee in the Civil Engineering Building (Nagle Hall) to determine what position should be assumed by the Alumni Association in the best interests of the college. As chairman, Moseley stated in his opening remarks that the objectives of the meeting were to "consider what attitude the Association should assume." Representative A. J. Kennedy, Senator Erwin H. Astin '99, and Judge R. E. Pennington '85, talked to the former students about the significance of the proposed amendment. Upon the conclusion of their remarks, letters were read from various members of the legislature which offered additional interpretations of the resolution. Generally it was agreed that the proposed legislation would have either an adverse or a fatal impact upon the A&M College. The delegates agreed that the former students should oppose the amendment with all the forces at their command.

Representative Kennedy advised that the "character of the fight . . . should be entirely above-board, open and clean, and not against any administration, institution or person." With this admonition in mind, a committee of five was named to "manage the campaign" before the public vote on the amendment on July 19, 1913.

Meanwhile, Alva Mitchell balanced the association's books to see what the "war chest" contained. Receipts for the year totaled $402.60. This amount, along with $113.96 carried over from 1912 and a loan of $200, gave the association a total working budget of $712.56.

Surging student enrollment resulted in the construction of "temporary" tent housing on the grounds in front of Old Main in 1906. This view of life in the tents, with Ross Hall in the background, is from 1908.

After paying bills for printing, the special train charter to Valley Junction, clerical work, music for the 1912 banquet, and the expenses of the legislative committee, Mitchell reported the association had a total of $154.61 cash on hand. This meager amount was all the association felt it needed to conduct its routine activities, but special collections would be needed for the work ahead.

During April and May, statewide debate on Senate Joint Resolution No. 18 became heated. A&M former students remained unalterably hostile to the resolution. After hastily voting the class of 1913 to membership and pausing to recognize the "roll of deceased members," former students attending the annual association meeting in June, 1913, approved the actions of both the Executive Committee and of the special committee of twenty-five working to counter the proposed amendment. In an effort to clarify the issues and meaning of the legislation, E. B. Cushing and Erwin H. Astin, former students and recent appointees to the Texas A&M Board of Directors, were called on to discuss the "agitation" brought about by SJR 18. Cushing delivered a stirring speech on the evils of the amendment. Upon the conclusion of his address, a committee was named to draft a "position stand."

The association's position statement was simple. The former students encouraged President Milner and the administration to fight the amendment by making the people of Texas aware of its possible adverse effect on higher education in the state. The association based its fight against the measure on the grounds that the amendment was "ambiguous," expensive to implement, a hindrance to higher education, and legally unstable because "practically any construction" could be made of it. They felt that its passage would be "the death knell of the A&M College of Texas." Although opposed to SJR 18, the association was not hostile toward Governor O. B. Colquitt, who had continued to be a close friend of the college throughout the debate. With future funding in mind, the alumni were careful to add a final paragraph to their press release of June 9, 1913: "Resolved Further: That we regret that in defending the very life of the A&M College, it is necessary for us to oppose a measure advocated by an administration which has heretofore been uniformly friendly to the College."

Debate in the Texas press reached a peak during July. Letters and editorials for and against filled the newspapers. The association succeeded in placing many pro-A&M articles in newspapers and also collected numerous petitions, which were submitted to the press and the legislature. As election day approached, entire pages were purchased to help sway the electorate. Headlines such as "Friendship for A&M College Questioned," "Houston A&M Club Raised Points of Objection," "Joe Utay of A&M Alumni Said Implied Subscription Prevented," and "A&M Friends Must Choose Horns of Dilemma."

The efforts of the former students bore fruit. On July 20 and 21 papers carried the news of the resounding defeat of SJR 18 by a margin of more than two to one. Walter Wipprecht, chairman of the Brazos County A&M Club, released a strong statement to the Associated Press in which he applauded the efforts of the former students and all citizens in their defeat of a bill which he termed was "only a means to rob Texans." In an article entitled "Swatting 18" it was reported that Brazos County, homeland of the college, voted 9 for and 1,314 against. Statewide the vote was 37,831 against to 13,233 for. Nevertheless, pressure from Austin over the separation of the institutions and division of the university fund was just beginning, and in the years ahead storm clouds continued to hover over the A&M College. But, as during the dark decade of the 1880's and the throes of the "Great Trouble," hard times inspired new allegiance and support among A&M former students. Trials and tribulations ultimately brought growth and development instead of defeat and decline.

Members of the class of '13 on campus for a football game.

Campus scene, about 1915.

86 WE ARE THE AGGIES

7. Farmers Fight

Texas A&M weathered the political storms of 1913 and 1914 in part because of the unshakable loyalty of alumni and friends, who believed that the college had much to offer Texas youth. Former student support continued to grow in proportion to the rising heat of the battle between the university and the college and the greater number of Aggie victories on the gridiron. Under the guidance of the indefatigable Charles B. Moran, who came to win, the Aggies amassed thirty-eight wins, eight losses, and four ties in six seasons. Moran's teams included the "immortals" Caesar ("Dutch") Hohn and Tyree Bell, among others. By June, 1914, the YMCA Building was entering the final stages of construction. Bernard Sbisa Dining Hall and the new main building were also well on their way to completion. The college and the Alumni Association seemed to be entering a new era of development and expansion. Former student participation in the activities of the association increased markedly.

The increased activities of the alumni association placed a great burden on the small number of volunteers and elected officers who directed association activities. Since the turn of the century the association's Executive Committee (composed of the president, secretary-treasurer, and one appointed member) directed the affairs of the association. Because of the increased demands on their time, in 1914 the Executive Committee was reorganized to comprise nine members: the president, the vice-president, the secretary-treasurer, the last living president, and five other members appointed by the current president. This nine-member group was empowered to exercise leadership and direct the affairs of the association "in the interim between the annual meetings." Only five members of the council were necessary to constitute a quorum. The new Executive Committee soon found itself immersed with the question of the political and financial separation of the A&M College and the University of Texas.

Executive Committee Reorganized

At an unprecedented meeting held on June 4, 1914, in Houston between the members of the "alumni associations of the A&M College and the State University," representatives for both schools attempted to arrive at a settlement favorable to both institutions without the further involvement of the Texas legislature. Two points of controversy were heavily debated. First, the two committees could not agree on "the powers of the two institutions" as set forth in the Texas Constitution. The argument on this point revolved around the nature and scope of courses to be taught at each institution. Did Texas A&M have exclusive authority in areas of engineering and agriculture? University of Texas supporters thought not. The second point of contention was over the "division of the joint permanent fund." This issue had been the basis of SJR 18. Both sides presented their cases at length, but no understanding was reached concerning the division of the fund. The meeting, which the two alumni groups had hoped would produce an understanding

A&M and UT Alumni Meet

before the legislature reconvened in Austin, resulted only in a stalemate. Alumni meetings around the state attended by delegates from both institutions similarly failed to reach an accord. Aggies and University of Texas alumni had proposed and counterproposed throughout the past two years without reaching any substantive agreements. The question of separation remained unsettled.

The Houston Committee

A&M former students and the directors of the college anticipated continuing discord between the institutions and among politicians. In 1914 the association named a permanent legislative committee known as the "Houston Committee" to represent the A&M position before the legislature. The committee, consisting of Cushing, Rowell, Stewart, Amsler, Giddings, Cravens, Moser, E. J. Smith, Rogan, and Downs, was extended "plenary powers" with the following guidelines:

1. The College should be separated from the University.
2. There should be an equal division of the University funds.
3. The amendment to be submitted looking toward the separation should be as brief as it can possibly be made and deal with only those matters which are absolutely necessary to accomplish the desired results and that all legislative detail and all matter foreign to the question of separation be strictly excluded from the amendment.
4. That prohibition against the appropriations for buildings at the University be repealed.
5. That no bonding provision whatsoever be included in the amendment.
6. That it is the opinion of this meeting that the committee should endeavor as far as possible to prevent the duplication at Austin of the legitimate work of the institution.

Voters to Decide on Separation

As anticipated by some association members, the legislature soon took action, but instead of approving a measure that would settle the funding issue, the legislature called for a state election on the question of separating the two institutions. Resolution No. 34, or the "Sackett resolution," appeared on the July ballot. It provided for the separation of the institutions with an equal apportionment of the joint permanent funds. There was intense debate on the legislation, which was viewed as generally favorable to Texas A&M. Editorials under the heading of "A. and M. College and University Divorcement" greeted Texas readers daily. One such article gave the following statement concerning the "indisputable reasons for separation": "A union that is forced by law where compatibility is lacking will never be a harmonious union, and will naturally lead to friction and domestic troubles. The autonomy of the A. and M. College is impossible as long as it is a 'branch'. No institution of learning can hope to achieve the best results whose very existence is hampered by the fact that the organic law of the State declares it a branch of another school. The constitution cannot make the child father to the man."

Separation Fails at the Polls

The hopes of many A&M College supporters were thoroughly dampened in late July, 1915, with the public defeat of the resolution. While emotions and political maneuvering over the university-college separation plan cooled, the distant fires of war in Europe began to flare on the horizon. The *Bryan Daily Eagle* of July 26, 1915, reported Resolution No. 34 a possible defeat under a mid–front page heading of "Sackett Resolution Is Still In Doubt." However, the story was completely overshadowed by bold print running the width of the top of the page: "U.S. STEAMER SUNK BY SUBMARINE." As Bryan readers hastened to find the voting results for Brazos County and the state in the newspaper, few gave much thought to the distant war and the warning headlines. In fact, foot-

The cadet block T on Kyle Field. The 13—0 in the student section is a reminder of A&M's victory over the University of Texas in 1915.

ball fever suddenly seemed to overwhelm the battle of the universities as well as war in Europe.

Football Again

After three years of bad feelings and severed athletic relations between Texas A&M and the University of Texas, football play again resumed between the archrivals in November, 1915. Before 1912, when play was suspended, games had been played at neutral sites, either in Dallas, San Antonio, or Houston. With the creation of the Southwest Intercollegiate Athletic Conference (SWC) in December, 1914, schedules, rules, and guidelines for regulated intercollegiate activities were firmly established. In scheduling the games for the 1915 season, Texas A&M and the University of Texas, according to SWC rules, agreed to play home-and-home games, abandoning the use of the neutral sites. Under the new conference guidelines, A&M won the toss, and the first game ever to be played against the University of Texas on Kyle Field was scheduled for November 19, 1915.

Excitement among the alumni of both institutions was enormous. Having battled for the funding and survival of A&M, alumni felt this game to be an extension of the rivalry between Texas' two major schools. Happily, A&M "administered a 13 to 0 drubbing to Texas" before a College Station crowd of over seven thousand. This momentous victory was witnessed by "at least forty percent of the alumni, many of whom had come back fearing that their own clan would be drubbed!" A&M's 1915 victory set a happy precedent the next decade. Of the first thirteen meetings of the two teams at Kyle Field, Texas A&M won twelve.

The First Thanksgiving Day Game

In November, 1916, the Aggies journeyed to Austin still full of memories of the 1915 victory. Three special trains transported the Corps of Cadets, twelve hundred strong, and

Farmers Fight   89

Bevo — Thanksgiving, 1916.

Five A&M students engineered the 1916 branding of Bevo. *Standing, left to right:* Merlin Mitchell '17, Ed Johnson '18, Hans H. Rothe '17, and Jim Crow '17. *Kneeling:* O. K. Johnson '17 and Carl Brannig.

Bevo — November 6, 1972. The University of Texas mascot was photographed on the A&M campus after being "rustled" by the freshmen members of cadet unit Huslin' One.

the alumni to Austin. The *Alumni Quarterly* said it was "the largest crowd that ever saw a football game in Texas." Although haunted by their 1915 defeat in College Station, the Longhorns avenged their first SWC loss to A&M with a 21–7 victory before more than fifteen thousand fans in Clark Field on Thanksgiving Day. Thereafter the home-and-home Thanksgiving Day rivalry endured until 1977, when the game was changed to a Saturday.

Before the 1916 Thanksgiving game six cadets branded the University of Texas mascot, a Texas longhorn steer, with the score of the 1915 victory, 13–0, to taunt the university supporters. To save face, the University of Texas students altered the brand by making a letter *B* out of the 13 and an *E* out of the dash. The letter *V* was inserted between the *E* and *O*, and thus the name Bevo was made. The adjustment of the brand was inspired by the *bevo*, which denoted a soda drink that tasted like beer. (Somewhat reminiscent of the 1915 Bevo branding was the November, 1972, kidnapping of Bevo from under the watchful eyes of its caretakers, the Silver Spurs, during the Austin Bevo Rodeo. Freshmen members of the centennial class of 1976, from Squadron One of the Corps of Cadets, engineered the modern-day feat in spite of attempts by the Texas Rangers and others to spoil their efforts. The steer was eventually returned healthy and unharmed.)

Despite athletics and the ominous war in Europe, the college and alumni in 1916 went about their routine activities, although now more watchful of events across the sea.

Bevo

Affairs at the College

Students and alumni alike began to feel that the United States could not long remain aloof. "We knew it was only a matter of time before we [the United States] would be involved in some fashion with the European War," commented Stewart C. Hervey '17. Meanwhile, the college steadily grew with the completion of the YMCA Building, the Academic Building, Sbisa Dining Hall, a dairy, new roads, and a new hospital. In the spring of 1916 the corps numbered 1,100 cadets. In the fall of 1916 the college experienced a modest increase to 1,242 cadets. As a part of this expansion the school of veterinary medicine formally opened classes during the 1916–1917 school year under the able direction of Dr. Mark Francis.

Plans for an Alumni Magazine

Alumni activities increased along with the growth of A&M and the expansion of the sports program. Political conflict between the University of Texas and A&M diminished only to manifest itself on the football gridiron. The rivalry, now a yearly Thanksgiving event, captured the attention of Texans statewide. Alumni of each institution rallied to their respective colors only to spend the ensuing year debating the merits of the contest just fought while at the same time looking toward the next clash. By the close of 1916 the battle of the universities had moved from the legislature to the gridiron.

More and more former students were returning to the campus for football games and commencement exercises. The association desperately needed its own official journal to keep former students better informed. Claude M. Evans '08 of the local Brazos County A&M Club recommended the establishment of an association magazine. After careful review of Evans' proposal, it was determined that the financial means to accomplish the task were simply unavailable. The publication was approved on the condition that it was not to be printed until sufficient funds were available to insure its continuing success. Pending the publication of its own journal, the association decided to run a column outlining association activities in the "regular quarterly college bulletin." Additionally, publication of association events would be reinstated in the *Battalion* via a weekly alumni column.

Finally, in April, 1916, after years of sketchy planning and faulty financing, the *Alumni Quarterly* made its appearance as the official voice of the college and the alumni. But this publication was *not* funded by the Alumni Association. It was established with state funds by President Bizzell and was to be maintained by the college, not by the association. The masthead to each edition read, "Published quarterly by the College Alumni Secretary, Agricultural and Mechanical College of Texas, College Station, Texas, in behalf of the alumni and former students of the college." The alumni and former students are referred to separately despite their union in 1911. This in no way should be viewed as a split within the association. The intention was to clarify the past affiliation of each group with the college.

College Alumni Secretary

President Bizzell worked closely with the Alumni Association in establishing the *Alumni Quarterly*. Since it was to be funded by the college, Bizzell appointed Nester M. McGinnis '98 as the first college alumni secretary. His position on the college staff had nothing whatsoever to do with the position of secretary-treasurer of the association, who in past years had handled all association publications. McGinnis' job was to edit the *Quarterly* and "keep in touch with the alumni and in general, revive the interest of all in the college." His first task was to obtain the addresses of the more than four hundred men who had not been heard from in many years.

During the first year there was considerable confusion about McGinnis' position and

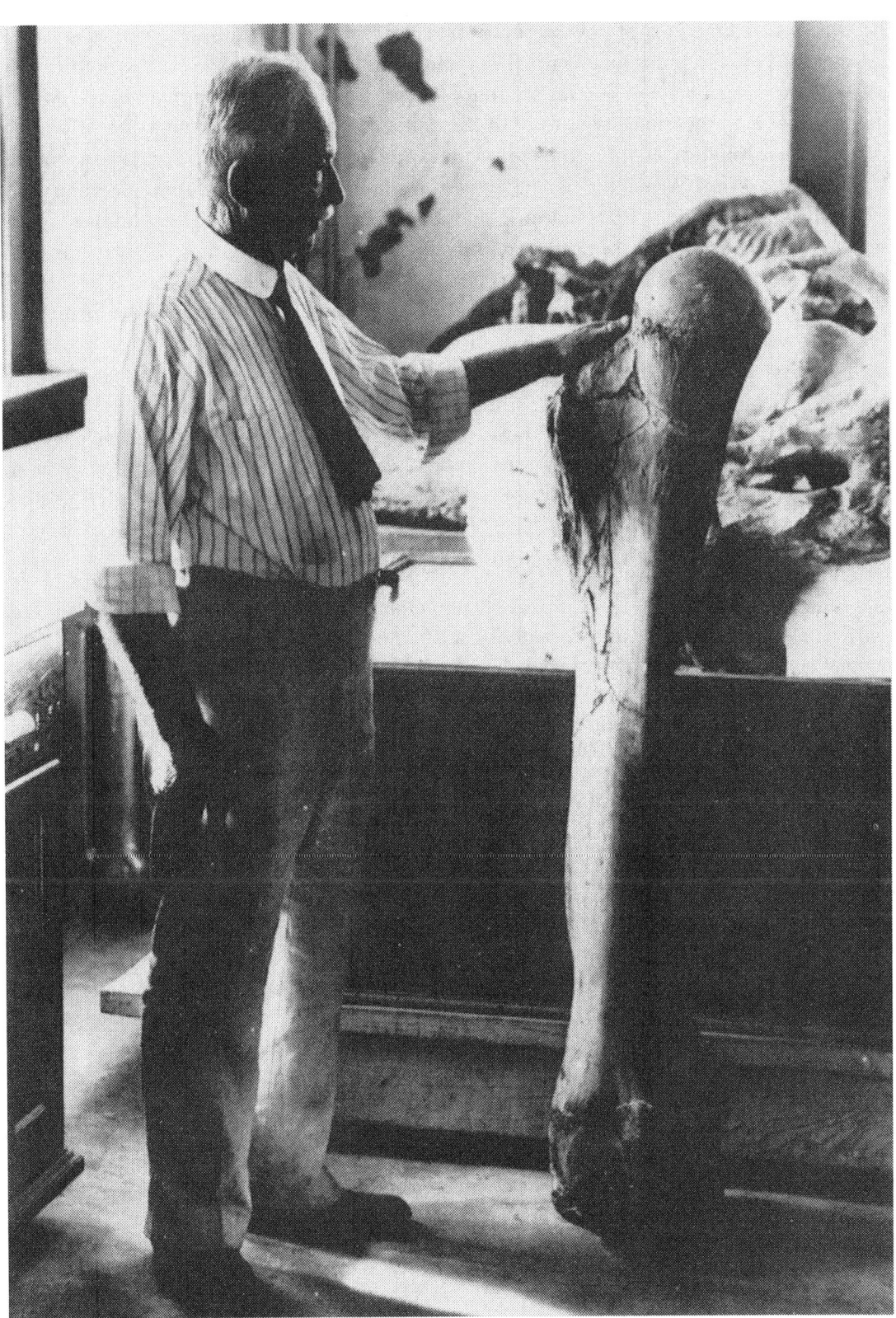
Famed veterinarian Dr. Mark Francis with a fossil bone found near the Brazos River.

the duties and functions of the secretary-treasurer of the association. Many questioned the necessity of the position and its direct affiliation with the college. These doubts were not held by the majority of former students and most alumni, who applauded the *Alumni Quarterly* as a tremendous asset to both the college and the association. In an attempt to clarify any misunderstanding, the following appeared in the June, 1916, issue of the *Alumni Quarterly*: "Again let us say, that the office of College Alumni Secretary was established by President Bizzell and is maintained by the College. The Alumni Association, as an organization, is in no way connected with it. Please do not confuse this office with that of F. J. Skeeler, secretary-treasurer of the Alumni Association." Despite the reassurances, the college alumni secretary represented an effort to provide the former students' association with a sorely needed, full-time professional staff person.

Home Coming 1916

The first issue of the *Alumni Quarterly*, consisting of only seven pages, appeared in April, 1916. It extended to all former students and alumni an invitation to attend the grand "Home Coming" scheduled for the June, 1916, commencement. On the cover page Dr. Bizzell encouraged the "old boys of gray" to be on campus for the fortieth commencement and "renew the acquaintances of former years." Publicity encouraging a good turnout filled the *Alumni Quarterly* and appeared in various state newspapers. McGinnis vividly recounted the early years of the college in his editorial:

Those fellows of a few years ago who sloshed around in the mud up to their knees, kindled their own fires in Austin and other such dormitories, ate in the temporary mess hall and grumbled about an unattractive hospital from a sick bed, will find much to encourage them when they return to the Home Coming exercises at the College this June. In place of the old mud walks there are thousands of feet of cement walks, the military walk is paved from the chapel to the Bernard Sbisa mess hall and the college roads are constructed of gravel and mudshell.

The strongest summons came from C. Otto Moser '04 of Dallas, 1915–1916 president of the association:

WARNING.

Capias,   Dallas, Texas, May 20, 1916
To the Alumni and Ex-Students of the A. and M. College, Everywhere.
Greetings:

This will serve as a personal warrant that you are to appear at College Station June 11, 12, and 13, before the tribunal of the Alumni Association, account of Commencement and Home Coming. You are charged with having failed to appear on previous occasions in the past as often as your indebtedness to your Alma Mater justly deserves. Any failure to answer this summons in person, or make a reasonable excuse will be followed by a vigorous prosecution by the Constable. We guarantee you that you will not be fined if you come, but can hold out nothing good for you if you do not show sufficient interest in your old successes of the College. You will be met at the train and hauled to the Calaboose in the Hoodlum Wagon. Combine pleasure and duty by making this great Home Coming the success which we anticipate. Reports from all sections say "Everybody is going to Commencement." You will miss it if you miss it.

F. J. SKEELER   C. O. MOSER
Constable   Sheriff

The appeals of Bizzell, Moser, McGinnis, and others proved effective. Nearly four hundred former students participated in the four days of activities which culminated with

Left, Nester M. McGinnis '98, college alumni secretary, 1915–1918. *Right*, William B. Bizzell (center), president of Texas A&M, 1914–1925. Dr. Bizzell was instrumental in creating the *Alumni Quarterly* and in fostering alumni support for various school programs.

the conferring of degrees to 120 cadets on Tuesday, June 13. Monday, June 12, was proclaimed "Alumni Day" by Bizzell. The faculty and staff hosted a reception in honor of the association in the YMCA, and the corps presented a special Alumni Day review in honor of former students. The activities of the 1916 alumni day and commencement were viewed by many as one of the high points in both the college's and the association's history. Dr. William Bennett Bizzell captured eloquently the spirit of A&M when he addressed the former students:

Forty years is a comparatively long period of time from the standpoint of human reckoning, but many of you have followed the career of the College through its many years of difficulties and achievements. Your observations have taught you what many men have not learned—that the building of a great college is not the work of a day, or the simple experience of an evening's pastime. It costs great human endeavor, great educational faith, and large human vision to build a really great college. From the beginning this institution has had the guidance and sympathetic support of many men of this character.

These remarks resulted in exuberant applause from those in the overcrowded YMCA auditorium. Board President John I. Guion's remarks, following Bizzell's address, were scarcely heard over the excitement. Bizzell, unknowingly, set the mood not only for the 1916 commencement but also for a period of growth and expansion which would span the next fifteen-year period. Perhaps inspired by Bizzell, former students launched a vigorous effort to resolve two long-standing financial problems: the first concerned the creation of a Students' Loan Fund, and the second encompassed an effort to generate more revenue via the association dues system.

The inception and initial drive behind the Students' Loan Fund concept, a program to assist Aggie students with tuition and fees, came from Edward B. Cushing, who wanted to establish a revolving fund to help needy students pay their way through college. In 1914 a special committee was named to examine the feasibility of this idea and report to

Students' Loan Fund

Farmers Fight 95

Military walk looking southward toward Guion Hall, 1917.

the association's executive committee, but American entry into World War I interrupted deliberations until 1918, when the original idea was revived. Finally, in 1922 Francis Marion Law '95, Will C. Hogg, Walter G. Lacy '96, Charles Rogan '79, L. J. Hart, Charles A. DeWare '09, Erwin H. Astin '99, J. Webb Howell '94, Charles Puryear, Bonny Youngblood '02, and William B. Cook '20 obtained a charter from the State of Texas for a corporation known as the Students' Memorial Loan Fund of the Agricultural and Mechanical College of Texas. The purpose of this loan fund was "to establish and maintain an educational undertaking in the form of a Students' Loan Fund of one million dollars ($1,000,000.00), or more, or such part thereof as may be found practicable, as a memorial to the killed, wounded, and maimed heroes of Texas A&M . . . former students who have nobly served, whether in war or in peace."

The Students' Loan Fund was to be governed by a board of directors including the president of Texas A&M, the president of the Board of Directors of Texas A&M, the deans of the agricultural and mechanical colleges, the president of the Association of Former Students, the secretary of the association, and the superintendent of public instruction of the State of Texas. All members of the Association of Former Students, friends of the college, or "any organization of whatever known name shall be welcome through their contribution" as members. Donations could be paid in installments. A committee of awards was established to recommend applicants for loans. Preferential consideration was given first "to soldiers from Texas whether maimed or not, who had participated in the great European war," and second to applicants who "unmistakably avow their intention to pursue their studies to a college degree in their chosen field." The committee of awards was to be headed by the secretary of the Association of Former Students.

An Unselfish Spirit

The official public announcement of the Students' Loan Fund in March, 1922, brought numerous donations. Edward D. Hopkins '19, at the time an engineer working in Tabasco, Mexico, with the International Petroleum Co., was the first former student to contribute to the fund. In his letter to the association he wrote: "Please find enclosed, a check for fifty dollars ($50.00), same to go to the Students' Memorial Loan Fund. I wish I could see my way clear to a real contribution. The fund is certainly an expression of the old A. and M. pep or spirit. You can't beat it." Hopkins read about the establishment of the loan fund in the March 15, 1922, *The Texas Aggie* tabloid.

At the June, 1922, annual meeting of the association, a unique contribution was made. Val Bennett '22, president of his class, was invited before the business meeting to tell how the class had started a loan fund for students. While enrolled, his class collected over one thousand dollars. Andrew C. Love, who chaired the Students' Loan Fund committee, hoped to demonstrate, by Bennett's testimonial, that the program was feasible. To this end Love introduced a resolution commending the class of '22 and urging the utmost support of the program. Love urged the association to work with college authorities "in creating a Students' Loan Fund of sufficient size to meet the needs of the college in assisting worthy students in acquiring a college education." He stressed in his proposal "co-operation" with the Board of Directors of A&M and with the college administration in this endeavor. His resolution was seconded by Tyree Bell.

Action on Love's proposal was delayed until the evening banquet in Sbisa Mess Hall. At this gathering, with the members of the class of 1922 as honored guests, Colonel Cushing reported that the Students' Loan Program was unconditionally approved. He expressed his thanks to the class of 1922 and to all the individual contributors who had made the program an initial success.

By March, 1924, the loan fund amounted to ten thousand dollars. It was estimated that five times that amount was needed for loans in September to aid students in the fall semester. Enrollment was expected to reach twenty-three hundred. Of this number an estimated eight hundred were expected to apply for loans. A drive was conducted throughout the spring and summer to raise the fund to fifty thousand dollars.

Mothers Clubs Contribute

In May the Dallas A. and M. Mothers' Club donated what they termed a "nest egg" of one hundred dollars to the loan fund. Dallas boys were to have first call on the loan funds. In order to raise money, the mothers gave teas at which each mother present was assessed a fee according to her height or waistline. The invitation to these affairs was both humorous and timely:

> The Dallas A. and M. Mothers are giving a tea,
> May the thirteenth, on Tuesday at three
>
> For a Students Loan Fund, our plan is unique,
> On this occasion your presence we seek.
>
> We A. and M. Mothers will greet friends one and all;
> Those large around and those who are tall;

Farmers Fight 97

Officers of the A&M Mothers' Club on the steps of Sbisa Dining Hall, 1928. *Bottom row, left to right:* Mrs. Travis Smith, corresponding secretary; Mrs. J. G. Toland, president; and Mrs. M. M. Shumate, treasurer. *Top row:* Mrs. M. M. Moore, recording secretary; T. O. Walton, president of A&M College; and Mrs. W. B. Lewis, second vice-president.

> A penny an inch for circumference or height;
> Be careful your measurements are right.
>
> Your giving this mite should bring you much joy;
> For your pennies will help some mother's boy.

A special guest at one of these Dallas teas was Ike Ashburn, secretary of the association during the early 1920's and a man of over two hundred pounds. Ike commented, "I could not figure at first whether to measure height or waist but eventually decided that the height would be cheapest and sent a check for seventy-five cents."

Just before the 1924 commencement, the Ross Volunteer Company presented the secretary of the association with $85 to be available "for any student." Cadet Captain Frank S. McGee '24, Cadet Lieutenant John V. Drisdale '24, and Frederick L. Downs, Jr., '24 made the presentation of this gift from money which remained after the R.V. Spring Banquet. Other student organizations also gave token amounts to help bolster the loan fund. During the 1924 association business meeting, special recognition was given to the Dallas A. and M. Mothers' Club, the Ross Volunteers, the Texas Aggie Minstrels, and the Campus Confectioners for their generous support of the loan fund. Of the loan fund, the secretary recorded, ". . . these sacred Funds shall be honestly and efficiently handled, zealously guarded and conserved, and expanded only for the high purpose for which they

The Aggie "T" and "AMC" during the early 1920's.

have been contributed—the students of Texas A&M." During the fall of 1924 approximately $8,621 in loans were made. While this was short of the goal of $50,000, the Students' Loan Program was hailed a great success.

In August, 1925, the Students' Loan Fund received a contribution that assured its continued existence at Texas A&M. In early 1925, A. Kidd Short '00, director of the Sears-Roebuck Agricultural Foundation, contacted the association about a possible corporation gift to the Students' Loan Fund. In May, Short entered into conference with Ike Ashburn, Everett E. McQuillen '20, and Marion S. Church '05 to arrange the donation of twenty-five thousand dollars to the loan fund. The donation was originally conceived by Short, who for many years had been assistant director of the Agricultural Extension Service before being employed by Sears-Roebuck.

Sears-Roebuck Donation

The funds were earmarked for loans to "agricultural students who are sons of farmers." With this donation by Sears-Roebuck, the available Students' Loan Fund jumped from three thousand dollars to just under forty thousand dollars in less than three years. Of this rapid growth *The Texas Aggie* of August 18, 1925, commented: "It is perhaps the most outstanding piece of work the Association of Former Students has put over. Five hundred boys will secure financial assistance from our organization this coming year most of whom would be unable to get a college education without this assistance. The splendid work has been brought about by the combined spirit of cooperation and work that exists among the ex-students of A. and M. and makes possible the functioning of the Association." Since 1925 the Former Students Association, through its loan funds, more recently by scholarships funded by practically every local A&M club, and through the President's Endowed Scholarship Program, has created a unique opportunity for tens of thousands of young men and women to obtain an education at Texas A&M. Thus, one of the great traditions established by former students at an early time in their development as an organization was that best expressed by the words, "We care."

Left, H. H. Tracy '98, W. T. Carter '98, and R. L. Barclay '98 pictured during their class reunion in 1915. *Right*, P. L. Downs, Jr., '06 and the distinctive Aggie Gig 'em. Downs, a member of A&M's Board of Directors during the 1920's, was famed for his appearances at All-College Night and Bonfire during the 1950's and 1960's.

A Declaration of War

Then, perhaps not unexpectedly, A&M's world changed—never to be the same again. On April 6, 1917, President Woodrow Wilson declared war against the Central Powers and vowed support to the Allied Powers embattled in France. By June, General John J. ("Blackjack") Pershing and the First Infantry were dispatched to France. The call for troops superseded all events and daily routines at the A&M College. Texas A&M became a war school. By 1920, A&M men recalled days at the Marne, Belleau Woods, and Verdun. The Aggie citizen-soldiers proved to be able warriors and proud representatives of their nation and their alma mater.

8. Warring for the World and for A&M

The war in Europe transformed life and times at A&M. Shortly after the declaration of war, college administrators canceled the 1917 commencement. Texas A&M released all seniors for active duty in April. The class of '17 received degrees in early June in a special off-campus ceremony at Camp Funston at Leon Springs, Texas, where nearly every member of the class had gone for military training. By May 9, command and leadership positions, ordinarily held by seniors, were filled by juniors of the class of '18.

College administrators, as early as January, 1917, before the United States entered the war, realized that Texas A&M could be called upon to provide not only its graduates but also its facilities to help train soldiers in wartime skills. Texas A&M petitioned the state legislature in January for funds to improve the college by adding an armory, new dormitories, and a gymnasium. Dr. Bizzell visited the War Department in Washington, D.C., in an effort to obtain assistance for war training programs at Texas A&M. The *Alumni Quarterly* said, "The college stands high in the esteem of the War Department, having ranked for many years as a distinguished institution." Funds were soon provided by both the state and the federal governments.

War Training Programs

To meet wartime training commitments the college added three new branches: the School of Radio Mechanics, the School of Auto and Motor Truck Mechanics, and the School of Meteorology. Personnel and equipment were commandeered from existing academic departments to service the new programs. In addition to these technical fields, instruction was offered in blacksmithing, carpentering, and horseshoeing. By August, 1918, more than 2,350 military personnel received training at College Station, while the Aggies themselves had gone off to war.

Aggies flocked to the colors. Every class was represented by men in uniform. As Dr. Bizzell said, "These men were trained to be farmers and engineers; but in time of national crises they have become statesmen, producers and soldiers as well." Numerous former students accepted direct commissions in the armed services in ranks ranging from second lieutenant to colonel. Among the most notable alumni leaders to serve in Europe were Colonel Edward B. Cushing '80; Second Lieutenant Victor Anthony Barraco '12; Captain G. P. F. Jouine '07, who served from the onset of the conflict as a tank commander in the French army; Captains Marion Somerville Church '05 and Hal Moseley '01; and Lieutenants Carl Clifton Krueger '12, Charles C. Todd '97, Andrew Davis Bruce '16, and Tyree L. Bell, Jr., '13.

By late January, 1918, college enrollment declined from more than four thousand to only one thousand students. Few students were attending regular classes. Because of the war and the drastic enrollment drop, the A&M administration seriously considered dispensing with commencement exercises in 1918 but finally decided to hold commence-

Cadets train during 1919–1920 with the latest armaments.

Tractor classes were transformed into motor truck mechanic courses during World War I.

Air Corps training became a routine affair on campus by 1918. In the background is the Academic Building.

ment on May 25. Upon receiving news that commencement was still planned, the class of '98, A&M's first "war class," planned for their twentieth reunion in conjunction with the May commencement.

Local alumni, including Edwin Jackson Kyle, Walter Wipprecht, Arthur Tillman Potts, Nester Massie McGinnis, and Ernest Langford made plans to house the visiting former students and guests in newly constructed Bizzell Hall during the three-day ceremonies. The opening ceremonies were to include the dedication of Guion Hall, the modern and massive auditorium which was completed in early 1918. On Monday, May 27, the Alumni Association held its first meeting in over two years in the YMCA. Robert Joseph Potts presided over more than one hundred in attendance. Among the group were fifteen of the twenty-three members of the class of '98. This was the first organized, on-campus reunion by a class in the history of association activities. Members of the classes of 1917 and 1918 were elected to full membership in the association. In recognition of their service to their country, the college awarded Honor War Certificates for each student who had departed the college before earning a degree. The meeting concluded with the election of Charles Rogan '79, "the first student to register at A. and M.," as president for the ensuing year and Wanzel Louis Stangel '15, of College Station, as secretary-treasurer. All of the commencement activities were reported as "a splended success" by the local press.

Nester M. McGinnis, editor of the *Alumni Quarterly*, estimated in February, 1918, that "25 percent of the graduates were known to be in service, and yet the list we use is only a partial one." McGinnis figured that more than 500 of the 1,425 living Aggies were on active duty. These figures did not include nongraduate former students. A New York statistical company tabulated that 37.5 percent of all living Texas A&M graduates were in the armed forces, thus making A. and M. "the undisputed leader among the larger colleges and universities."

The First Class Reunion

Top left, Captain G. P. F. Jouine '07, highly decorated tank commander, served with the French Army during the early part of the First World War. *Right,* C. C. ("Polly") Krueger '12. *Bottom left,* Edwin J. Kyle '99.

The A&M Service Flag

In honor of the men of Texas A&M in the service of their country, the Alumni Association proposed that a large service flag be made to represent Texas A&M's participation in the war. McGinnis, alumni coordinator for the administration, supported the idea, saying, ". . . none can boast of a better record than the Agricultural and Mechanical College of Texas." On May 27, 1918, at special ceremonies the World War I memorial flag was raised in the rotunda of the Academic Building to hang vertically from the fourth floor. It measured 15 × 26 feet and provided room on its wool muslin sides for 2,110 stars, each memorializing an individual Aggie. These ceremonies were presided over by Alumni President Robert J. Potts, Dr. William B. Bizzell, and Judge John I. Guion, president of the Board of Directors. The cover of the August, 1918, *Alumni Quarterly* displayed a

The World War I Service Flag hung in the rotunda of the Academic Building through the mid-1940's.

color picture, a first in itself, of the flag with a field of 1,800 stars. The local newspaper hailed the raising of the flag as the "chief feature at Alumni Day at the 42nd annual commencement." In late May it was reported that a total of 1,963 Aggies were in the military service. The list included 648 graduates and 1,315 former students.

Private Daniel R. Edwards '12 was awarded the Congressional Medal of Honor in July, 1918, for bravery near Soissons, France. (*Drawing by Loraine Blount.*)

A&M's First Medal of Honor Winner

In mid-July, 1918, Daniel R. Edwards became the first former student to be honored with our nation's highest military award for bravery, the Congressional Medal of Honor. On July 18, on the outskirts of Soissons, France, Private First Class Edwards of the Third Machine Gun Battalion, although severely wounded, rallied his unit to push back an intensive attack by the enemy. "The Texan is one of the greatest living heroes of the World War," reported the *Fort Worth Star-Telegram*. Edwards was one of the few men to receive the Congressional Medal of Honor and the Distinguished Service Cross. He was also decorated by Great Britain, France, and Belgium.

Edwards attended Texas A&M for only a year and one-half in 1909 and 1910. While working his way through school he was a quarterback on the football team and third baseman on the baseball team. After the war he organized a "Comeback Club" for disabled veterans while attending Columbia University. In his later years he dedicated his life to vocational education and veterans' affairs, as did William G. Harrell, who was awarded the Congressional Medal of Honor for service in World War II.

Accounts of Aggie experiences in France during 1918 indicated that the men of A&M were in the thick of the fighting. Major W. H. H. Morris, formerly assistant commandant for the Corps of Cadets in 1916–1917, assigned to the Ninetieth Division, wrote:

Combat in France

September 26, 1918

Dear Dr. Bizzell:

Just a few lines to let you know that I am still alive after the first engagement with the enemy.

The Ninetieth Division was in the St. Mihiel drive and my regiment, the 360th Infantry, was on the right flank of the whole thing. My battalion led the regiment "over the top" twice and took Bois Le Pretre and Hill 327, which the French have not been able to take in four years. Lieutenants Harry J. Burkett '17 and William Bebb Francis '15, old A. and M. men, were with my battalion in the drive. The work of Burkett can not be too highly praised and Francis was the bravest little fellow of them all and showed absolutely no fear of death whatsoever. I wish you would tell Dr. Francis that I said no officer could show more bravery and sand than he did.

I suppose that you have heard that Captain Sam Craig '17, was killed and blown to pieces by a high explosive shell. I hear that Major Ike Ashburn was wounded twice in the neck and once in the leg. Several officers were killed and others wounded; for myself, I was just lucky.

My battalion took both objectives assigned to it, the first in an hour and forty-seven minutes, the second in an hour and fifty minutes. We went through the hardest kind of high explosive barrage, gas and machine gun fire. We stayed in the front lines during the offensive for seven days before we were relieved. It rained most of the time and the shelling was very heavy. Before that time we had been in the lines twelve days; so we practically faced the enemy nineteen days before being relieved.

It takes a battle to show what an officer is made of. Several officers were relieved from command, including captains, majors and colonels, for inability to command. One captain is being tried for cowardice but he is not from A. and M. Strength of character and leadership are the two requirements of an officer. It takes a long time to determine these two things and a battle is the supreme test.

Ditmar is in my battalion and he is a wonderful officer. Mike Hogg, son of the former governor of Texas, is also a captain in my battalion.

Two more days and we are off to the front again.

Give my best to all, especially the boys.

W. H. H. Morris

Back home in Texas, in a move spearheaded by the Dallas A&M Club, former students of the college organized a regiment of infantry composed entirely of former students of the college. Joe Utay '08, Thomas H. Barton '01, and Francis Kamp McGinnis '00 were appointed to meet with Governor William P. Hobby in order to obtain a Texas National Guard designation for the proposed unit. They met with the governor on February 2, 1918, and "generated much interest in the proposed regiment, but he [the governor] could not make promises at the time." Subsequent meetings with the adjutant general resulted in the formation of an officially recognized unit by late July. The unit was designated as the

The A&M Regiment

Governor Pat Morris Neff keynoting the memorial services dedicating A&M's World War I Memorial. Note that the monument is draped with the World War I Service Flag. On the platform (*left to right*) are Dean Charles Puryear (with hat in front of face); Dean F. C. Bolton; Colonel Ike S. Ashburn, executive secretary of the Association of Former Students; Dean E. J. Kyle '99; Colonel C. C. Todd '01, commandant; and Colonel F. H. Turner, assistant commandant.

Third Regiment of the First Brigade but was to be known as the A. and M. College Regiment. Regimental headquarters was set up in Dallas under the direction of the Dallas A&M Club.

The Dallas A&M Club appointed a "steering and finance committee" to help organize and assemble the unit. L. E. McGee '14 was named chairman or temporary commander. Much of the organization and work of this committee was performed by Joe Utay and Marion Church. Since the state provided no funding, the regiment hoped that it would soon be federalized and "trained for overseas duty."

The seriousness of this venture was stressed in the following passage from the August, 1918, *Alumni Quarterly*: "It should be borne in mind that this regiment is not an 'air bubble' or 'play thing', but a real fighting unit and one that all loyal A. and M. men should support for all they are worth." By early October they were at full strength, "had passed inspection, and were ready to be taken over by the U.S. Government at any time." Colonel Abe Gross '97 of Waco was designated regimental commander over three battalions headed by Major Joe Utay '08, Dallas; Major John D. McCall, Austin; and Major Richard H.

Standifer '08, Fort Worth. Lieutenant Colonel Marion S. Church '05 was named deputy commander of the regiment.

In late October, 1918, Utay and Church made a special trip to Washington to confer with Secretary of War Newton D. Baker and Chief of Staff Peyton C. March about a timetable for mobilization and training. The regiment was eager to travel to France. However, before final mobilization plans were made, the armistice was signed on November 11, 1918, thus ending hostilities in Europe. "Since the A. and M. Regiment had wanted to enter the war effort to only fight we declined an offer to serve as an occupational force after the armistice," said Utay.

Kamp McGinnis wrote, "The armistice has been signed. Peace seems to be very near. When the history of battles is written the writers will set forth many deeds of courage and gallantry of A. and M. men everywhere who went into the business of winning the war with a zeal and a determination instilled within them by the training given at our Alma Mater."

Calling for a victory homecoming and a "fitting memorial service," Dr. W. B. Bizzell said:

Memorial Services

> I am persuaded that this memorial should assume a form that will permit it to preserve to succeeding generations the names, pictures and record in service of the men who counted not their own lives dear unto themselves but gave them up freely that those of us who remained at home, along with the peoples of all other nations, might forever enjoy the blessings of liberty.
>
> I am convinced that this memorial should serve some other useful purpose on the Campus, so I am considering a proposition of incorporating in such memorial a building that can be used for some much needed purpose.

Thirty-eight former students were initially reported dead as of February, 1919. By March the list numbered forty-six.

In memorial services on March 2, 1919, held in Guion Hall, William E. Livingston, president of the class of '19, read slowly the list of forty-six fallen Aggies from the "Roll of Honor." Reverend Glenn Lawson Sneed '98 reminded all in attendance that this loss of lives was not in vain, since they died "for the cause of political liberty and social justice." The ceremony closed with the singing of the "Star Spangled Banner." During the silence that followed, "Silver Taps was sounded."

Additional special ceremonies were held in the months that followed the armistice. Mindful of the contributions of A&M sons in the war, the administration felt it would be fitting to complete a memorial project which had been delayed for over twenty years. On May 14, 1919, before a gathering of one thousand faculty, friends, and students, the statue of Lawrence Sullivan Ross was unveiled in front of the Academic Building. Judge Norman G. Kittrell of Houston gave the keynote address, and L. J. Hart of San Antonio, president of the Board of Directors, presided over the unveiling. On February 23, 1920, an additional ceremony was held. The Corps of Cadets massed on the main drill field in full military dress as the Board of Directors and Dr. W. B. Bizzell presided over the planting of fifty-three trees. The oaks encircling the drill field were representative of the honor roll of Aggie citizen-soldiers who had died in the war.

Sul Ross Statue and Memorial Oaks

Although World War I generated a new bond among Aggies, it also depleted association coffers. In late 1918 more than ten thousand dollars was owed the association in unpaid dues. The association urgently requested that all dues be paid so it would be able to assist

Left, Student members of Alpha Phi Omega service organization replacing World War I memorial markers at the bases of the trees around the main drill field. *Right,* World War I Memorial, now standing near West Gate, given by the classes of '23, '24, '25, and '26.

Alumni Reorganization

in the "readjustment of the former students as well as taking the lead in assisting the college in getting back to its normal place." Notwithstanding these financial problems, a special alumni committee, with the assistance of the Brazos County A&M Club, made plans for the largest alumni gathering in the history of the institution at the June commencement. The 1919 homecoming was to be dedicated to all returning former students, but most especially to the classes of 9's—1879, 1889, 1899, 1909—thus continuing the "tradition" of the class reunion.

The May, 1919, issue of the *Alumni Quarterly* informed its readers that "special matters vitally affecting the College and the Alumni Association will be discussed and passed upon at the business meeting" to be held on Monday afternoon, June 23. The "special matters" concerned a plan to substantially broaden the role and scope of the Alumni Association. A reorganization of the association had been attempted in 1910 and again in 1916. Efforts in 1910 and 1911 to reorganize and expand the activities of the association failed because of poor membership participation and inadequate finances. In mid-1916 association activities and membership requirements were again reviewed, and plans were made to restructure the association. This second reorganization attempt was delayed when the United States entered the war. Now, anticipating the return of numerous former students for the June, 1919, meeting, Charles Rogan, the association president for 1918–1919, and W. L. Stangel '15 planned to restructure and revitalize the association. But in March, Aggies were suddenly distracted by another battle for higher education.

Separate A&M from the University?

The Texas legislature submitted for consideration to the voters a resolution to amend the higher education provision, Article 7 of the Texas Constitution. The major provisions of this complicated bill, House Joint Resolution No. 29, were:

1. To completely separate Texas A. and M. from the University of Texas

The statue of Lawrence Sullivan Ross, known as "Sully," erected in May, 1919. *(Photograph by Jerry C. Cooper '63.)*

Left, Bonney Youngblood '02. *Right,* W. L. Stangel '15, executive secretary of the Association of Former Students, 1918–1920.

2. To provide that the permanent endowment be divided in the ratio of 66⅔% to the University of Texas and 33⅓% to Texas A. and M.
3. To allow the investment of such funds as each institution saw fit.

Only four years earlier in 1915 this same type of resolution went before the Texas voters only to meet defeat.

Former students felt strongly about the HJR 29. The view held by the administration, board members, and former students was that its passage would only seal in law what was in fact the relationship between Texas A&M and the University of Texas. In the past the two institutions had disagreed over the ramifications of such legislation. Now, in an unprecedented joint action, both institutions supported the amendment. On June 7, 1919, the Ex-Students' Association of the University of Texas, at their annual meeting, passed a special resolution to "servedly approve and endorse this amendment" in "cooperation with a like committee from the Agricultural and Mechanical College."

Aggies and Texas Exes Cooperate

In a like manner, the Texas A&M Alumni Association approved almost an identical resolution to "cooperate" with the University of Texas ex-students in support of passage of HJR 29. The Alumni Association's statement read in part: "for many years it has been the desire of the friends and especially the ex-students of the Agricultural and Mechanical College that it should be divorced from the State University and be made an independent institution." Representatives of both institutions felt that the time was right for voter approval. A special committee of twenty-one A&M former students and administrators was named to "bring the amendment before the voters." Leonard Tillotson was named chair-

Corps parade in Waco during the early 1920's.

man of the committee, and Joe Utay '08 served as secretary. President Bizzell "emphasized the necessity of putting forth a combined effort towards passing this amendment."

McGinnis urged everyone to earnestly work for the passage of the amendment. He cautioned *Alumni Quarterly* readers, "If this amendment fails to carry it will not be many years before your Alma Mater will be struggling to keep her head above the water." Bizzell, fellow administrators, and former students from both A&M and the university canvassed the state urging voters to give an approving vote to the bill on November 4, 1919. Early returns on November 5 were divided over the amendment; by late evening on November 6, with nearly all the votes counted, the bill was officially declared defeated by the voters of Texas. Once again alumni efforts to insure the independent status of Texas A&M met with defeat.

Separation Fails Again

Controversy over the separation issue very nearly derailed plans to reorganize the Alumni Association. Charles Rogan salvaged the reorganization in a last-minute, late-banquet meeting of the alumni held at the college during the June, 1919, commencement. Rogan proposed that "we organize an ex-Cadets' Association, and anyone attending the College one year be eligible to membership." The initial officers of this "ex-cadets' association" were to be filled by the elected 1919–1920 slate headed by Erwin Hugh Astin '99 and including J. O. Newton '79, first vice-president; William S. Wurzback '88, second vice-president; W. J. Bryan '79, third vice-president; and Wanzel L. Stangel '15, secretary-treasurer. Both motions, "after much discussion," carried.

The Association of Former Students

Rogan then urged Astin to appoint a committee to draft bylaws and a constitution for the "ex-cadets association." This was accomplished with the selection of W. A. Wurzback,

Warring for the World and for A&M

Sully — snowbound.

114 WE ARE THE AGGIES

San Antonio; M. S. Church '05, Dallas; Elmer L. Martin '99, Dallas; J. Allen Kyle, Houston; and Thomas W. Blake '04. Then, just as the dust seemed to have settled: "Youngblood moved that the name be changed from Ex-Cadets' Association to the Association of Former Students of the A. and M. College of Texas. Motion carried. Meeting adjourned."

This sudden and apparently unexpected motion by Bonney Youngblood '02, director of the Agricultural Experiment Station, marked the birth of the present Association of Former Students and the end of the old schism between "ex-cadets" and graduates. The *Bryan Daily Eagle* commented that the association change was ". . . one of the most far reaching decisions that has been made . . . in many years."

The committee selected to draft a new constitution and bylaws met throughout the fall of 1919 and early spring of 1920 in an effort to have a "definite report not later than May." Charles E. Friley '19, the newly appointed editor of the *Alumni Quarterly*, editorialized on the magnitude of this landmark change and its effect upon the college:

In addition to the 1,700 graduates of A. and M., there are at least 10,000 ex-students whose influence could and should be a most important factor in the building of a greater A. and M. These ex-students deserve every consideration; many of them have already shown their interest in, and their love for A. and M. in various and substantial ways. The college is entering upon a new period in its history and the people of Texas will look to it more and more for leadership and guidance in developing the wonderful resources of the State. The Ex-Students' Association can become a vital factor in this development, and in doing so they will benefit not only the College, but themselves as well.

The proposed constitution of the new Association of Former Students was read and discussed on May 24, 1920. Friley suggested and won approval of an amendment to the membership clause of the proposed constitution. As first presented and approved, membership was open to all students who had attended A&M at least one year and had left in good standing. Friley's amendment opened membership to all former students "who have attended the College at least one session and left in good standing." After some discussion, Astin declared this final touch to the new constitution of the Association of Former Students "unanimously adopted."

Tent city during the winter of 1918.

Left, Aggie Athletic Hall of Fame member Jack Mahan '21 and Coach D. X. Bible. *Right*, R. G. Higginbotham '20 goes over the line to score the winning touchdown against the University of Texas in 1919. Higginbotham also coached A&M's first SWC baseball title—winning team in 1931.

9. *Hullabaloo, Caneck! Caneck!*

War's end found Texas A&M, along with the rest of the nation, about to embark on that fantastic journey into the modern world. The roaring twenties brought unprecedented growth and prosperity to the nation—and to Texas A&M. Aggies, or some of them, now came to school in Model T's and, after 1926, on a paved road. The faculty found automobiles "time-consuming" and "otherwise objectionable" and banned their use by students. But students came in trains, busses, and cars—and by hitch-hiking—in greater numbers than ever before. Student enrollment doubled from prewar levels, with enrollments exceeding twenty-five hundred by 1925.

The old tent city gave way to other temporary, makeshift housing called the Hollywood Shacks, and new construction on campus continued throughout the twenties. Radio, flush toilets, and some women students appeared on campus. Mary Evelyn Crawford was the first woman to earn a regular degree at A&M in 1926, but for the most part women continued to be excluded from the school. There were some raccoon coats, and once in a while a "flapper" or "jellybean" appeared on the scene, but they were not Aggies. The men of A&M all, without exception, were members of the Corps of Cadets and proud of it. To be sure there were some other activities around—like the social clubs with funny names: Fat Men's Club, Bowlegged Men's Club, Swastikas, and the K.K.'s. Most of the things that happened at A&M in the 1920's were good. Aggies got a radio station, a fight song, a winning football team, a change in team colors from the "red and white" to the "maroon and white" (quite by accident, to be sure), and the Association of Former Students got its first full-time secretary and, for the first time, a healthy bank account.

President William Bennett Bizzell in May, 1921, urged former students to "get in touch with the college" and "stand in readiness" to support its programs, students, and administration. John Webb Howell '94 of Bryan sponsored a resolution to increase dues from two dollars to five dollars, while at the same time warning those gathered that this token increase would never fully satisfy the financial needs of the association.

Charles DeWare '09 became president of the association for the 1921–1922 year. DeWare, a former athlete and avid sports fan, stressed alumni support for the athletic programs of the college. That support was easy to get. Aggies, if they had not been so before, became rabid football fans in the twenties. In 1919, Dana X. Bible's team was undefeated and unscored on. A&M lost only to Texas (7–3) in 1920, and in 1921 A&M became Southern Champions by defeating the "Praying Colonels" of Centre College, Kentucky, in the Dixie Classic (known today as the Cotton Bowl), one of the nation's first postseason bowl games, held in Dallas. An account in *The Texas Aggie* expresses vividly the excitement of the A&M victory:

Southern Champions

The original "Twelfth Man," E. King Gill '24, and 1975 Association President John W. Caple '52 at the Sul Ross reunion in 1974. Gill was also an all-SWC basketball standout in 1923–1924.

Another small college was put on the football map yesterday when Texas A. and M. defeated the famous Centre College eleven by the score of 22 to 14.

It was the biggest surprise ever experienced in this or any other section since the United States adopted that alleged Eighteenth Amendment. The entire State of Texas is delirious with joy today and many of the citizens are trying to corroborate the score by interviewing the eye-witnesses.

It was a surprise, but in no way can the victory be called a fluke. The 15,000 spectators at the new stadium saw the native sons run rough shod over the Southern Champions, saw them outplay and out-general the conquerors of Harvard, Auburn, Tulane, Arizona, and Washington and Lee, and were amazed at the wonderful exhibition of football from a team which had not been given an outside chance to win.

The Twelfth Man

At the Dixie Classic game, the famed Aggie Twelfth Man tradition was born. During the course of the contest, Texas A&M suffered numerous injured players. To augment the depleted Aggie squad, a student, E. King Gill '24, a basketball player and former football player, was called from the stands to suit up in case a substitute was needed. Since 1922 the Aggie student body stands during each gridiron contest to indicate their readiness to serve as the twelfth man.

Football fans enjoyed winning seasons each year until 1930. The twenties closed with construction beginning on the new Kyle Field stadium. Winning teams fed a rising school spirit captured by the lyrics of the "Aggie War Hymn."

The Aggie War Hymn

James Vernon ("Pinky") Wilson '20 composed the hymn while standing guard duty on the Rhine River during World War I. Reviewing in his mind the various Aggie yells and the fierce rivalry of the annual Texas-Texas A&M Thanksgiving game, lyrics slowly took shape. Revised once, then twice, the initial fourteen lines were first sung as a quartet ballad by a group of American soldiers stationed in Germany.

Left, The "Twelfth Man" during a mid-1920's football game. *Right,* J. V. ("Pinky") Wilson '20.

>Hullabaloo, Caneck! Caneck!
>Hullabaloo, Caneck! Caneck!
>Good-bye to Texas University,
>So long to the Orange and White.
>Good luck to the dear old Texas Aggies,
>They are the boys that show the fight.
>"The Eyes of Texas Are Upon You,"
>That is the song they sing so well—
>So good-bye to Texas University,
>We're goin' to beat you all to—
>>Chig-gar-roo-gar-rem!
>>Chig-gar-roo-gar-rem!
>>Rough! Tough!
>>Real Stuff! Texas A. and M.

Wilson, returning from Europe, re-enrolled at Texas A&M to finish his education. While a student, he formed a new quartet which featured among its selections the "Aggie War Hymn." Aggie yell leaders first heard the "War Hymn" in ballad form at a short recital by Wilson's quartet during the intermission of a movie at the Palace Theater in downtown Bryan. "We made an agreement with the theater manager to sing a few songs during intermission in exchange for free passes to the picture show," Wilson recalled. Yell leaders in attendance at the movie liked what they heard and encouraged Wilson to "jazz up" the lyrics to provide the Aggies with a fight song for the November clash with the University of Texas. George Fairleigh, the Aggie band director, helped Wilson compose the music in time for the 1921 Thanksgiving game.

"In 1926 the Former Students Association and yell leaders pestered me to write a second verse that could be more readily used at all athletic events," Wilson said. "I felt at the time, as I do now, that the student body has a mind of their own and would, regardless

Corps trip to Houston by train in the early 1920's.

of how many verses are added, continue to sing the first and most meaningful rendition!" Notwithstanding Wilson's feelings, the urgings of the yell leaders won out, and the second verse was composed in late 1926:

> Hullabaloo, Caneck! Caneck!
> Hullabaloo, Caneck! Caneck!
> All hail to dear old Texas A&M,
> Rally around Maroon and White;
> Good luck to the dear old Texas Aggies,
> They are the boys who show the fight.
> That good old Aggie spirit thrills us,
> And makes us yell and yell and yell;—
> So let's fight for dear old Texas A&M,
> We're goin' to beat you all to—
>   Chig-gar-roo-gar-rem!
>   Chig-gar-roo-gar-rem!
>   Rough! Tough!
>   Real stuff! Texas A&M

On numerous occasions, most recently in the fall of 1969, the second verse has been introduced to different incoming fish classes only to fail to win student acceptance. As Wilson guessed, the first verse had become that inexplicable moving experience which any number of supplemental verses could never duplicate.

The Maroon and White

The 1920's also witnessed an obvious but unheralded change in A&M's school colors. A poem praising former Aggie football coach Charlie B. Moran appeared on the front page of the November 1, 1921, *The Texas Aggie* as a means of congratulating him for being selected to the Coaches Hall of Fame:

This cornerstone for an alumni memorial stadium to be built on Kyle Field was part of an optimistic campaign to raise forty thousand dollars in 1920. Difficulties in raising the money caused the project to be cancelled. A stadium was constructed by the college nine years later. (*Photograph by Jerry C. Cooper '63.*)

>He's a grand old man,
>   Though we don't like to brag.
>And his worth he will prove to you soon;
>   He's the idol of the team we love,
>That fights for the dear old maroon,
>   Rah! Rah!
>And we stand by him,
>   Though we lose or win,
>And our faith in him will stand,
>Though other coaches may be good,
>Take your hat off to Coach Moran.

The most unique feature of this poem is the rhyme of *maroon* with *soon*. Before that time the school color maroon had been scarcely used at Texas A&M, although some A&M teams wore a band of maroon and white around their grey jerseys during the early 1920's. Before 1920, team jerseys were usually of grey, with dark-colored pants. The rallying colors of the Corps of Cadets at athletic events, banquets, and commencement were red and white, and in newspaper articles, yell books, *Longhorn* annuals and general correspondence the college colors of Texas A&M were unmistakable red and white.

In September, 1923, James Sullivan, business manager of athletics, ordered "plain maroon colored jerseys" for the football squad. Like the Corps of Cadets, who changed from the West Point–style gray uniform to the olive drab attire of World War I, Sullivan hoped to give the team a new look for the 1923 season. Of the change Sullivan commented, "The darker solid colors will add to the appearance of the team in that it will make it look heavier and more uniform." He failed to mention that maroon also better concealed the oxblood-colored football when it was carried close to the chest. But the change

The Golden Egg

in jersey colors, by accident or design, for all time changed the school colors from red and white to maroon and white.

William B. Cook '02, secretary of the association and first editor of the semimonthly newspaper *The Texas Aggie*, thoroughly covered sports events and association activities in the journal. Hardly an issue was printed without a call by him or other former students and administration leaders for more, "much more," participation in college and association activities. In the 1922 New Year's Day edition of *The Texas Aggie*, Cook outlined the purpose and objectives of the newly reorganized association:

THE ASSOCIATION OF FORMER STUDENTS OF THE A. AND M. COLLEGE OF TEXAS

WHAT IT IS

1. An organization composed of the Alumni and Ex-Students of the A. and M. College of Texas. The Alumni Association no longer exists. This is the Alumni Association enlarged to accommodate all men who have ever attended the A. and M. College.
2. Every man who ever attended the A. and M. College of Texas is eligible to membership. There are approximately 15,000 men eligible to membership in the Association.

ITS OBJECT

1. To employ a secretary to devote his full time to the interest of the Association and edit the Association paper.
2. To locate A. and M. men and in time compile a complete directory of A. and M. Ex-Students and Alumni.
3. To publish an Ex-Students' paper that will be a credit to the Association and the College, and to aid in the general publicity of the College.
4. To build a creditable home for the Association on the College campus to be owned, controlled and operated for the benefit and convenience of the Ex-Students and Alumni of the College.
5. To create a suitable students' loan fund for the benefit of young men who do not have sufficient funds to attend A. and M. College.
6. To assist in finding employment for students attending A. and M. College and for graduates and Ex-Students leaving the College.
7. To secure endowments from philanthropists.

Cook, in his capacity as editor of *The Texas Aggie*, also served as the first continuous on-campus secretary of the association. For his efforts he received no pay. He handled class reunion mail-outs and attempted to update the card file of former students which he inherited from the *Alumni Quarterly* editors Nester M. McGinnis and Charles Friley. Cook encouraged and fostered an expanded membership drive to help inform former students and to develop a base by which a financial support could be augmented. His efforts set the stage for the massive fund drives which soon followed under the leadership of Marion S. Church '05 and Carl Clifton Krueger '12.

Not all of the correspondence from former students to Cook was complimentary of association activities. One former student, Louis Edward Holloway '15, after reading the 1922 New Year's Day edition of *The Texas Aggie*, was unhappy with new reorganization and the fund-raising drive. To express his discontent with the objectives and intent of the

Left, P. L. Downs, Jr., '06 leading yell practice in the Grove. *Right*, Famed Texas artist and former student E. M. ("Buck") Schiwetz '21 did the artwork for the 1919, 1920, and 1921 *Longhorn* yearbooks. This drawing is from the 1920 edition.

new association, Holloway wrote the following note to Bill Cook as a satire on association efforts:

THE GOLDEN GOOSE EGG ASSOCIATION OF THE A. AND M. COLLEGE OF TEXAS

WHAT IT IS

1. An organization formed at the insistence of the president and faculty of the A. and M. College of Texas as a source of political pressure to be used to coerce the legislature and as a fount of easy "kale" for such moneys as not provided by regular appropriations.
2. This organization is peculiarly subject to dictation at the hands of the president of the College thru his personal representative, the secretary, and such members of the Association who are his employees.

ITS OBJECT

1. To assist in the over-development of semi-professional athletics as an acceptable sacrifice on the altar of the Golden Calf of Publicity.
2. To support a lobby at the state capitol.
3. To furnish funds for any and every business manager who starts yelling, "Calf Rope."
4. To build a suitable club house for the benefit of the ex-students who live within easy motoring distance of the College.
5. To send developed athletes from high schools to A. and M. so that the company leagues may be scrapped as of no further use to our coaches.

Hullabaloo, Caneck! Caneck!

Left, Bill Cook '20, executive secretary of the Association of Former Students, 1920–1923. *Right,* 1921 *Longhorn* cartoon by Buck Schiwetz '21.

6. To create a suitable students' loan fund for further attraction of crack athletes so badly needed by our coaches.

7. In general, whenever our College is concerned to waste no effort to secure size and to hell with quality.

Cook's reaction to this and other letters was to print them in *The Texas Aggie* in order to give all an equal voice. His policy of airing grievances helped dispel discontent. Such letters as Holloway's also revealed the inherent dangers of an alumni association becoming but a tool and voice of the incumbent administration. In this the A&M Association of Former Students has remained distinctive among alumni groups as a self-governing and truly independent body.

Association Goals

During the early part of 1922, Bill Cook and association President Charles DeWare encouraged three main programs: (1) the student loan fund, (2) the expansion of membership, and (3) a celebration day by each club statewide on April 21 "in order to rally former students." It was believed that if the second and third programs were successful, then the student loan fund would become a reality.

The annual meeting in June, 1922, was both productive and controversial. After welcoming remarks by Dr. Bizzell, DeWare opened the floor to some of the hottest debates in association history. Issues concerning the student loan fund, social fraternities, secret on-campus societies, finances, and class reunions were covered in great detail.

Students' Loan Fund

The student loan fund, as already seen, was greatly aided by large gifts donated by the class of '22 for student scholarships. Debate on the loan fund centered around the scope and magnitude of the new program. After much discussion, a "committee of five was appointed to cooperate with the board of directors of the College in formulating plans and devising methods for raising the necessary funds." With the loan fund question in

Association of Former Students staff for 1945. *Standing, left to right:* Lonnie B. Locke '22, who served as assistant secretary for forty years; unidentified; Beulah Bukowski; Natalie Boriskie; Marie ("Jane") Kalinec; and E. E. McQuillen '20. *Seated:* Thelma Rau; Mrs. Holick; and Willie Mae Shepperd, class programs secretary for twenty-six years.

committee, the gathering moved on to one of the hottest debates in association history.

For a period of several years there had been campus friction between the Ross Volunteer Company and certain secret societies such as the "K.K.'s," the "Swastikas," the "T.T.'s," and other fraternities, both social and honorary. Caesar Hohn '12, in a fiery speech, urged that all "fraternities" be barred from campus. Gustave A. Mistrot '12 of Houston seconded this motion, stating that "all forms of social and secret societies" only worked to divide the cadets and former students. Opinion was divided. Tyree Bell '13 protested that Hohn's and Mistrot's actions were "primarily aimed at the R.V.'s."

A degree of reason in this increasingly heated argument was interjected by DeWare and Everett E. McQuillen '20. In a soft-spoken but meaningful speech, DeWare reminded those gathered that Texas A&M was basically a "poor man school," having no place for "rich man's" organizations. McQuillen offered a motion that the association adopt a policy supporting "honorary fraternities" only. DeWare's and McQuillen's oratory produced a resolution giving support to "fraternities sponsoring scholarship at A&M without the use of Greek letter organizations or secret societies." A committee was named to meet with the Ross Volunteers, Swastikas, K.K.'s, and T.T.'s to impress upon these organizations the concern of the association for harmony among the students. Rivalry among the campus organizations soon diminished, and for the most part, except perhaps for the mysterious T.T.'s, or "True Texans," secret societies soon disappeared. Not for half a century would social fraternities and sororities appear on the A&M scene.

Four class reunions were held during the 1922 commencement week for the classes of 2's: 1882, 1892, 1902, 1912. Caesar Hohn, at the evening banquet, welcomed the class

Secret Societies

Class Reunions

of '22 to association membership. Hohn's remarks were acknowledged by Cadet C. W. Thomas '22 of La Grange, class valedictorian and Texas A&M's first Oxford Scholar elect. The class of '22 was the largest to that date, with 216 members.

William A. Wurzbach '88 won association support for a revised reunion schedule which would reunite more former students on a regular basis. Association class reunions were scheduled to be held every five years in lieu of the old system of every ten years. Bill Cook began at once to establish a rotating schedule for all classes, past and future. In early 1923 a new elaborate five-year reunion schedule was published in *The Texas Aggie*.

The new reunion schedule increased the reunion activities sixfold. Bill Cook said of the new program, "Instead of holding reunions every ten years as has been done in the past, it was decided that classes would return to the campus at five year periods and would be grouped so that the four classes that were in college at the same time can meet together." During the first year of the new program twenty-three class reunions were scheduled.

Under the new plan, one-half of all the classes ever graduated by Texas A&M were to meet in reunion each June. Cook, optimistic of the program, wrote, "No one should stand back because he thinks there will be too much for the College to comfortably care for. We shall be able to care for as many as come." This extensive reunion schedule was used until the early 1930's.

The New 1923 Revised Reunion Schedule

Class	Year									
	1923	1924	1925	1926	1927	1928	1929	1930	1931	1932
1922	—	—	—	1922	—	—	—	—	1922	—
1921	—	—	—	1921	—	—	—	—	1921	—
1920	1920	—	—	1920	—	—	—	—	1920	—
1919	1919	—	—	—	1919	—	—	—	1919	—
1918	1918	—	—	—	1918	—	—	—	—	1918
1917	1917	—	—	—	1917	—	—	—	—	1917
1916	1916	—	—	—	1916	—	—	—	—	1916
1915	1915	—	—	—	—	1915	—	—	—	1915
1914	1914	—	—	—	—	1914	—	—	—	—
1913	1913	—	—	—	—	1913	—	—	—	—
1912	—	1912	—	—	—	1912	—	—	—	—
1911	—	1911	—	—	—	—	1911	—	—	—
1910	—	1910	—	—	—	—	1910	—	—	—
1909	—	1909	—	—	—	—	1909	—	—	—
1908	—	—	1908	—	—	—	1908	—	—	—
1907	—	—	1907	—	—	—	—	1907	—	—
1906	1906	—	1906	—	—	—	—	1906	—	—
1905	1905	—	1905	—	—	—	—	1905	—	—
1904	1904	—	—	1904	—	—	—	1904	—	—
1903	1903	—	—	1903	—	—	—	—	1903	—
1902	—	—	—	1902	—	—	—	—	1902	—
1901	—	—	—	1901	—	—	—	—	1901	—

Class	1923	1924	1925	1926	1927	1928	1929	1930	1931	1932
1900	—	—	—	—	1900	—	—	—	1900	—
1899	—	—	—	—	1899	—	—	—	—	1899
1898	—	—	—	—	1898	—	—	—	—	1898
1897	1897	—	—	—	1897	—	—	—	—	1897
1896	1896	—	—	—	—	1896	—	—	—	1896
1895	1895	—	—	—	—	1895	—	—	—	—
1894	1894	—	—	—	—	1894	—	—	—	—
1893	1893	—	—	—	—	1893	—	—	—	—
1892	—	1892	—	—	—	—	1892	—	—	—
1891	—	1891	—	—	—	—	1891	—	—	—
1890	—	1890	—	—	—	—	1890	—	—	—
1889	—	—	1889	—	—	—	1889	—	—	—
1888	—	—	1888	—	—	—	—	1888	—	—
1887	—	—	1887	—	—	—	—	1887	—	—
1886	—	—	1886	—	—	—	—	1886	—	—
1885	—	—	—	1885	—	—	—	1885	—	—
1884	—	—	—	1884	—	—	—	—	1884	—
1883	1883	—	—	1883	—	—	—	—	1883	—
1882	1882	—	—	1882	—	—	—	—	1882	—
1881	1881	—	—	—	1881	—	—	—	1881	—
1880	1880	—	—	—	1880	—	—	—	—	1880
1879	1879	—	—	—	1879	—	—	—	—	1879
1878	1878	—	—	—	1878	—	—	—	—	1878

The Texas Aggie magazine opened its columns to an even wider variety of topics of interest to the former students. Special events such as annual musters and Memorial Day activities, reunion schedules, sports (mainly football and basketball), club activities, and former student job placement notices, under the heading of "Round Pegs for Square Holes," filled the semimonthly issues. Circulation was estimated to be about ten thousand in mid-1925. In addition to job placement notices, items such as public service announcements and the schedule of the student radio station, WTAW, founded in early December, 1922, were listed for alumni consumption.

In early March, association President Elton P. Hunter '00 launched a drive, with the assistance of Cook, Church, and Krueger, to have a statewide muster on April 21, 1923. A special muster broadcast over WTAW on the campus was beamed to Aggies statewide. More than twenty formal musters were held around Texas. To recapture the spirit of comradeship developed during muster, Hunter urged all former students to return to the campus during commencement. Alumni response was overwhelming, and Cook added new recruits to association rosters. The membership drive and fund-raising efforts by Hunter broadened the range and scope of association activity. The new reunion schedule brought twenty-four classes together on the campus in 1923. The 1923 homecoming was

Reunion of the class of 1879 during commencement week, 1924.

Association Fund Drive

all, and more, than it was billed to be. Hunter was able to capitalize on the momentum of the year's activities to put the association on the road toward a sound fiscal base.

Hunter presented the complete details of the association's finances before the annual meeting in 1923 in an effort to solve the perennial money problem. His approach was subtle yet firm, and his frankness was candid, not insulting. The following items were presented as the major needs, problems, and shortcomings of the association: (1) the association was in debt $4,219.67, (2) income from dues was "uncertain and inadequate," (3) the yearly cost of The Texas Aggie for 1923–1924 would require a budget of "at least" $7,500, and (4) Bill Cook had resigned as The Texas Aggie editor just before the meeting, and a new editor and executive secretary were "imperative."

With ample leadership available, Hunter proposed that the dues structure be abandoned in favor of a "pledges or subscription" financial foundation. While not a novel idea, it did place the burden on association members and not on the leadership to make the organization financially solvent. Yearly, the association leadership had been required to balance the budget with crash fund-raising drives or bank loans. To implement this new system, Hunter suggested that the state be divided into fifteen districts. Each district was to provide a member for the finance committee, and this district chairman was to solicit subscriptions to be due on or before October 1 each year. Subscriptions could be obtained from individuals, business firms, mothers' clubs, or A&M clubs. After the budget was met, any excess funds would be placed in the Students' Loan Fund.

The Aggie Band, 1924–1925.

No one could have found a more receptive audience. Scarcely had he concluded his remarks when former student after former student stood to applaud his ideas and to pledge "their fair share." Within thirty minutes 125 Aggies had pledged a resounding $15,000. The amount was increased "following the barbecue Monday night and it was expected that over $25,000 would be pledged before the exes leave campus." These pledges were referred to as funds for the "endowment fund." They were the nucleus of what is today the "annual giving" concept.

During both the general morning session and the barbecue, inspirational speeches were made by Marion Church, W. A. Wurzbach, P. L. Downs, Jr., and others. It was decided to wage a campaign "throughout the land of A&M graduate dwellers and create an endowment of $100,000." This income was envisioned to have four distinct purposes: (1) to make the association solvent, (2) to make funds available to employ a "competent" full-time executive secretary, (3) to support activities that were in the best interest of the college, and (4) to make more loans available to the students. Under the title of "A Rejuvenated Association," the following statement appeared in *The Texas Aggie*:

> The Association of Former Students of the A. and M. College is alive. New spirit, new enterprise, and a permanent foundation, financially were breathed into that organization at the commencement meeting at the College. Public spirited, loyal sons of the institution adopted plans for financing the organization which will make it possible for that organization to do a big piece of work for the College.
>
> Get in behind your district chairman. Make as large a gift to the organization as you possibly can. Concern yourself with its welfare. Work for students, for popular esteem for your Alma Mater. Makes its interests yours and see to it that the people of your district are convinced of the worthwhileness of your institution to the extent that they will see to it that it shall not suffer.
>
> WHAT HELPS THE A. AND M. COLLEGE OF TEXAS HELPS
> YOU AS A FORMER STUDENT OF THE INSTITUTION.

With the idea firmly implanted, the burden was on the entire membership to fulfill their pledges. The organization drive behind the plan was more important than the plan itself. To initiate Hunter's blueprint, Marion S. Church '05 was elected president for the 1923–1924 term. Church's first vice-president-elect was C. C. ("Polly") Krueger '12.

It was decided to wait until the fund-raising campaign was well established before selecting a new executive secretary. The association constitution was altered so that future executive secretaries would not be elected by the association but would be employed by the executive board. As Luke L. Ballard wrote in an editorial in August, 1923, "it was the sense of the Association that a man of great capacity in handling delicate affairs of public interest affecting an institution with such wide ramifications as this college, should be saluted and that such a man need not necessarily be an alumnus." The executive secretary's position was to remain vacant through the summer and fall of 1923 as a suitable candidate was sought. In the interim, Church, Krueger, Tom Blake, and A. C. Love absorbed the secretary's duties.

Marion Church

Marion Church was a real leader and a dedicated Aggie. During his student days he was manager of the football team, captain of the baseball team, valedictorian of his class, member of the Athletic Council, president of the senior class, cadet major of the battalion, and commander of the Houston Rifles, today known as the Ross Volunteer Company. After graduating, he was state feed inspector before entering the study of law at the University of Texas. It is interesting to note that Church was a star third baseman on the University of Texas baseball team as he had been at Texas A&M. Krueger recalled, "To the surprise of the Texas University coach, Church refused to play in the games against Texas A&M. There was no greater Aggie."

Unaffected by the vacancy of the secretary's position, "Parson" Church, as he was commonly called, launched a full-scale statewide fund-raising and membership drive in the late fall of 1923. *The Texas Aggie* of August 15, 1923, carried a front-page picture of Church accompanied by a lengthy editorial on the progress of the fund-raising efforts. The headline running the width of the front page read: "FIGHTING AGGIE SPIRIT MARKS CAMPAIGN." Completely ignoring his Dallas law firm, Church stumped the state relentlessly. His emotion-packed speech, entitled "One's Loyalty to His Alma Mater," became household news to all Aggies.

The Texas Aggie said of Church's inspired leadership, "Marion Church has been conducting revival meetings ever since his election and Aggie 'amens' of 'Farmers Fight' have been reechoing from Houston and the Magic Valley and San Antonio, all the way up to Wichita Falls. The notes are rolling in." C. C. ("Polly") Krueger wrote of Church's fund-raising ability:

> One of Marion Church's favorite stories was about the poor farm boy who longed to go to Texas A&M. He was given the family cow which he led to College. He lived in a tent south of the campus and sold the milk to the families of faculty members in the neighborhood to defray his expenses. I must confess that I never saw the boy nor the cow, but when Church told the story in his tear-producing manner, very few men ever left the meeting room without signing a pledge to donate to the Association for the students' loan fund.

By late September, 1923, the fund-raising drive had amassed 284 individual former student donations in the amount of approximately $31,200. As Church and other former students canvassed the state to raise money, the college boasted the largest enrollment to date, 2,066. Of the large increase in enrollment, *The Texas Aggie* commented: "Splendid

The 1919 Yell Leaders. *Left to right:* D. M. ("Cop") Forsyth '21, A. L. Robertson '19, Robert B. Goodman '19, Maynard Landa '19, Red Thompson '21, and H. F. Womack '23.

tribute to the name and fame of A. and M. is paid by this increasing attendance. Knowledge of inadequate living conditions; knowledge that Young Son probably would be bunked in a tent did not lead father and mother into sending their boy elsewhere. In other words, the 900 Freshmen who wanted to enroll and the 1200 old boys who returned to the fold were willing to pay the price of over-crowded conditions and inadequate accommodations to be present at Old Aggieland." The enrollment, while labeled a "splendid tribute," caused monumental difficulties for the administration. To house this influx, the tents were discarded in favor of "bungalettes," known commonly by the students as "the Hollywood Shacks." More than three hundred cadets were housed in these 16' × 16' box buildings, which came complete with a door, three windows, a pot-bellied stove, and "running water in each building."

In mid-November, Ike S. Ashburn was nominated to be the first full-time executive secretary of the association. Although not a former student of Texas A&M, he was held in high regard by both the administration and the association. He fulfilled, beyond a doubt, the association's expectations as a "man of great capability." In January, 1913, he had begun his relationship with Texas A&M as publicity secretary and secretary to the Board of Directors. He had resigned from the college staff to enter military service in April, 1917, and was among the first group of Texans to attend the first Leon Springs training camp in mid-1917.

Camp conditions at Leon Springs were primitive, due to the urgency of training as many men as possible to be commissioned for service in France. Many in attendance complained of the dust, chiggers, poor food, and snoring. Every barracks had its own snoring champ, and the Ninth Company claimed the champion of champions—Ike Ashburn. "Ike

Ike Ashburn: Secretary

Hullabaloo, Caneck! Caneck! 131

Colonel Ike Ashburn, executive secretary of the Association of Former Students, 1923–1926.

Kyle Field construction, September, 1929.

could snore," they said, "with the rumbling reverberations of a mighty pipe organ. It must be admitted that his size gave some justification to that comparison."

Ashburn survived the camp and earned a captain's commission. During World War I he became a renowned hero and was decorated three times by the United States and France for bravery. In 1919 he returned to Texas A&M to become commandant of cadets, a post he held until his appointment as executive secretary of the Association of Former Students on January 1, 1924. The selection of Ashburn by the executive committee composed of M. S. Church, C. C. Krueger, T. W. Blake, A. C. Love, L. L. Ballard, J. L. Lockridge, and M. J. Miller proved to be the ideal addition to the already prosperous activities of the association.

By March, 1924, *The Texas Aggie* reported that 609 former students had signed pledges totaling $58,527.50. These pledges were to cover a five-year period. Many notes of $5 per year were pledged by the recent graduates of the college, and other contributions ranged up to $200 per year for a total of $1,000 for the five-year period. Still not satisfied with success of the fund-raising drive, Church planned "a whirlwind finish to his administration . . . in order to secure notes in excess of $75,000" by the annual commencement and association meeting in early June.

More than 150 former students were in attendance in June. Marion Church rose to deliver one of his most "inspiring and stirring" messages. He candidly reviewed the past twelve months of the association and pointed out that upon receiving the presidency of the association in June, 1923, he had inherited an organization with an indebtedness of $5,000, no executive secretary, no complete records, and "a general lack of interest in, and sympathy with the organization." Not belaboring the problems of the association, he thanked the membership for its unending efforts to "rejuvenate" the association. In closing, he announced that as of early morning, 975 "loyal A&M men" had signed pledges for $75,243.50. The "Parson" had put the association on a sound financial footing it continues to enjoy to this day.

Artillery practice in the early 1930's.

10. Vintage Years

The financial successes of the Association of Former Students led to its incorporation in 1925 as a nonprofit institution under the laws of Texas. Mindful of the legal ramifications associated with the collection of large donations, Marion S. Church, with Ike Ashburn, Tom W. Blake '04, Andrew C. Love '99, Elton P. Hunter '01, Luke L. Ballard '05, Charles Rogan '79, Joe Utay '08, Carl C. ("Polly") Krueger '12, and William A. Wurzbach '88 formed a committee authorized by the association to petition the State of Texas for the incorporation of the association. The Association of Former Students of the Agricultural and Mechanical College of Texas was chartered "for a term of 50 years," but in 1964 an amendment to the charter changed the term to "in perpetuity." Under the charter a board of directors of twenty-five men was elected annually to transact the business of the association. One director was selected from each of the eighteen congressional districts of Texas. The remaining seven were to be elected at large. The purposes of the association as drafted in the new charter were to "aid the students of Texas A&M, promote social, literary and scientific pursuits and perpetuate and strengthen the ties of affection and esteem formed in college days."

Articles of Incorporation

Membership was open to all persons who had been students and all students regularly enrolled or "who may become enrolled as students at the college." The new legal status of the association facilitated fund-raising efforts which C. C. Krueger, association president for 1924–1925, continued to expand. The heavier workload of correspondence and accounts required the addition of staff personnel. In January, 1925, Everett E. McQuillen '20 came to work at the association office as assistant secretary to work under Ike Ashburn. A full-time clerical worker was also employed. The association was enjoying growing pains. Moreover, former students became increasingly conspicuous in the management of the affairs of the college.

Staff Expansion

In 1925, five prominent former students of Texas A&M served on the eight-man Board of Directors of the college: Francis Marion Law '05, Pinckney Lovick Downs '06, Walter G. Lacy '95, Henry C. Schuhmacher '88, and William A. Wurzbach '88. For a time Texas A&M was unique among public institutions of higher learning in that its alumni directed administrative policy. While the alumni have always exercised a strong influence on the administration of a college, the influence of the former students on Texas A&M was perhaps never so direct, or so great, as in the 1920's and 1930's.

Dr. W. B. Bizzell, president of Texas A&M for ten years, resigned in 1925 to assume the position of president of the University of Oklahoma. Under Bizzell's direction the academic programs and the student body had improved in quantity and quality. On September 3, 1925, Thomas Otto Walton was named by the Texas A&M Board of Directors to replace Bizzell as president of Texas A&M.

The class of '00 in reunion during commencement, 1930. *First row, left to right:* F. K. McGinnis '00, T. W. Griffiths '00, R. B. Boettcher '00, J. E. Abrahams '00, W. J. Walden '00, Alumni Secretary E. E. McQuillen '20, and Hal Moseley '00. *Second row:* S. H. Simpson '00, O. W. Myers '00, A. K. Short '00, A. Winkler '00, President T. O. Walton, W. I. Bryan '00, and E. P. Hunter '01. *Top center:* W. W. Sterling '10.

Reception for T. O. Walton

Former students were quite pleased with the selection of T. O. Walton as president of the college. Walton assumed the office after having served as director of the Agricultural Extension Service for eight years. Shortly after the appointment, Ike Ashburn and D. X. Bible hosted numerous receptions statewide at various Texas A&M clubs in order to introduce "the new fish prexy" to the former students. Walton was warmly greeted wherever he visited. The "Houston Gang" gave by far one of the wildest receptions at the Rice Hotel on September 8, 1925. "Dutch" Hohn, serving as toastmaster, made the evening an unforgettable occasion.

Dutch, in welcoming President and Mrs. Walton, planned to present the new president with a token of the club's appreciation. En route to the party, Hohn stopped by the local Woolworth store and hastily purchased a punch bowl for the Waltons. The ensuing events, as reported in the *Houston Post-Dispatch*, were observed by more than 250 Aggies:

PREXY'S HOPES OF CONVIVIAL CORN CROP SHATTERED
WHEN DROPSY DUTCH HOHN SPILLED THE PUNCH
AT HOUSTON AGGIE BANQUET AT RICE HOTEL

The feelings of scores of persons were severely hurt and property valued at 15 cents was totally destroyed Tuesday night in a head-on collision between T. O. (Texas, not Oklahoma) Walton, A. & M. president, and Dutch Hohn, alias Dropsy Dutch.

The collision occurred at the banquet fed by A. and M. ex-students to "Prexy" Walton, the jefe of the college.

136 WE ARE THE AGGIES

President T. O. Walton (*left*) and Francis Marion Law '95, president of the Board of Directors, during the semicentennial celebration in 1926.

The priceless Woolworthian glass punch bowl, purchased through funds obtained by popular extortion for presentation to Professor Walton as a token of esteem, was shattered.

In some unknown manner Hohn dropped the bowl. It fell. There was a crash. The bowl was demolished.

By early June, 1925, under Polly Krueger's leadership, over $108,000 was pledged to association activities and the Students' Loan Fund. Krueger had effectively directed the association in the wake of its tremendous "rejuvenation" initiated by Church. The energy of Krueger and Church would prove difficult to match in future years. Each succeeding group of association leaders hoped to build on the stable base so expertly established between 1923 and 1925. Many new association programs needed expansion and assistance.

In order to capitalize on the momentum, Luke C. Ballard, elected to the presidency of the association for the 1925–1926 term, worked with Ike Ashburn, E. E. McQuillen, and A. C. Ward, all of College Station, and William A. Orth '12 of San Antonio and Carlton Meredith '15 of Dallas to reorganize the Texas A&M clubs statewide. Hoping to attract more Aggies to club meetings, leaders considered "a ritual for introducing Aggies into A. and M. Clubs." Such a ritual was not adopted, although clubs statewide did reorganize and become more active during 1925–1926 with support from association officers and staff.

A&M Club Activities

Other club activities, including local journals and newsletters, were generated to attract more former students into the activities of the association. Under the editorship of Asa Hunt '22, the *Dal-AGGIE*, "a weekly publication devoted to the interest of the Dallas A&M Club," was inaugurated. Hunt adopted the idea of a weekly newspaper from the Houston A&M Club, which published the *Houston Aggie*. Issues of both publications were especially popular during football season because of the excellent coverage of campus and association activities. Efforts to reorganize and rejuvenate old clubs led to the

Vintage Years 137

The President's Home during the 1930's.

formation of new clubs in Navarro and Bell counties, Texas; a club in Guatemala; and the South Plains Club and Oklahoma City Club in Oklahoma.

As a special project for the numerous Texas A&M clubs, Ballard urged state and nationwide reunions on April 21 to celebrate San Jacinto and to "relive the good ole' days at A&M": "From Guatemala to Chicago, A. and M. Men Are Making Plans to Celebrate San Jacinto Day." Plans were made by Ashburn and McQuillen to host fifteen class reunions during the fiftieth annual commencement of the college.

Semicentennial Celebration

During the October, 1926, semicentennial celebration, President T. O. Walton was formally inaugurated in a colorful ceremony witnessed by the representatives of more than 125 institutions from throughout America and Europe. All but one of the living past presidents of the college attended the celebration. On hand were former presidents Colonel John G. James (1879–1883), Major L. L. McInnis (1888–1890), Henry H. Harrington (1905–1908), and Dr. W. B. Bizzell (1914–1925). One of the highlights of Texas A&M's golden anniversary was the reunion of the "old time Aggies, members of the classes of '76, '77, '78, and '79." Aubrey L. Banks of Denton, one of the first students to register at the college, Colonel George Washington Hardy '79 of Shreveport, Colonel P. L. Downs '79, Herbert Albert Paine '79 of Bryan, Senator Irving Harvey Bryant '78 of Austin, General Thomas Jefferson Hardeman '79 of Galveston, and Reuben D. Bowers '78 of New Orleans were the A&M "pioneers" present at the ceremonies. Texas A&M and the Association of Former Students at the semicentennial celebrations stood on the threshold of great achievements—and more immediately on the threshold of the Great Depression.

The class of 1899 and their wives on campus for the thirty-fifth-year reunion, April 15, 1934. *First row, left to right:* Mrs. R. D. Ragsdale, Mrs. Charles D. Evans, Mrs. E. J. Kyle, and E. L. Martin. *Second row:* Charles D. Evans, Josh Sterns, A. C. Love, J. M. Adams, and Dr. L. F. Blaud. *Top row:* R. D. Ragsdale, E. J. Kyle, and E. H. Asten.

Ike Ashburn resigned his position as executive secretary of the association in November, 1926, to accept employment in Houston. The Executive Committee promoted Everett E. McQuillen '20 to the top position. Ashburn reflected upon the achievements of Texas A&M and the association and pointed to the great opportunities ahead:

Ashburn Leaves A&M

In tendering my resignation as Executive Secretary of the Association of Former Students of the College, effective January 1, 1927, I sever relations with an institution with which I have been connected since January, 1913.

I sincerely believe that the A. & M. College makes a finer contribution to the manhood of its men than any other educational institution in the United States. It is my genuine conviction that the men who go out from this college have less to unlearn when they go out into the world.

No one not intimately in touch with the work can appreciate the importance of the work being carried on by the Association of Former Students. It was conceived by men who had the deep desire to serve their college and the organization has taken on the fine ideals of those men. The surface has barely been scratched. There is no end to the possibilities that lie before the Association from the standpoint of helping the College.

While the Great Depression dimmed the vision and dampened opportunities, it uncovered new wellsprings of strength, resourcefulness, and dedication among students and former students of the "A. and M. C." The repercussions of the stock-market crash of October, 1929, sent shock waves all across the United States and Texas. Enrollment at Texas A&M, which had reached a high of twenty-eight hundred in the fall of 1929, began to decline in 1929 and sank to a little over two thousand in 1932 and 1933, but then spurted

The Great Depression

The reading room of Cushing Memorial Library, mid-1930's.

dramatically after 1934 and rose to over sixty-five hundred by 1940. In many ways Texas A&M weathered the Great Depression better than most institutions of higher learning, thanks largely to three unique situations.

Oil Royalties

One of these situations had to do with Texas A&M's participation in the oil royalties from Texas' University Land Endowment. Oil was discovered on the two-million-acre endowment in 1926. During the depression decade, Texas A&M received one-third of the more than twenty million dollars in oil revenues derived from university lands. These funds were used in maintaining facilities and in new construction.

Project Houses

A second factor which made it possible for more students to attend college than might otherwise have been possible was the development at Texas A&M of "project houses," or student housing cooperatives. This unique program, developed by Professor Dan Russell in 1932, enabled students to rent a house, bring food and provisions from home, do their own cooking and cleaning, and live more cheaply than they could otherwise. Students brought cows, chickens, butter, canned goods, and household goods and pooled their money and bought groceries wholesale. The Texas A&M experiment mushroomed and spread to other colleges and universities throughout the nation. In 1936 the A&M Board of Directors arranged to have the Association of Former Students build project houses on the campus to be managed under college auspices. Some of the houses were built by local A&M clubs for students from their communities. The Board of Directors also financed construction of fourteen houses from college funds. By the end of 1937 more than fifty project houses were in operation on and off campus. In part because of the care and concern of the Association of Former Students, thousands of young people who otherwise

Left, Walter W. Wipprecht '84 inspecting a large mesquite tree that stood near the West Gate for many years. *Right*, Three stalwarts of the A&M College during the 1930's. *Left to right:* Dr. Mark Francis, Professor Robert F. Smith, and Dean Charles Puryear.

would have been unable to do so were able to obtain a college education during the depression.

Association support of A&M students extended as well to individual financial aid through the association's student loan program. Individual loans to students varied from five dollars to one hundred dollars. The association jealously guarded its loan fund. Lonnie Locke, who joined the association staff in 1928 and who administered the loans, commented years later that "the interest accrued from the monies loaned through the students' loan fund were sacred," and despite the financial straits of the association, those funds "could not be used for salaries and expenses." Without exception, the student loans were always repaid. Indeed, today A&M students are unusually responsible in the repayment of student loans, whether to the Association of Former Students or to U.S. government loan programs. Aggies have the lowest loan default record of any student body in the nation. Because the former students care enough to give those who are in need the opportunity for an education at Texas A&M, A&M students, like those before them, have developed a sense of responsibility and a commitment to those who follow. Thus, out of the hard times of the depression there developed an unusual love and dedication among former students for Texas A&M. So a man such as W. T. ("Bill") Moore '40, a depression Aggie, could profess in 1974 "to an unsurpassed love for this institution because of what it did for me."

As economic hardships began to diminish association revenues, association officers found it necessary to reduce expenditures. The staff was cut to three employees, including E. E. McQuillen, Lonnie Locke, and Daisy Brogdon. In an attempt to reduce expenses as much as possible, both McQuillen and Locke periodically took voluntary reductions in salaries between 1929 and 1937. Similarly, all state employees, including A&M College faculty and staff, received a 25 percent reduction in salary in 1933. Both the college ad-

Students' Loan Fund

Vintage Years 141

The class of '08 in reunion during commencement, 1938.

ministration and the Association of Former Students struggled to protect their cash assets and maintain needed revenues. The association dues structure failed to produce adequate income to finance the various programs of the organization. Expenditures of the 1933–1934 term were reported by E. E. McQuillen in his annual secretary's report to total $8,350, including salaries of $5,500, publication of *The Texas Aggie* at $1,500, postage at $650, and office supplies at $250, with the remaining $450 budgeted for entertainment, travel, insurance, and miscellaneous expenses. Income from dues was approximately $2,500 less than the expenditures. But the association found relief from an unexpected source.

The Tailor Shop

An activity that helped relieve financial shortages was the association-owned tailor shop. The tailor shop was opened in early 1928 as a campus service to former students, students, and faculty and was located on the second floor of the Old Exchange Store across from Milner Hall. It provided both cleaning and tailoring services. When dues failed to meet its financial needs, the association drew from the profits of the tailor shop in order to balance the budget. The shop, in the mid-1930's, netted the association "approximately $2,500 annually." Locke was in charge of the shop, which employed three shop assistants and twenty-six "solicitors," who used their earnings to support their education. The auditor's review of 1931 reported to the association that "The Shop was found to be in very tidy condition." Throughout the 1930's the shop showed a substantial profit. In the mid-1930's, after a series of positive reports were submitted by the auditors, it was suggested in jest that because of the success of the tailor shop the association should change the name of the organization to the "Campus Cleaners Association."

In 1931, Julian B. Thomas '11 was elected as president of the association for the 1931–1932 term. He was followed by A. Kidd Short '00 (1932–1933) and Thomas K. Warden '03, who served two terms (1933–1935). Warden called for ". . . team play of the highest order of all A. & M. men as being requisite for the best service of their institution and the welfare of the Association." Much to the surprise of Locke, McQuillen, and Warden, former students flocked to the campus in May, 1934, for the annual meeting. During 1934 it was reported that "successful class reunions were held for the classes of 1884, 1894, 1904, 1909, 1914, 1919, and 1924." But accommodations for visiting guests on the campus continued to remain a problem. Locke recalls having to house visiting former students in the "campus hospital, on cots in DeWare Field House and at private homes in the neighborhood."

Irwin A. Uhr '17 of San Antonio helped to regain some of the momentum of the mid-1920's during his term as association president from 1935 to 1936. In an effort to stimulate more active participation by former students, Uhr in early April, 1935, attempted to change Texas A&M's April 21 annual muster to a new rally day, October 4. This new celebration was to be known as Founder's Day. Although narrowly approved by the association's board of directors, the idea provoked an unfavorable reaction from nearly every former student. Muster had become an Aggie "tradition." Finally, in March, 1937, the association board decided that the annual mustering day be "moved back from its fall date, to April 21, or San Jacinto Day." Never again was there an attempt to alter the annual muster celebration.

Founder's Day

Although the Founder's Day idea was unsuccessful, even the negative response seems to have reawakened former student support. Uhr continued his proselytizing with a "Pull 'Em In" campaign. He visited A&M clubs in Dallas, Houston, Fort Worth, Athens, Beaumont, Brady, Austin, San Antonio, Corpus Christi, and Harlingen in an effort to raise the "A&M spirit." The full effects of Uhr's "Pull 'Em In" campaign were not felt until late 1936. E. E. McQuillen in his annual report commented, "The success of the campaign must be credited to the great work done by the local clubs. . . . The Beaumont A&M Club raised its active Association membership from 20 to 150—the most astonishing and complete work along this line that has ever been recorded." As the association returned to a more stable financial basis, the salaries of McQuillen and his staff were raised to their pre-1930 level. This readjustment was possible in large part to a more than "50 percent increase in dues payments" between 1934 and 1937. During the 1935–1936 term, 1,880 members paid dues, as opposed to more than 1,080 in the previous year.

Pull 'Em In

Irwin A. Uhr in his annual report for the fiscal year 1935–1936 outlined in clear terms the financial conditions of the organization: "Let me call your attention to the total assets of our organization at this time. They reach the respectable figure of $222,354.64 which includes student loan funds and other trust funds. This figure is significant in that it means our organization must be a stable one, carefully managed and supervised. Our Association has heavy responsibilities in the conservation, the handling, and the use of these funds. We are no fly-by-night, two-bit concern, but a Texas Corporation with assets, program, and accomplishments that should make us proud to be members of our Association." During the 1936 annual meeting, Charles A. Thanheiser '01 was elected president for the ensuing 1936–1937 year. By mid-1937, 3,080 men were bonafide, dues-paying members of the association, and the Students' Loan Fund totaled in excess of $235,000.

In late 1937 a study was completed by association President F. Dudley Perkins '97 (1937–1938) to create a long-range program for membership recruitment. Perkins proposed that comprehensive programs be devised first to attract the former students and second to develop among the student body an awareness of the purpose, functions, and

Vintage Years 143

The 1939 National Football Champions. *Left to right, first row:* Herbie Smith, Marland Jeffrey, Ed Robnett, Cotton Price, Marion Pugh, Frank Wood, Bill Henderson, Les Richardson, and Joe Rothe. *Second row:* Mack Browder, Muley White, Charles Henke, Marshall Robnett, Tommie Vaughn, Euel Wesson, Jim Thomason, John Kimbrough, Bud Force, and 'Bama Smith. *Third row:* Cullen Rogers, Bill Conatser, Derace Moser, Odell Herman, Bill Miller, Hugh Boyd, Bill Buchanan, Jim Sterling, Cotton Williams, Bubba Reeves, and Martin Ruby. *Fourth row:* Ernie Pannell, Marshall Spivey, Bill Duncan, John Abbott, Zolus Motley, Bill Blessing, Leon Rahn, Harold Cowley, Dog Dawson, and Rock Audish. *Fifth row:* Leonard Joeris, Joe Parish, Howard Shelton, Jo Jo White, Jack Kimbrough, Chip Routt, Carl Geer, Chester Heimann, Joe Boyd, Gus Bates, and Willard Clark. *Sixth row:* Roy Bucek, Henry Hauser, and Pinky Williams. *Seventh row:* Charles DeWare, Marty Karow, Bill James, Hub McQuillen, Homer Norton, Lil Dimmitt, Manning Smith, Harry Faulkner, and Dough Rollins.

Membership Drive

goals of the association. The recruitment of former students was to be handled at the local Texas A&M club level. The most far-reaching and intriguing program was the plan of action known as the "second phase of the 10 year program":

We must build our Ex-Students Association among the student body at Texas A. & M. During the next 19 years at least 5,000 young men will become Ex-students from our school—4,000 of them actual graduates. In this group rests our opportunity for really substantial growth. If we wait, however, until these men become Ex-Students, then we face the same difficulties with them that we now face with some 5,000 A. & M. men. Five thousand loyal and more or less interested A. & M. men—but for some reason 5,000 men we can't get into our Association.

The aim of this part of our program, will be to nourish and cultivate this coming 5,000 Ex-students to the end that everyone of them will be active Association members in 1948. Important, too, is our hope that these young members will join us because they WANT to, because they feel it is their DUTY and because they regard it as their PRIVILEGE and their HONOR.

A special fund created by allocating fifty cents from every former student donation was established as a recruiting fund. This money was allocated to approximately twenty-five

Coach Homer Norton and All–Southwest Conference halfback James N. ("Jim") Thomason '41.

David Brooks Cofer (*center*) did much to preserve A&M heritage by fostering the creation and maintenance of the University Archives.

Vintage Years 145

"Wee-Willie's Dead Aim." Letting off steam in the late 1930's.

student organizations "at the will and selection of the dues payer." The college YMCA, the Aggie Band, the "T" Club, the Ross Volunteers, the Glee Club, the library, and the Saddle and Sirloin Club, to name but a few, would all benefit from this plan. It was expected that under the 1937 membership rules between one thousand and seventeen hundred dollars "would be scattered" among the student organizations. It was anticipated that this plan would interest former students in campus activities by providing a worthwhile and concrete contribution to the college. In summary, the plan would "provide real, tangible proof of Ex-student interest and aid in present student activities—and thus provide wonderful contact between today's and yesterday's A. & M. students. . . . additionally it would appeal to varying types of men—the Math shark as well as the football fan—the 'Y' Cabinet ex as well as the Hell-raiser."

In order to launch the program, Perkins outlined a goal that should be accomplished in what he termed "the immediate future." He envisioned by mid-1938 the inauguration of some ceremonial feature of commencement at which occasion graduating seniors would be welcomed, initiated, pledged, or inducted into the ranks of the former students.

Senior Banquet

Association Presidents Charles L. Babcock '20 of Beaumont (1938–1939), Calvin P. Dodson '11 of Decatur (1939–1940), A. G. Pfaff '25 of Tyler (1940–1941), and Tyree L. Bell '13 (1941–1942) pursued the goals of the 1937 membership report energetically. During the early 1940's the association began holding banquets during or just before each commencement in order to welcome the seniors of each graduating class into the ranks of the former students. This program continues and has proved to be highly successful. In more recent years graduates have received a year's free subscription to *The Texas Aggie* magazine and miniature laminated diplomas as a memento of their graduation.

The depression decade drew to a close with the Association of Former Students in a solvent financial state and spiritually more vigorous than ever before. The very special care and support for the welfare of the college and of the individual Aggies attending school helped develop that extra sense of loyalty via membership in the Association of Former Students.

Mounted Cadet Cavalry unit at the beginning of World War II.

George F. Moore '08, shown here as commandant of cadets, later became ranking Aggie on Corregidor during April, 1942.

11. The Military Legacy

The hard-fought battles against depression had not fully ceased when the even more desperate conflicts of World War II erupted. Aggies, much like Americans everywhere, had for the past years tried to ignore the tramping of the invader's boot over most of Europe and parts of Asia and had heard only faintly, in a wondering way, the roar of warplanes over the English Channel. That detachment, like American neutrality, ended in a blinding eruption and a tangled mass of steel and men at Pearl Harbor on December 7, 1941. As the *Centennial History of Texas A&M University* records it: "The A&M campus was quiet that Sunday afternoon. Many students were at the campus theater watching 'A Yank in the R.A.F.' The film snapped and amidst the proverbial catcalls and boos the theater manager, Charlie Tiegner, announced, 'If you would care to know, Japanese forces have just bombed Pearl Harbor.' There was shock and disbelief, followed by yells, 'Beat the hell out of Japan,' and 'Let's make a Corps trip to Tokyo.' Many Aggies were already close to the Japanese Empire—prominently at Corregidor, Bataan, Mindanao, and Midway."

Corregidor Muster

In the early months of the conflict, the eyes of the world focused on the men of Corregidor who fought to hold that island fortress against the Japanese onslaught in the Philippines. Under command of former Corps of Cadets Commandant General George F. Moore '08, the Americans resisted against enormous odds. Amid the fury of battle, the Aggies on the island gathered at the mouth of the main cave to hold a traditional San Jacinto Day Aggie Muster on April 21, 1942. This muster was attended by twenty-five former students of the college, including General Moore. Within days, all had been captured or killed. News of this gathering under wartime conditions inspired Aggies worldwide and continues to do so. Since this famous Corregidor Muster, Aggies have gathered worldwide annually to reflect on "the good ole' days at A&M and the memory of departed comrades."

On September 15, 1942, the following telegram was sent to the *Houston Post* from the commander of American forces in the Pacific:

From CG GHQ SWPA Q999 Texas A and M is writing its own military history in the blood of its graduates not only in the Philippines campaign but on the active fronts of the Southwest Pacific. Texans daily emblazon the record with outstanding feats of courage on land and on the sea and in the air no name stands out more brilliantly than the heroic defender of Corregidor General George F. Moore. Whenever I see a Texas man in my command, I have a feeling of confidence.

MacArthur

Because of the shock and impact of the reports arriving daily from the Pacific during the first few months of the war, those times were emotional ones for all Americans. Never

The class of '42 taking the commissioning oath in Guion Hall, May, 1942.

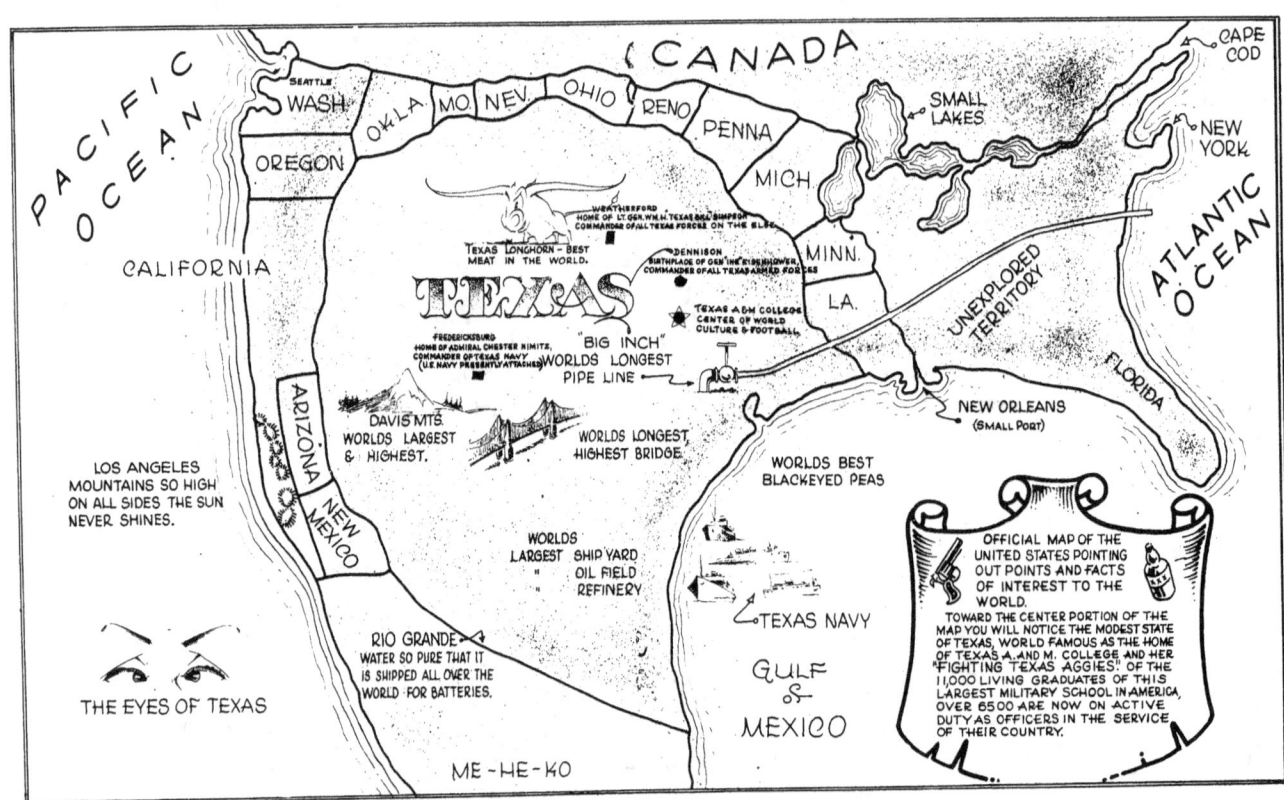
Map of Texas from the program for the Aggie Muster on the Elbe River, Germany, April, 1945. (*Courtesy T. B. ("Gype") Sebastian '33.*)

Participants in the April, 1943, Aggie Muster in Guadalcanal. *First row, left to right:* Pfc. Richard S. Terry '36, 1st Lt. Lewis G. Compton, Jr., '34, Capt. Walter D. Bellamy '33, Capt. Thomas H. McDowell '32, Maj. Vernon L. Wimberly '31, Col. Stewart D. Hervey '17, Maj. Frank A. Shepardson '30, Maj. James D. Edgar '32, Maj. Henry C. Bohnenkamp '32, Maj. Max A. Mosesman '36. *Second row, left to right:* Ensign Grover L. Berryhill '42, 1st Lt. James M. Browning '40, Capt. August M. Schmidt '38, 1st Lt. Eugene F. Shiels '41, 1st Lt. M. B. Huffman '40, Capt. Robert T. Shiels, Jr., '40, Capt. James J. Riley '41, 1st Lt. Charles E. Staudt '38, Capt. Philip L. Daffron '37. *Third row, left to right:* 1st Lt. George F. Bentinck '41, 1st Lt. Clinton H. Herron '40, 1st Lt. Richard R. White '39, 1st Lt. G. B. Beeler '41, 1st Lt. P. B. Bennett '40, 1st Lt. John C. McDuffie '42, 1st Lt. B. B. Fowler '41, 1st Lt. Robert L. Spencer '40. *Seated in front:* 1st Lt. Jack W. Howard, University of Texas '40.

before had so much of America's lifeblood been pumped into such faraway places in defense of democratic ideals. By January, 1943, most able-bodied men were in uniform at training posts, on ships at sea, or at scattered outposts worldwide. On the home front E. E. McQuillen struggled amidst a boot-camp campus environment to keep Aggies around the world in touch. Over his desk he became the relay point for news between roommates and more often than not between Aggies and their families. Common of the many requests received by McQuillen was the following sent from Manila by Captain James T. Danklefs '43: ". . . By the way have the circulation section of the paper send the 'Aggie' to my home

Left, Lieutenant William P. Brown, Jr., '46 being awarded the Air Medal by Colonel John C. Munn. Brown was credited with shooting down seven enemy planes during the Okinawa campaign. *Right,* The Camp Claiborne Texas A&M Club was formed in the fall of 1944. Captain T. A. Kincaid, Jr., '28 and Captain S. H. Whitehurst '38 are pictured at the club's headquarters.

address. Mother likes to glance through it and then she airmails it on to me. Box 144, Garwood, Texas. Thanks." Although his staff was drastically reduced, McQuillen maintained a solid, up-to-date record file amid the pulse of all that embodied Aggie activity. The formal structuring of Aggie Musters, in the same spirit that resulted in the Corregidor gathering, was one of McQuillen's chief goals.

The roots of A&M observances of San Jacinto Day, April 21, commemorating the victory of Sam Houston's Texans over Santa Anna's army and the liberation of Texas from Mexico, date back to before the 1900's. In the 1880's literary presentations often highlighted the special observance of San Jacinto Day, and in 1883 the "Roll Call for the Absent" was first used. In the 1890's the Corps of Cadets made annual visits to the San Jacinto battlefield to participate in mock battles and maneuvers followed by a parade down Main Street in Houston. About the turn of the century the day was set aside for "Track and Field Day," when competitive intramural athletic events were staged. President David F. Houston proposed to cancel the April 21 activities in 1903, but "a determined student body, 300 strong, marched in orderly military precision" to the president's home "to insist upon some observance of the anniversary of the battle that won Texas' independence." Houston relented. These early students not only memorialized Texas heroes, but also honored those students and former students with the "roll call," during which a living comrade would answer "here" for the one whose name was called. During World War I, Aggies mustered in the trenches and towns of France and pledged A&M and "all our brothers overthere and overhere in the wine of France."

In 1923 Aggie Muster was institutionalized by decree of the Association of Former Students as an annual event when Aggies, wherever they were, should "get together, eat a little, and live over the days you spent at the A&M College of Texas." During the 1923

The April 21, 1945, muster on Guam. Organizer of the meeting was Colonel Victor A. Barraco '15.

Muster, radio station WTAW broadcast a program including A&M songs, greetings from the coach, Dana X. Bible, and Aggie yells by the corps. By the close of the 1920's and into the 1930's muster had become not just a practice, but a part of Aggie tradition. During this period before World War II, musters were very informal and were primarily held only throughout Texas, and there is no record of any campus gatherings.

In February, 1943, E. E. McQuillen, reflecting on the events at Corregidor during its finest hour in mid-April, 1942, and being reinforced by numerous reminders and letters from Aggies worldwide, assembled the first written muster packets for distribution to the various Texas A&M clubs, mothers' clubs, and military installations around the world. The first universal use of the word *muster* and the first organized efforts to establish the Aggie tradition on an annual basis can only be credited to the efforts of McQuillen. The muster packets contained a program featuring the "Roll Call for the Absent" and a muster poem by Professor John Ashton '06 of the A&M faculty. At locations across America and on all war fronts where Texas Aggies served, musters were held. Those who attended one of the hundreds of ceremonies for a short time were brought away from the war and close to the memories of their state, alma mater, and fellow alumni.

In April, 1943, the feature activity of the muster was a nationwide radio program over the Columbia Network from Washington, D.C., featuring Secretary of Commerce Jesse H. Jones and Texas Senator Tom Connally. The program included the "Cavalcade of the Fighting Aggies," which highlighted A&M songs and yells. In announcing the program in the April 15, 1943, *The Texas Aggie*, McQuillen commented: "The size of the muster is not important. The spirit that brings A&M men together this one night of the year is a vital element."

The first student-coordinated campus muster was held in April, 1945. According to McQuillen, that event was quite a "coup on the part of the cadets." It was organized by senior cadet Hank Avery '44. More than fifteen hundred cadets held "strictly a student affair with cadet leaders presenting the program." The special guest of the cadets was Lt. Clifton Chamberlain '40 of Marlin, who had been one of the A&M men present on "The Rock" in 1942. Chamberlain had recently returned to Texas in February, 1945, after being held prisoner of war for 999 days on Luzon Island in the Philippines by the Japanese. The campus muster committee had learned of Chamberlain's release from a letter his parents in Marlin had forwarded to McQuillen: "Dear Mother, Reborn January 30, 1945, at 7:30 A.M. Am well and so happy I can't describe how I feel. After three years of uncertainty to be back with your own people is heaven."

The full impact of McQuillen's efforts and of the enthusiastic April gatherings was dramatically augmented by the appearance of General Dwight D. Eisenhower at the Homecoming victory muster of April, 1946. In response to an Aggie invitation to attend the 1946 Corregidor muster, the Manila A&M Club and A&M President Gibb Gilchrist received the following letter from General MacArthur:

Sons of Texas A&M
on Corregidor—21 April 1946.

In this hallowed soil lie the mortal remains of many men who here died that liberty might live. Among the bravest of these brave are twenty officers, sons of Texas A&M, unable themselves to answer this year's annual muster. It is for us, therefore, to do so for them—to answer for them in clear and firm voice—Dead on battleswept Corregidor where their eternal spirit will never die but will march on forever, inspiring in those who follow the courage and the will to preserve well that for which they bled.

Of them and those of their fellow alumni who lie in hallowed soil of other lands and those who survive them, may it truly be said that in the noble teachings of their Alma Mater—in the tradition of the great American leader, Sam Houston, who this day, one hundred and ten years ago, wrested Texas from foreign dominion by defeating Santa Ana on the historic battlefield of San Jacinto—they stood steadfast, unyielding and unafraid through those dark days of our country's gravest peril—and by inspiring example helped point the way.

Douglas MacArthur

April 21 through the years has been a time-honored day of reflection and commemoration of those whose initiative and gallant acts have made Texas a place of freedom. The muster tradition reunites more alumni in a single day than any program or event sponsored by any other college or university in the world.

Today, Aggies on campus, throughout the nation, and overseas make every effort to attend muster on April 21, when they live again their college days, renew their pledge of loyalty and friendship for each other and for the school, and recognize those who have departed by responding for them to the roll call—"here"!

Among the twenty thousand men of A&M in the armed services during World War II who exemplified the ultimate in service to their country and to their comrades were the seven who received the nation's highest decoration, the Congressional Medal of Honor.

Left, Lieutenant Colonel Raymond L. Murray '35 being awarded his second Silver Star by Admiral Chester W. Nimitz for bravery against the enemy on Tarawa. Murray was an All–Southwest Conference end in 1933. *Right*, In 1945 the first muster to be held on Corregidor after its reconquest was attended by only three Aggies. *Left to right:* Major R. N. Conolly '37, Lieutenant Colonel Ormond Simpson '36, and Lieutenant Tommie G. Martin '40. Japanese snipers were still present on the Rock at the time.

The April 21, 1946, Calcutta, India, Muster. *Front row, left to right:* 1st Lt. Henry F. O'Lexa '45, Capt. H. Albert Stroebele '42, 1st Lt. Ben B. Isbell '45, Capt. Thomas M. Smith '32, and Maj. Max McCullar '40. *Back row, left to right:* Pvt. Alvin R. Rees '47, 1st Lt. Billy C. Sanders '44, 1st Lt. Donald Weihs '45, 1st Lt. Charles L. Taggart '44, 1st Lt. James E. Gardner '45, and 1st Lt. Henry Wahrmund '44.

The Military Legacy 155

Left, 1946 Corregidor Aggie Muster program. (*Courtesy Willard A. Flowers '44.*) Right, Lowering the flags on Corregidor after the 1946 muster.

The April 21, 1946, Corregidor Aggie Muster. (*Photograph by James T. Danklefs '43.*)

Left, Major Luther A. Harrison, Jr., '38 being awarded the Legion of Merit for exceptionally meritorious service in the Africa–Middle East Theater, 1944–1945. *Right,* Lieutenant Cliff Chamberlain '40, speaker at the 1945 Campus Muster held in Guion Hall. Chamberlain was at the 1942 Corregidor Muster and had just been released from a Japanese POW camp after being held captive for 999 days.

Yell Practice at the Aggie Muster in the lobby of the Imperial Hotel, Tokyo, Japan, April 21, 1946.

The Military Legacy

Medal of Honor

Second Lieutenant Lloyd D. Hughes '43 of Corpus Christi was awarded the Medal of Honor posthumously for his heroic actions while flying a B-24 Liberator bomber in a strike against the Ploesti, Romania oil fields held by the Germans. At the Anzio beachhead Lieutenant Thomas W. Fowler '43, a tank platoon leader, won the Medal of Honor on May 23, 1944, "for conspicuous gallantry and intrepidity, at the risk of his life." During the assault of Mount Altruzzo in Italy, Sergeant George Dennis Keathley '35 earned posthumously the Medal of Honor. After being mortally wounded he rallied his men to repulse a heavy German attack.

Lieutenant Turney W. Leonard '42 took part in the landing at Omaha Beach as commander of a tank-destroyer company. After moving inland, his unit was trapped in the town of Kommerscheidt. Casualties were high, and every infantry officer was killed during a three-prong German attack. After personally scouting out the enemy's strength, Leonard reorganized his forces to prepare to stand off another attack. During the fierce fighting that followed, a direct shell hit took off the lower part of his arm, and Leonard tied a tourniquet around the stump and withdrew from action. That was the last time he was reported seen. For his leadership, bravery, and daring he was posthumously awarded the Medal of Honor.

While fighting with the Fifth Marine Division on Iwo Jima, Sergeant William Harrell, a student at Texas A&M during 1939 and 1941, won the Medal of Honor. On March 3, 1945, Harrell was on watch in the early morning when the Japanese attacked his position. "A grenade broke his thigh and tore off his left hand. With his right hand, he killed a Japanese poised over him with a saber, while another shoved a grenade under his head. Harrell pushed the grenade out with his good hand, killing another Japanese soldier with the grenade, but losing his other hand. He was found at dawn still alive with a dozen Japanese dead around him." The award was personally presented by President Harry S Truman on the White House lawn.

Horace S. Carswell, Jr., who attended Texas A&M in 1934–1935 before transferring to Texas Christian University in Fort Worth, earned the nation's highest award as a result of bravery displayed during a bombing mission over Japan. Carswell Air Force Base, near Fort Worth, was named in his honor.

The only living Aggie recipient of the Medal of Honor is Doctor Eli L. Whiteley '41, who became a professor of agronomy at Texas A&M. Whiteley was decorated for bravery as a result of the house-to-house fighting in Sigolsheim, Germany. After being wounded several times, he killed or captured numerous German SS troops in a successful attack which captured the village.

The bravery and dedication of the fighting Texas Aggies can never be fully known or adequately chronicled. Such men as James Earl Rudder '32, who led his Rangers up the cliffs of Pointe du Hoc to destroy German gun emplacements overlooking D-Day invasion beaches, and John S. Hilger '32, who flew the almost suicidal mission with General James Doolittle over Tokyo in 1942, as well as those who won the Medal of Honor, give testimony to the courage and devotion of those Aggies who fought for and served their country in its darkest hours. None gave so much as those 950 Aggies who never returned. The memory of these men is enshrined in plaques in the Memorial Student Center dedicated in 1951:

Medal of Honor Winners of

World War II

(*Drawings by Loraine Blount.*)

Lieutenant Lloyd H. Hughes '43

Lieutenant Thomas W. Fowler '43

Sergeant George D. Keathley '37

Lieutenant Turney W. Leonard '42

Lieutenant Eli L. Whiteley '41

Sergeant William G. Harrell '43

Major Horace S. Carswell, Jr., '38

The Military Legacy

Lieutenant Eli Whiteley '41 receiving the Congressional Medal of Honor from President Harry Truman. Dr. Whiteley, a professor with the Texas Agricultural Experiment Station at Texas A&M, is the only living Aggie recipient of the nation's highest award for bravery.

Left, "Through Unity Strength" — the arms of the Corps of Cadets. *Right*, The 1946 Aggie Bonfire stack on the main drill field. (*Courtesy Mr. and Mrs. William C. Lonquist, Jr., '48.*)

In humble reverence . . . to those men of A. & M. who gave their lives in defense of our country. Here is enshrined in spirit and in bronze enduring tribute to their valor and to their deep devotion. Here their memory shall remain forever fresh—their sacrifices shall not be forgotten.

Greater love hath no man than this, that a man lay down his life for his friends.

John 15:13

Academic routines were all but suspended on the A&M campus from 1942 to 1945. Facilities were converted to war training programs, including a preflight training school, an army specialized engineer training school, and a V-12 naval officer training school. One of the most unique "war contributions" of the Texas Aggies was a film for popular release, *We've Never Been Licked*, which chronicled the selfless saga of Brad Craig (Richard Quine), an Aggie who before war began was suspected by his comrades at A&M of being a Japanese sympathizer. Craig emerges when war begins as a propagandist in the employ of the Japanese. In the final, dramatic moments Craig reveals his true identity as an American agent, seizes control of a Japanese plane, and directs American fighters (led by his "old lady," Cyanide Jenkins, played by Noah Beery, Jr.) in an attack against the Japanese fleet. Craig is killed in the attack and posthumously receives the Medal of Honor at ceremonies in Kyle Field. When the war ended, a tank commanded by an Aggie and captioned "We've Never Been Licked" led American forces into Tokyo.

Among the many tributes to the military record of Texas A&M was that of General Omar Bradley, who told the 1950 graduating class: "The men of Texas A&M can stand up to any men in the world and compare favorably their education and training for leadership —leadership in the pursuits of peace, and if it comes to war, leadership in battle. This combination is significant, for the capability for a productive peace, coupled with the ability to defend your beliefs, as well as your resources, is essential to survival. . . ."

We've Never Been Licked

The Military Legacy

East Gate main entrance to the campus in the early 1950's.

12. Unselfish Devotion

Texas A&M reverberated with a new intensity of spirit after the war. Returning veterans, along with entering freshmen, flocked to the campus. Conditions became so crowded on the main campus in the fall of 1947 that 1,000 freshmen were moved to the old Bryan Air Force Base, known as the A&M Annex, visiting the main campus only on weekends of home football games. Total A&M enrollment surged to 8,538 by 1948. As the influx of veterans slowed, the campus returned to more normal conditions. By early 1950 the housing problem had eased, and freshmen were returned to the main campus. Enrollment stabilized at 6,000–7,000 students over the next decade.

Through the relatively "placid" decade of the 1950's, old Aggie traditions, customs, and attitudes provided a sense of continuity for the college that was becoming a university and for the Former Students' Association, which was becoming a more active agent and catalyst in Texas A&M's emergence as a university. The truth was, Texas A&M was in the throes of change, and the Association of Former Students played a major role in the process of creative and constructive development which helped prepare A&M for a broader and more dynamic educational role.

The Annual Fund Drive

Improved financial and managerial programs instituted within the Association of Former Students during and shortly after World War II would eventually provide the resources which enabled Texas A&M to achieve a greater flexibility and new dimensions in academic attainment. The concept of "annual giving," introduced by 1942 by Everett E. McQuillen '20, revolutionized the fund-raising and membership recruitment efforts of the association. McQuillen believed that "the amount of your gift is not important; what *is* important is *you*." By eliminating the old dues system, McQuillen opened the doors to larger gifts and easier membership recruitment. He announced the new plan in the June 15, 1942, *The Texas Aggie*: "There will no longer be MEMBERS or NON-MEMBERS of the Association of Former Students. There will be no membership dues. Every A. & M. man will be considered a member of the Association, as he has always been in fact whether he paid membership dues or not. In place of previous annual dues every A. & M. man will be asked to make a gift that year to the Development Fund."

The 1942 Development Fund annual giving drive was kicked off in September. The first year's fund goal of $50,000 was reached, with 6,277 former students donating $51,119.74. These funds were to be placed in war bonds "to be held for the duration" of the war. The theme and slogan of the appeals and messages mailed to all A&M men by association President W. J. ("Bill") Lawson '24 of Austin was "GOLDEN DREAMS (The Student Activities Center)—NAILED DOWN WITH STEEL BULLETS (War Bonds)." McQuillen's guidelines for the fund drive, as approved by the association board, were:

Unselfish Devotion

Sul Ross Reunion, June, 1948. *Left to right:* Harry P. Jordon '95, Travis L. Smith, Jr., '98, H. W. South '98, and G. Rollie White '95.

1. Every A. & M. man is now a member of the Association of Former Students.

2. In place of dues, every man is asked to make an Annual gift of whatever amount he wishes, to the Development Fund.

3. An annual honor roll fund report will list the name of every donor, but not the amount of his gift.

4. Every donor will receive THE TEXAS AGGIE.

5. A. & M. men will present a gift to the College through the Development Fund each year at commencement.

6. The Fund will endeavor to give A. & M. some of the things she needs—but cannot secure through state funds.

7. Fund objectives will be selected by joint committee (College Board, Faculty, Ex-Students); but each donor may restrict his gift to any objective he wishes.

8. Success of the fund depends as much upon the number of donors as upon the amount of their gifts. Emphasis is placed upon every A. & M. man giving something.

9. If you have not already done so, mail your gift today. It will buy STEEL BULLETS TO NAIL DOWN OUR GOLDEN DREAM.

In order to make the giving competitive, donation totals were reported by class, giving the former students an idea of what other segments of the alumni were donating.

McQuillen and in later years association Executive Directors Dick Hervey '42 and Richard ("Buck") Weirus '42 were to employ the most direct link with each class—the class agent or co-agents—as the central collecting agent for the class gifts. McQuillen coordinated the annual fund-giving through the association offices.

The Development Office, through 1953, made up of members of the association staff and the directors, allocated the expenditure of funds and planned special programs. This low-pressure, high-performance plan for generating financial support has over the years made Texas A&M alumni second only to those of Harvard University in annual support of their alma mater. The unstinting financial support of the former students has enabled the association to sustain and expand existing programs such as the Students' Loan Fund and to add useful new projects such as an alumni/student coordinator, class reunions, high school orientation programs, student scholarships, and faculty achievement awards.

Texas A&M Former Student Annual Giving

Year	Number of Contributions	Total Amount Given
1942–1943	6,277	$ 51,119.74
1943–1944	7,404	63,780.78
1944–1945	8,108	74,374.07
1945–1946	8,500	78,593.80
1947	7,356	68,057.58
1948	7,510	78,328.45
1949	10,968	94,000.94
1950	7,988	74,979.37
1951	9,437	93,879.81
1952	8,201	98,224.61
1953	8,509	106,967.45
1954	8,314	118,725.62
1955	8,452	138,874.97
1956	8,712	161,423.02
1957	15,284	186,615.84
1958	9,351	144,100.11
1959	9,610	196,031.51
1960	9,371	178,830.72
1961	13,094	304,574.75
1962	17,468	283,476.83
1963	14,744	316,954.82
1964	14,637	267,744.06
1965	15,121	575,242.00
1966	14,203	376,662.32
1967	20,129	383,396.80
1968	17,821	462,619.00
1969	17,932	694,499.21
1970	26,408	1,073,071.27
1971	20,175	1,066,326.25

Year	Number of Contributions	Total Amount Given
1972	21,867	.1,915,895.49
1973	23,195	1,787,039.30
1974	19,041	1,198,729.52
1975	22,118	1,380,871.23
1976	27,352	2,427,830.00
1977	20,883	2,248,823.36

Although McQuillen resigned as executive secretary of the Association of Former Students in late 1947 after nearly twenty years of service with the association, his novel fund-raising program remained the vital key to the association's postwar development. McQuillen assumed the directorship of the Texas A&M Development Fund, which had been vacated by R. Henderson Shuffler '29. The Executive Board of the association regretted the loss of McQuillen but appreciated his opportunity to render greater services to the college in his new position. The Executive Board "considered the advisability of adding two members to the staff of the Association." James B. ("Dick") Hervey '42 of Greenville was selected as the new executive secretary of the association on September 29, 1947. He was to devote his interests to general association affairs, A&M clubs, reunions, and annual giving. Hervey's imaginative efforts placed the association on a sound business footing. James T. Noton '41 was employed as editor of *The Texas Aggie* on September 20, 1947, "at a salary of $3,000 per year."

Post-War Goals

The association offices, located in the System Administration Building, housed Hervey, Noton, Lon B. Locke '22 (bookkeeper and student loan officer), Willie Mae Sheppard (class reunion coordinator), a records section, and a mailroom. In the postwar years association Presidents Carroll M. Gaines, Sr., '12 (1946–1947), Adolph E. Hinman '25 (1947–1948), George G. Smith '30 (1948–1949), and Louis A. Hartung '29 (1949–1950) worked closely with the staff, class agents, and local A&M club officers in an effort to implement three major programs: (1) the annual fund drive, (2) the expansion of Texas A&M clubs throughout the state, and (3) a special fund drive to build the Memorial Student Center (MSC). Complementing these major goals were the enhancement of class reunion programs, the development of the high school relations program, an expanded directory of former students, and construction of All Faiths Chapel on campus.

The Development Foundation

The Gifts and Bequests Office to which E. E. McQuillen moved in 1947 was an administrative branch of the A&M College which managed wills and bequests left in the name of Texas A&M. McQuillen now worked closely with the association in its annual fund drive and solicited and managed unusually large donations or bequests. The success of A&M's and the association's fund-raising efforts necessitated the development of a legal trust foundation to serve as a custodian and manager of funds. Subsequently, under the leadership of Herman F. Heep '20, and with sizable gifts from Heep, W. T. ("Doc") Doherty '22, and the class of '22, the Texas A&M College Development Foundation was established as a private trust foundation on September 12, 1953. Charter members of the foundation included a distinguished group of alumni and A&M friends:

R. Wofford Cain '13   E. E. McQuillen '20
David H. Morgan (A&M president, 1953–1956)   E. F. Mitchell '09

Guy W. Adriance '15
C. W. Crawford '19
Gibb Gilchrist '13
Dale F. Leipper
W. C. Freeman '40
Frank Bolton, Jr. '34
Olin E. Teague '32
Oscar T. Hotchkiss, Jr. '24
S. C. Evans '21

Herman F. Heep '20
W. P. Machemehl '33
J. W. Porter '22
Tyree L. Bell '13
M. T. Harrington '22
R. F. Allen (A&M director, 1951–1957)
J. H. Dunn '25
H. C. Heldenfels '35

The purposes of the foundation were simple: to solicit donations from all sources both individual and corporate within the guidelines of the charter and to use those funds to support major college needs. McQuillen served as director of the foundation until his retirement in 1963. He was succeeded by Dorsey E. McCrory '39, who served until Robert L. Walker '58 assumed the post in 1973. Walker, named vice-president for development in 1977, and his expanded staff have added a new, progressive dimension to the traditional trustee role of the foundation. During its first twenty-five years of existence donors entrusted over $12 million to the foundation for Texas A&M. Of this total, over 93 percent has been given since 1974. The goal of the foundation is to amass $100 million by 1985. The foundation and the unselfish devotion of A&M former students have helped assure the opportunity for continuing development and academic enrichment to the modern Texas A&M University.

One significant method of funding scholarship programs in the 1950's and 1960's was through "ABC transactions" in the oil business, by which a nonprofit institution was permitted to serve as an intermediary in a transaction. Such a device was created by the formation of the AMC Corporation by three prominent former students—James W. Aston '33, E. E. Monteith, Jr., '43, and J. A. Crichton '37. Funds from AMC Corporation provided significant help in scholarship and faculty enrichment programs.

The annual giving concept contributed to a reinvigorated Association of Former Students. Intensive campaigns were launched in the major metropolitan areas to encourage former student participation in A&M club activities and their support of annual giving. Each year, local A&M club leaders headed the local annual fund drive, which not only brought financial support but also created a more active membership. The giving of a donation, as opposed to the paying of a membership fee, proved a double blessing.

Texas A&M University Development Foundation

Year	Total Assets	Total Contributions	Disbursements
1953	$ 2,112.00	$ 2,210.00	
1954	2,149.50	7,900.00	$ 7,925.00
1955	2,177.38	5,822.06	5,897.06
1956	28,539.95	41,276.00	15,375.00
1957	55,331.61	42,725.00	17,650.00
1958	156,726.65	110,503.40	11,850.00
1959	195,254.30	48,199.00	13,300.00
1960	199,522.99	1,525.00	3,700.00

Year	Total Assets	Total Contributions	Disbursements
1961	211,520.29	11,200.00	4,800.00
1962	214,893.39	9,200.00	11,500.00
1963	221,949.57	1,200.00	5,500.00
1964	223,152.02	1,700.00	7,500.00
1965	276,976.53	55,700.00	12,800.00
1966	289,186.95	1,700.00	27,774.81
1967	293,128.39	6,200.00	17,111.29
1968	292,285.24	2,200.00	15,000.00
1969	305,135.28	10,699.71	12,000.00
1970	312,772.17	8,068.97	16,590.00
1971	381,203.38	68,747.20	18,600.00
1972	402,432.69	20,105.00	19,100.00
1973	791,355.34	368,851.79	4,400.00
1974	2,696,559.24	1,935,670.32	55,460.30
1975	3,782,683.34	1,188,112.80	167,605.45
1976	7,509,059.44	3,793,285.00	332,600.10
1977	12,254,055.42	3,923,614.58	551,742.13

The Gifts and Bequests Office, and the Development Foundation which succeeded it (the trustees of which are appointed by the association board), have enabled former students to provide unique services over the years to Texas A&M. In addition to partial funding for the Memorial Student Center and construction of the All Faith Chapel, contributions by former students and friends of A&M have made possible the Gold Star Fund, which has provided educational assistance to the children of A&M men who died in military service, and in 1944 the Opportunity Award Scholarship Fund. In 1949 development funds financed a new *Directory of Former Students*, provided twenty-five thousand dollars for a campus golf course, and supplied new scholarship money as well as dress rifles for the Ross Volunteers. A ten-thousand-dollar allocation in 1950 established the Texas A&M Archives program. The following year, development funds financed the writing of *The Story of Texas A. & M.* by George Sessions Perry and provided housing for the Metzger Gun Collection. More recently, the Cain Olympic swimming pool, Forsyth Alumni Center, Cain Hall, University Library expansion, and Visitors Information Center have been stimulated or made possible by association support.

The Directory of Former Students

The modern-day version of the *Directory of Former Students* was first assembled and published while Louis A. Hartung '29 was president of the association. This 1949 directory of more than six hundred pages contained an alphabetical and geographical listing of over twenty thousand former students. Additionally it included lists of casualties of both World War I and World War II. As conceived, the directory was to be updated for publication every five years. As the membership grew more mobile and graduating classes increased in size, however, it became desirable after 1967 to print a new edition every three years, a frequency made possible because of computerized records instituted by Buck Weirus in the 1960's. The 1967 directory contained two unique features: it was the first former student directory to be compiled from computer records, a vast improvement over

Football Coach Ray George and co-captains Bob Smith '51, fullback from Houston, and Hugh Meyer '51, center from Gainesville.

the old manual processing of 3″ × 5″ cards, and in addition to the regular alphabetical and geographical listings, rosters of all living members by class were included in each volume. The computerization was largely the work of Robert L. Smith, Jr., '51 and Doug Yauger '61 in conjunction with the University Data Processing Center. Although the capital investment in computerized processing was considered excessive in many circles, such modern and sophisticated organization enabled the association to lead in the rapid expansion of the university that was yet to come. The 1976 centennial edition of the *Directory of Former Students* contains the names of over seventy thousand former students of Texas A&M.

Throughout the 1950's class reunions were held during commencement, home football games, and Aggie Musters, primarily as a result of the efforts of Willie Mae Sheppard. The elaborate reunion schedule devised during the mid-1920's was abandoned. Classes usually met every five or ten years, depending on how energetic the class agents and class members were. On October 4, 1951, to celebrate the seventy-fifth anniversary of the opening of A&M, the classes of 1907, 1922, 1937, and 1942 mustered on campus during the weekend of the Texas A&M–Kentucky football game. Due to the hostilities in Korea, many former students were unable to attend the campus gatherings. The contribution of Texas A&M in that conflict was evident. By December, 1952, twenty-five Aggies were known to have been killed in action.

In order to make more Texans aware of Texas A&M, the High School Day program

Class Reunions

Reviewing party for General Dwight D. Eisenhower's 1951 visit. *Left to right:* Cadet Colonel A. D. Martin '51, General Eisenhower, President M. T. Harrington '22, General Leroy Lutis, Colonel Ike Ashburn, Chancellor Gibb Gilchrist, C. C. ("Polly") Krueger '12, James W. Witherspoon, Tyree L. Bell '13, and Rufus R. Peeples '28.

The Deep East Texas A&M Club presenting check to E. E. McQuillen '20, executive director of the Association of Former Students, for a Student Opportunity Award, January, 1950.

Lieutenant Oscar Garcia '40 *(left)* and Colonel Eugene S. Coghill '11, youngest and oldest members at the April 21, 1951, Aggie Muster at the Bristol Hotel, Salzburg, Austria.

established in 1948 by the Association of Former Students was expanded in the spring of 1952 to give prospective students a view of the campus and its many educational programs. In 1952 an estimated 750 and in 1953 over 1,000 high school students visited the campus during April. They were given special tours of the campus, including dorms, the library, and the mess halls, and they were given a chance to see how the cadets lived on a day to day basis. Of the 750 who visited in 1952, it was estimated, more than half returned in the fall of that year to enroll as students. Former students, via local A&M clubs, began to canvass the local high schools in order to obtain quality students for Texas A&M. The fall enrollment in October, 1952, was 6,277, partly a result of alumni recruiting. The association-sponsored high school relations programs have continued. Under the leadership of 1972 association President J. R. ("Bob") Latimer, Jr., '44 these programs became more highly structured and budgeted and have contributed significantly to the recruitment by Texas A&M of top-flight high school students and to the university's growing academic excellence.

Today Texas A&M clubs in Texas and Louisiana designate former students to deal directly with high school relations programs and counselors. Many clubs also provide local scholarships for outstanding students bound for Texas A&M. The Brazos County A&M Club, for example, sponsors eight Opportunity Award Scholarships at $250 a semester for a total of $2,000 per student over a four-year period. It also gave a $10,000 Centennial Endowed Scholarship in 1976. The Dallas A&M Club and the Northern Louisiana A&M Club have established $25,000 President's Endowed Scholarships in addition to varying numbers of Opportunity Awards. The President's Endowed Scholarship program affords the recipient $1,500 per year of study. Scholarships and their amounts vary from club to

High School Day

Unselfish Devotion 171

 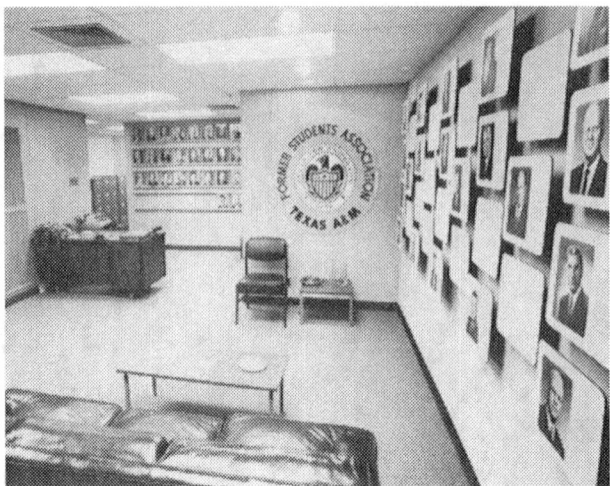

Left, E. E. McQuillen '20, E. Keith Langford '39, and J. B. ("Dick") Hervey '42. *Right*, The offices of the Association of Former Students during the 1960's.

Left, Student Body President John G. Thomas '59 receives an association donation for the funding of student activities. Alumni support of campus programs has always been a hallmark of the association's dedication to the enhancement of student involvement in campus activities. *Left to right:* Association Executive Secretary Dick Hervey '42, John G. Thomas '59, William G. Meyers '59, and W. L. Penberthy. *Right*, Sul Ross Reunion members, May, 1957. *Left to right:* C. A. Love '99, H. H. Tracy '98, H. E. Rawlins '98, and Travis L. Smith '98. All four attended the funeral of Governor Ross in 1898.

club, yet they have one goal in common—to foster academic excellence via recognition of outstanding student scholars. In 1978, a total of 151 Texas A&M clubs, civic groups, and mothers' clubs sponsored Opportunity Award Scholarships.

An additional function of each A&M club high school representative is to remain in contact with high school counselors at their schools in order to familiarize them with admissions procedures, student scholarship opportunities, and credit by examination as well as to give them a look at A&M student life. These association and local A&M club–sponsored programs have done much to reach students statewide.

Members of the class of '95 during their fifty-fifth anniversary. *First row, left to right:* Harry Jordan, G. R. White, D. D. Peden, and W. F. Hutson. *Second row, left to right:* A. W. Amthor, Mrs. Donna Coulter Carnes, Walter Coulter, J. A. Russell, A. J. Moursund, and A. G. Farmer.

An ancient and divisive issue reared its head again in the 1950's—that of coeducation. Many former students strongly desired to see the old traditional all-male, all-military complexion of Texas A&M preserved. But many others wanted their daughters to attend the college—and resented their exclusion. Still others, interested in seeing Texas A&M develop a broader academic position in support of its emerging status as a major, multifaceted university, regarded coeducation and voluntary enrollment in the Corps of Cadets as necessary concomitants to academic growth.

In March, 1953, State Senator William T. Moore '40 of Bryan submitted a resolution to the Texas legislature "to permit the enrollment of female students in the 76-year-old all-male college." The resolution was introduced on March 3 at a time when the Texas Senate was acting on routine matters, and it was approved by a voice vote "without objection or discussion." The resolution was termed a "bombshell" by both the Texas A&M administration and angry former students. Hundreds of telegrams from former students flooded President Marion T. Harrington's office, the association office, and the offices of the various state senators. On Thursday, March 5, "with lightning speed" the Senate recalled and killed the resolution by a vote of 26-1. Senator Moore cast the only negative vote. The question of women at Texas A&M was to be debated for over ten years in both

Coeducation

Unselfish Devotion 173

Left, "Of course there's always the possibility that you're just not cut out to be a tobacco chewer." Cadet Slouch, a part of Aggie life since the mid-1950's, was created by Dr. Jim Earle '54, head of the Texas A&M Engineering Design Graphics Department. *Right,* The 1957 officers of the San Antonio A&M Club. *Left to right:* Al Hawley '42, director; Charlie Allen '45, director; Buck Weirus '42, president; Bob Tankersley '52, vice-president; Ivan Moser, Jr., '50, secretary; and Harry Weiner '27, treasurer.

Left, J. R. ("Bob") Latimer '44 and Buck Weirus '42. Under Latimer's leadership the High School Relations Program was expanded and structured. *Right,* The New Orleans A&M Club hosted the Ross Volunteers in the early 1950's during one of the RV's annual trips to Mardi Gras.

Left, Coach Paul ("Bear") Bryant, William F. Oxford '42, and George B. Morgan '48 at the Beaumont A&M Club Barbecue, 1954. *Right,* Faculty Achievement Award winners, May, 1960. *Left to right:* President James Earl Rudder '32, James H. Bass, Charles J. Keese, Jr., '41, William T. Berry '42, Richard H. Davis, Jr., '40, Robert O. Reid, and Association President W. C. ("mAggie") McGee, Jr., '31.

the courts and the legislature. Finally, in mid-1963 Texas A&M opened its doors on a limited basis to women, and in 1971 it admitted all students without regard to sex. Subsequently, enrollments soared from 14,775 students in 1971 to 29,414, almost one-third of whom were women, in 1977. In 1965 enrollment in the Corps of Cadets became optional. Although membership in the corps declined markedly, the unity and spirit of the corps maintained it as the vibrant heart of the Aggie student body and guardian of Aggie traditions.

In the midst of the argument over coeducation at Texas A&M, many other events transpired. During early 1954, with former student encouragement and approval, Paul ("Bear") Bryant assumed the job as head football coach and athletic director of the college. In April of that same year the cadets, faculty, numerous visiting former students, and special guest General Matthew B. Ridgway, chief of staff of the army, packed Guion Hall to view the premiere showing of the documentary film *We Are the Aggies*. The annual fund continued to grow yearly, and by October, 1954, the amount of $84,017.06 had been contributed by 5,789 former students. The association also aided the administration's efforts to upgrade the academic departments of the college.

In order to attract and keep an excellent teaching faculty and staff, the Association of Former Students in 1955 created the Faculty Distinguished Achievement Award to be presented annually to outstanding members of the college faculty and staff. In the early 1950's Texas A&M and other schools of higher education in the state experienced a frightful "brain drain" of many outstanding professors and researchers away from Texas. The problem was so acute that the alumni and administrators at both Texas A&M and the University of Texas in Austin canvassed the state, meeting with community leaders, civic groups, and legislators in an effort to create a state-wide awareness of the crisis. In 1954–1955 the association board of directors placed primary emphasis on reversing this trend with the establishment of the Faculty Distinguished Achievement Awards. These awards

Distinguished Achievement Awards

Unselfish Devotion 175

Left, Texas A&M graduates Darwich Al-Haidara '31 *(left)* and Albert Meymarian '30 *(right)* review the joint Iraq–United States anti-locust program with Iraqi Dhia Ahmed. Hardara, Iraq's director general of Agriculture, and Meymarian, an entomologist, worked with the U.S. Point 4 Mission to control the annual desert locust invasions. *Right*, James Earl Rudder '32, commander of the Ninetieth Infantry Division, receiving congratulations from Brigadier General H. P. Watson *(left)* and Colonel Albert A. Horner *(right)* upon being promoted to the rank of Brigadier General in 1954. *(U.S. Army photograph.)*

initially were accompanied by a five-hundred-dollar cash gift. In 1956 the award was increased to one thousand dollars for each recipient. The first five awards were presented in Guion Hall in late November, 1955, to Travis J. Parker, professor of geology; Robert L. Skrabanek '42, associate professor of rural sociology; Fred E. Ekfelt, professor of English; Wayne C. Hall, associate professor of plant physiology; and Walton D. ("Pete") Hardesty '44, business manager of student activities. This program is continued today and recognizes distinguished achievement, research, and service among the ranks of the faculty and staff. President Marion T. Harrington in 1958 made the following comment about the Distinguished Achievement Award:

I believe that the Faculty Achievement Awards have been one of the outstanding contributions our Association has made to the Agricultural and Mechanical College of Texas. They have been important because they have aimed at the most important persons in our organization—our faculty members.

I am convinced, too, that the Awards have been of great value to our Association of Former Students—for, by participation in this program, we are brought to more active consideration of the importance of providing, for our faculty, incentives and marks of appreciation for jobs well done.

The Faculty Distinguished Achievement Awards program has grown from the original five awards presented in 1955 to fourteen yearly since 1977. The award now includes the one thousand dollars in cash, an engraved gold watch, and a framed certificate for each recipient. This alumni support of the faculty, in both a material and a spiritual sense, has contributed to the university's goal of attaining excellence in teaching, research, and extension and student service activities.

During the summer of 1953 numerous former students and Texas A&M officials stumped the state to create an awareness of the needs for higher education in Texas. Pictured here at the Menger Hotel in San Antonio are A&M Chancellor M. T. Harrington '22 with former chancellor Gibb Gilchrist; C. C. ("Polly") Krueger '12; J. Harold Dunn '25, president of the Association of Former Students; David H. Morgan, president of A&M; Ray George, head football coach; and C. L. Babcock '20, president of the Aggie Club.

Other association projects were similarly designed to benefit the students as well as the entire campus population. A major activity which occupied a five-year period, was the planning, design, fund raising, and construction of a chapel to be located on the campus. The idea was first presented to the association in March, 1952. In August of that year it was decided that this special project would be financed with funds raised in the annual giving drive. On October 1, 1955, Oscar T. Hotchkiss, Jr., '24 and W. Lambert Ballard '22, association president, presented Wilfred T. Doherty '22, chairman of the A&M College Board of Directors, a check for fifty thousand dollars and a letter of commitment for an additional fifty thousand dollars if needed to complete construction. The All Faiths Chapel was designed in mid-1955 by Richard Vrooman '52, a professor in the Department of Architecture. The chapel was dedicated for student use in the fall of 1957.

Throughout the 1950's and early 1960's the association mustered able, energetic leadership at all levels of the organization. The overall programs, however, continued to reflect the unique enthusiasm and energy of each association president. W. Lambert Ballard '22 (1957–1958), R. N. ("Dick") Connolly '37 (1958–1959), Tom A. Murrah '38 (1959–1960), and W. C. ("mAggie") McGee, Jr., '31 (1960–1961) helped prepare the association and the college for the diverse, intensified expansion which was to mark the 1960's. During McGee's term the association president's term was altered to coincide with the calendar year instead of the college's academic year, and James W. Aston '33 was elected to serve throughout 1961.

In January, 1958, James Earl Rudder '32 resigned from the Texas Land Commission to become vice-president of Texas A&M. His primary job was to be the chief administrative assistant to Dr. Marion T. Harrington. Rudder, a renowned soldier, proven leader, and statesman, was to figure heavily in the modernization of Texas A&M as it was transformed from a state college into a nationally known university.

During the late 1950's stress was placed on attracting top-level administrators and professors to the campus. There had been a drain of key faculty personnel away from Texas A&M due to low salaries. This problem was not unique to Texas A&M. In 1958 state leaders and educators began to map out a course of action to upgrade and sustain quality

The All Faiths Chapel

Campaigning for higher education and Texas A&M in 1953 were: *(left to right)* W. C. Penberthy, J. Harold Dunn '25, J. B. ("Dick") Hervey '42, Bones Irvin '26, M. T. Harrington '22, E. E. McQuillen '20, and David Morgan.

Over the past twenty-five years the Association of Former Students has won numerous awards for excellence and alumni fund giving. *Left to right:* the American Alumni Council Award, 1966, given by the Sears-Roebuck Foundation; the U.S. Steel Foundation Grand Award, 1959; and the 1963 Alumni Service Award.

Left, A class that doesn't meet on Friday? That's the only limitation you have? *Right*, Tackle Charlie Krueger '58, All-American in 1956 and 1957.

higher education in Texas. In this vein Dr. Harrington called on the former students to "help inform the tax-paying-and-voting people of Texas, including the members of the Legislature, of the absolute necessity for an increase in our appropriation." Harrington warned, "New buildings and modern facilities will not do the work of education and research—they are merely the necessary tools. Qualified manpower is the deciding factor in determining if Texas A&M will have progress or stagnation. This is the area in which our problem is most acute." With mAggie McGee, Herman Heep '20, Jimmy Aston '33, and Pat Zachry '22 aiding them, Tom Harrington '22, Harry Ransom (University of Texas president), J. B. ("Dick") Hervey '42, and Earl Rudder canvassed the state in support of higher education and teaching excellence. As a result of these and other activities in Austin, the Commission on Higher Education in Texas, known today as the Coordinating Board, was created.

Through association interaction, faculty salaries were raised in the 1960's. In an effort to aid the various departments and the president's office, unrestricted funds were allocated to offset faculty recruiting costs and incentive programs. By 1962 salaries began to increase and remain competitive with those of other major colleges and universities.

The demand for greater funds for special projects caused the association to place greater emphasis on the annual fund drive. Contributions from individuals had been steady through the 1950's. A marked increase in member contributions in 1957 earned for the Association of Former Students a ten-thousand-dollar cash award from the American Alumni Council at its forty-fifth annual meeting held in Kansas City, Kansas, on January 6, 1959. A remarkable 15,284 contributors, or 48.9 percent of Texas A&M's 31,200 former students, gave $186,615.84 to the 1957 fund drive. At the Kansas City meeting the Alumni Council announced that "the participation figure of 48.9 percent is the highest ever compiled for alumni fund efforts of a major tax supported institution." The large number of donations were in part a response to the many worthy projects pursued by the association during the 1950's; a campus chapel, Opportunity Award Scholarships, Faculty Achievement Awards, the President's Emergency Fund, dean's funds, the *Directory of Former Students*, class reunions, high school relations programs, and the regular operation of the association offices. The Alumni Council's award, sponsored by the United States Steel Foundation, was accepted by President M. T. Harrington '22, E. E. McQuillen '20,

National Recognition

Unselfish Devotion 179

Sully getting his annual "fish" shining.

 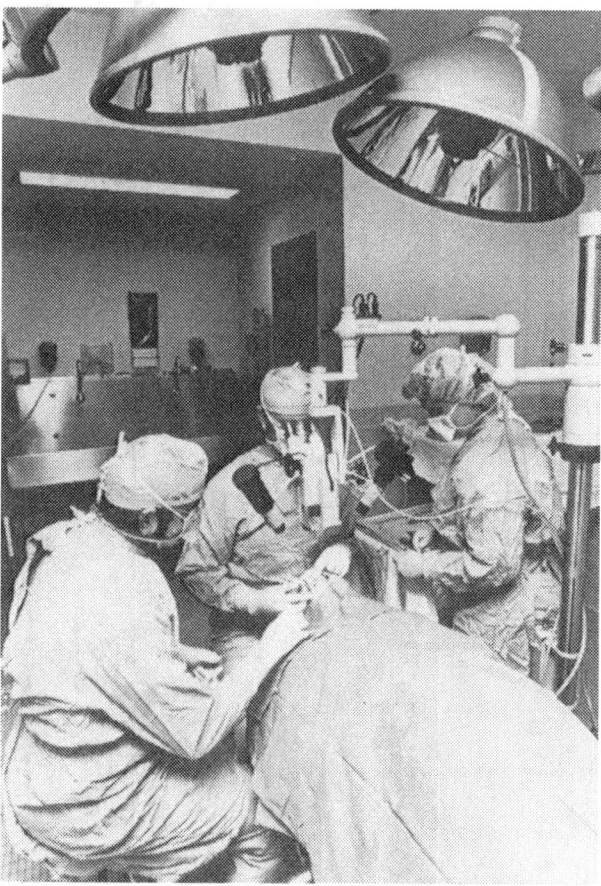

Left, J. B. ("Dick") Hervey '42, executive secretary of the Association of Former Students, 1947–1964. *Right*, The College of Veterinary Medicine at Texas A&M yearly produces outstanding graduates trained in all phases of animal care.

and Dick Hervey '42. More than three hundred colleges, universities, and independent secondary schools competed for this award.

The postwar years and the decade of the 1950's witnessed the establishment of the association on a firm footing as a concerned body mindful of the need, costs, and vigilance a truly outstanding program of higher education demands. The efforts of the 1950's were not in vain, for they laid the seed bed for a thorough evaluation of association and university programs during the 1960's, culminating in the emergence of Texas A&M as a nationally recognized university of the first class by the time of its centennial celebration in 1976.

Unselfish Devotion 181

The Texas Aggie from tabloid to full-color magazine.

182 WE ARE THE AGGIES

13. A Partnership in Higher Education

One of Texas A&M's most important assets throughout the past century has been the unselfish love and loyalty of its alumni. The general organizational outline of the Association of Former Students was essentially perfected during the first half-century of Texas A&M's development. The commitment of former students to their old college seemed to be heightened by the experiences of World War I and World War II and by the fact that their A&M experience had prepared them well for their professions in both peace and in war. By 1960 the association had channeled this commitment into an effective program of financial aid and assistance to the college through the Development Foundation programs and annual giving. In the 1960's and 1970's the Association of Former Students moved into a more effective partnership in the pursuit of excellence in education and public services at Texas A&M.

Ninety percent of all Aggies who ever lived are alive today, with nearly one-fourth of them currently enrolled in Texas A&M. The future of Texas A&M and the growth and development of its partner in progress, the Association of Former Students, have never been so promising. The university has profited immeasurably from the support and concern of former students, and they, in turn, have felt the reward and satisfaction of knowing that their values and investments have made Texas A&M, and perhaps the world, a better place to live and learn.

Through the efforts of the university, Texas Aggies have achieved positions of leadership and responsibility in every phase of life's endeavors. A recent survey indicates that approximately 54 percent of A&M's former students are engaged in business and industry, 16 percent in government services (including the military), 16 percent as self-employed professionals, 8 percent in education, and 6 percent in farming and agribusiness. In Texas, 80 percent of the water districts are supervised by Aggies, twenty-two of the twenty-eight district highway engineers are A&M men, and more than 60 percent of the city engineers, directors of public works, and city planners are Aggies. Seventy-five percent of the Texas county agents received training at A&M. Aggies are found in the managerial offices of nearly every major oil company, and thousands have achieved distinction as lawyers, judges, physicians and dentists, veterinarians, ministers, teachers, and good citizens in our democratic society. The work of A&M and of the Association of Former Students, nonetheless, is never done.

In March, 1960, James Earl Rudder '32 was inaugurated as the fourteenth president of Texas A&M. Texas A&M and the Association of Former Students began the development of planning committees to guide the college through the next fifteen-year period before the centennial celebration in 1976. Two studies, directed largely by former students, set the mood and direction in which the association and the university would move

Plans for the Future

Left, J. Harold Dunn '25. *Right*, Dave Fitch '42, first secretary of the Aggie Club, reviews goals of the organization with Dick Hervey '42.

to further develop the institution into a renowned major university. Those studies were made by the Long Range Planning Committee of the association, chaired by Tyree L. Bell '13, and the Texas A&M Century Study, chaired by J. Harold Dunn '25.

Long Range Planning Committee

The Long Range Planning Committee, created in mid-1959, also included J. Harold Dunn '25, vice-chairman; Dick Hervey '42, ex-officio member and secretary; and members Harold Bockhorn '39, Tom Murrah '38, Guy F. Harrison '40, Gene Howard '45, Roy Caldwell '40, O. T. Hotchkiss, Jr., '24, and Pat H. Wood '54. The committee labored for over two years in reviewing the progress of the association. After numerous meetings and subcommittee reports, Tyree Bell presented the final report of the committee to the Executive Council of the association on February 11, 1961. His report contained the blueprints for today's association and many of the programs which have helped advance the goals of both the association and Texas A&M.

The Long Range Planning Committee recommended that the record-keeping process be updated and computerization expanded to handle the expected influx of new members during the next fifteen years. It was recommended that the association staff be increased to include a full-time fund-raising director and a full-time editor of *The Texas Aggie*, transforming it from a tabloid into a magazine. *The Texas Aggie* through the years has become a truly unique association publication. Major changes began in 1955 when Karl Elmquist, A&M professor of English, became editor. He initiated the conversion of the publication from a newspaper to an oversize magazine in February, 1965, and then to the present standard size in March, 1966. Elmquist was followed in September, 1966, by Joe J. Buser '59, who served as editor until September, 1968, and by R. C. ("Connie") Eckard '55, who was editor from October, 1968, through July, 1971. Presently Jerry C. Cooper '63 is editor in chief of *The Texas Aggie*, which releases eight issues per year.

One unique recommendation of the Bell committee was the establishment of the Distinguished Alumni Award Program to recognize and honor outstanding former stu-

Left, Can you beat that? My chili unstopped our sink! *Right*, Richard ("Buck") Weirus '42, executive secretary of the Association of Former Students, 1964–present.

Board of Directors of the Association of Former Students, October 1, 1960, in San Antonio, Texas. *Standing, left to right:* J. B. ("Dick") Hervey '42, executive secretary; Joe H. Ashy '29, Beaumont; Tom Murrah '38, San Antonio; Phil Bible '43, Austin; F. E. Roberts '31, Carthage; E. C. Clark, Jr., '38, Corpus Christi; John H. Cuthrell '29, New Orleans; and Wayne Durham '40, Abilene. *Seated, left to right:* W. C. ("mAggie") McGee '31, Houston; James W. Aston '33, Dallas; Nelson Rees '32, Odessa; A. C. Elliott '33, Midland; Louis F. Fields '49, Fort Worth; E. Barker Chapman '49, Waco; and Richard ("Buck") Weirus '42, San Antonio.

A Partnership in Higher Education 185

Left, The Dallas A&M Club is one of many that sponsor legislative dinners during election periods to foster support for the university and its programs. (*Photograph by Jerry C. Cooper '63.*) *Left*, Royce E. Wisenbaker '39 and A&M President Williams upon the endowment of the Jack K. Williams Scholarship. Wisenbaker, the father of the President's Endowed Scholars Program at Texas A&M, has established four such scholarships.

Distinguished Alumni Awards

dents for their achievements of state, national, and international significance. Bell said, "Such a program would do more than honor such men. It would spotlight the accomplishments of the college, it would increase our pride, and our student body and faculty's pride in our institution." Recipients of the award are evidence of that unselfish devotion shared by the tens of thousands of Aggies who care.

Tyree Bell stressed that the key to each of these programs rested on expanded participation and increased giving to the annual fund. To this end the addition of an assistant secretary to the staff was approved to work primarily with the fund-raising efforts. On July 1, 1961, Richard ("Buck") Weirus '42 joined the association staff as associate director. His work proved immediately productive. The Development Fund received gifts of $304,574.75 in 1961 and $283,476.83 in 1962.

The Long Range Planning Committee suggested that in order to attract top high school students, scholarships be established to endow continued financial support for higher education at Texas A&M. It was further suggested "a Wills and Bequests program in long-range support of the Association and college goals" be established to insure lasting support. As a result, the Development Foundation in 1973 was expanded under the direction of Robert Walker '58, who had succeeded Weirus as director of the association's annual fund when Weirus became executive director of the association in 1963.

Also conceived during the 1960–1961 study of the Long Range Planning Committee was the creation of a multimember committee to review the objectives and future development of the college. Upon association urging, the college Board of Directors approved a joint board-association committee to be known as the Century Council. This body was to number one hundred of Texas' most outstanding citizens in a joint effort to chart the future of higher education at Texas A&M. J. Harold Dunn '25 was selected chairman of the Century Council, and the Association of Former Students provided fifty thousand dollars to finance this study. The observations and recommendations of the Century Council prescribed progressive programs which helped transform Texas A&M into a more diversified institution of higher learning:

1. The highest possible *quality instruction* to both undergraduate and graduate student.
2. *Selectivity of program* development with emphasis on agricultural and engineering sciences, veterinary medicine, physical and natural sciences, and carefully selected areas of the arts and sciences.
3. Development of a strong program in *research*.
4. Carefully conceived programs of *extension activity*, particularly in agriculture and engineering.
5. Development of an institution of *"university"* structure supported by solid programs in the humanities, the social sciences, and the natural sciences.
6. Development of a strong *graduate program* in selected areas.
7. *Improvement of faculty* by the employment of men of nationally recognized attainments and professional competence, and through strengthening the present faculty members.
8. *Emphasis upon "excellence"* as the criterion for evaluating all programs and activities.
9. *Development of a physical plant* and equipment consistent with the program of excellence.
10. Long-range programs to attract *students of high intellectual capacity, integrity, and ambition*.
11. Establishment of a program to develop *"sources of financial support"* above and beyond the funds anticipated from public revenues.

Proclaiming completion of the Century Council study, *The Texas Aggie* of January, 1962, ran headlines reading, "GREAT DAYS AHEAD FOR A&M." And indeed they were. In 1963, by act of the Texas legislature, the old Agricultural and Mechanical College of Texas became Texas A&M University, the "A&M" designating only the great traditions, the spirit, and the achievements of the past.

In 1963 Buck Weirus succeeded Dick Hervey as executive director of the Association of Former Students. While a student at Texas A&M, Weirus was in the Third Headquarters, Field Artillery unit of the Corps of Cadets, lettered on the A&M swim team, and was a member of the Singing Cadets and the Aggieland Orchestra. While employed by the State of Texas and the City of San Antonio, he was an energetic A&M club worker, holding most of the volunteer positions from club president to association board member. His energy, enthusiasm, unselfish devotion, and resourcefulness contributed to a phenomenal growth in the membership and financial welfare of the association.

Alumni programming requires enormous tact, determination, and composure. The modern Association of Former Students, as complex and diverse as the university itself, requires the commitment of director and staff and the time, money, and planning of thousands of Aggies. During the tumultuous years between 1963 and 1978 the university experienced massive alterations in its size and structure. But even as student enrollment rose from 8,174 students in the fall of 1963, to 29,414 in the fall of 1977, the university improved in the quality of its students, the size and efficiency of its physical plant, and the excellence of its faculty. Moreover, amidst all the expansion, the old traditions and values of the student body and alumni were maintained.

During the 1960's, leadership and the energy behind these studies, as well as the

Left, The President's Endowed Scholars program is the keystone to attracting outstanding student scholars to Texas A&M. *Right,* The Award for Excellence presented to the Corpus Christi A&M Club. *Left to right:* Lamar Walker '50, Ken Cox '59, Lloyd Neal '59, and J. Charles Wilson, Jr., '58. *(Photograph by Jerry C. Cooper '63.)*

achievement of their results, can be credited in large measure to the various association administrations of James W. Aston '33 (1961), Frank B. Harvey '41 (1962), Leland F. Peterson '36 (1963), John H. Lindsey '33 (1964), John F. Younger '37 (1965), Royce E. Wisenbaker '39 (1966), John A. Crichton '37 (1967), Jeff Montgomery '41 (1968), Ford D. Albritton, Jr., '43 (1969), and their co-workers.

The New Organization 1968– Present

Although the early 1960's witnessed numerous progressive achievements, association leaders expressed concern over the future stature of both their organization and the university in particular. In order to map out a blueprint for the future, according to J. R. ("Bob") Latimer, Jr., a long-range planning group was named in 1966 under the direction of James L. Sewell '27. The key result of the long-range study was a new association organizational plan which was implemented at the November, 1967, annual meeting. Officers of the new organization took office on January 1, 1968.

The new organizational structure of the association had the concept of a board of directors consisting of the president, the president-elect, six "program" vice-presidents, and six regional vice-presidents. This board was directed by the president and the Executive Committee, which consisted of the president, the immediate past president, the president-elect, and the executive director of the association. The initial board took office in January, 1968, with each of the officers under President Jeff Montgomery obliged to develop a format and duties for his office. The board met in February, April, June, August, and November of that year, and there were many interim meetings during which all facets of the association's activities were considered. This timely reorganization was to prove most effective since the ranks of the former students were both growing and becoming more active in the support of association programs. To further expand the association's contact with former students statewide, Harry J. Green, Jr., '52 joined the staff as field director from 1969 to 1973.

President's Scholars

In 1967 the university scholarship program made a significant expansion. Ten scholarships of one thousand dollars each were established by the university Board of Directors with provisions for the establishment of ten more each year until forty were being funded annually. Recipients are known as President's Scholars and are selected on the basis of

Left, President Jack K. Williams *(right)* and Bob Walker '58, director of development, on the occasion of Dr. Williams' induction into the Century Club during A&M's centennial year 1976. *Right*, A&M President James Earl Rudder '32 lies in state in the Systems Administration Building in 1970. *(Photograph by Tom Nelson.)*

academic and leadership qualities without regard to their family's financial condition. In 1968 the association board voted to provide annual stipends for ten additional President's Scholars. After ten years this yearly grant was transferred to the Opportunity Awards Program since the Endowed Scholars Program was on such firm footing.

Under the leadership of Royce Wisenbaker the President's Endowed Scholarships were created in 1968 to allow individuals, clubs, classes, or organizations to endow scholarships for outstanding students by means of a donation of twenty-five thousand dollars. Wisenbaker gave the first scholarship in the name of university President Earl Rudder. As a result of this bold association initiative, by early 1970 more than fifty of these endowments had been established. Today they total more than two hundred, benefiting students from all areas of the state.

The university was preparing itself for the dynamic future. Not content with token accomplishment, the association reviewed the objectives of the 1961 plan in 1966 and again in 1967 and 1977. The outcome of the 1967 long-range planning committee, chaired by James Sewell '27 of Dallas, was to reaffirm the association's committees. In 1965 the Annual Fund gained additional support with the creation of the Century Club. This program, which required a one-hundred-dollar donation for Century Club membership each year, was initially conceived by Buck Weirus after a visit to the Big Ten Conference annual meeting of fund raisers in 1964. By late 1968 the Century Club program was a well-established fund-raising tool of the association.

By distinguishing gifts in dollar categories it was felt that there would be a greater willingness among former students to increase their annual giving in order to assist the financing of the many programs of the association. During the first five years of the Century Club concept, gifts of only $100 or more were solicited from individual former students and friends of the university. During this incubation period, the number of these pledges increased from 370 in 1965 to 1,339 in 1970. The Century Club program gained added momentum when additional donor categories were established in 1970: Silver Century, $250 or more; Gold Century, $500 or more; and Diamond Century, $1,000 and up.

The Century Club

A Partnership in Higher Education 189

Mr. and Mrs. J. M. ("Cop") Forsyth '12, Dr. Jack K. Williams, and Buck Weirus '42 during the opening ceremony of the Forsyth Alumni Center.

In the Centennial Celebration year 1976, more than 8,350 former students and friends of A&M made gifts of $100 or more.

Total Century Club gifts by former students in recent years have averaged over one million dollars annually. This generous giving has allowed the association to expand its already broad base of university support programs. During the past few years funds have

Century Club Memberships
for the Years 1965–1977
as of September 10, 1977

	1965	1966	1967*	1968	1969	1970*	1971	1972	1973*	1974	1975	1976*	1977
Bronze	370	980	572	1,056	1,339	1,664	2,352	2,679	3,605	3,829	4,479	7,644	6,536
Silver†						90‡	131	144	193	222	292	401	443
Gold†						20‡	38	45	64	95	102	123	136
Diamond†						17‡	26	64	81	108	140	187	232
Total	370	980	572	1,056	1,339	1,791	2,547	2,932	3,943	4,254	5,013	8,355	7,347
Yearly Change		+610	−408	+484	+283	+452	+756	+385	+1,011	+311	+759	+3,342	−1,008
Percentage of Yearly Change		+165%	−42%	+85%	+27%	+34%	+42%	+15%	+34%	+8%	+18%	+67%	

*The *Directory of Former Students* was published during these years.
†The upper levels of Century Club membership began mid-1970.
‡Accurate counts were not kept for the upper levels during 1970. While the total number of Century Club members for the year is correct, there may have been more upper level memberships than indicated here.

The Forsyth Alumni Center.

been used for varied programs of educational support, including academic department enrichment funds, the establishment of a visitors' information center, a fund to help in the recruitment of new faculty, and other special projects. These funds have also been used in an effort to expand the awards programs recognizing research and teaching excellence. In 1965 the Association of Former Students, in conjunction with the Graduate College, began honoring outstanding graduate students in the areas of academic excellence, research, and teaching. In May, 1978, Graduate Dean Dr. George W. Kunze '45 noted that the association contributed more than thirty thousand dollars during the previous year to assist college recruiting and the support of graduate students.

In July, 1978, the United States Steel Foundation, via the Council for the Advancement and Support of Education (CASE), presented the Association of Former Students the first-place award for public institutions in the improvement category in recognition of 27,353 former student contributions representing $13 million in 1976. As a result of fundraising programs coordinated by Buck Weirus and Randy Matson '67, associate executive director, this is the fourth time the association has won a CASE award.

In addition to the Association of Former Students there are numerous special-interest organizations that give of their time and resources to support campus activities. Most notable among these groups are the Aggie Club and the Federation of Texas A&M Mothers' Clubs. The Aggie Club was established in the early 1950's to provide athletic scholarships, funds for athletic facilities, and overall support for the vast sports program at Texas A&M. The Aggie Club allows for a concentrated fund-raising base that is not in competition with the larger Association of Former Students. The mothers' clubs, first organized in Dallas

A Partnership in Higher Education   191

Left, The centennial gift of the class of 1976. *Right*, Joe H. and Betty Moore '38 and Frank Wardlaw, first director of the Texas A&M University Press, at the press building.

during the early 1920's, are a unique service organization of Aggie "moms" dedicated to the support of on-campus student activities. As a result of the mothers' clubs' close contact with Texas A&M, a special parents' weekend is held on campus each year in the spring. Other organizations of former students, such as the Aggie Band Association, the Lettermen's Association, the Ross Volunteer Association, and the Former Fish Drill Team Association, yearly enhance their corresponding campus organizations.

President Earl Rudder died in March, 1970, and was succeeded after the interim administration of Major General Alvin Roubal Luedecke '32 by Jack Kenny Williams, who became president of the Texas A&M University System. During Williams' administration, Texas A&M continued to expand and improve its academic breadth and quality, and it became a Sea Grant College in September, 1971. The university also inaugurated the development of a full four-year academic program at the Moody College of Marine Sciences and Maritime Resources in Galveston, Texas. The new College of Medicine, which first admitted students in August, 1977, the Center for Energy and Mineral Resources, and the Center for Education and Research in Free Enterprise, initially funded by the association, provided a new dimension in A&M's services to the state and nation. In 1976–1977 Texas A&M's funded research in the amount of $51.8 million made up 40 percent of the total research conducted by Texas' public senior colleges and universities. Under Williams' leadership the quality of academic life at Texas A&M University has been greatly enriched.

Association leadership during the 1970's has been equally attuned to the fast-paced rise of both the association and the university. The able guidance and insight of Presidents James L. Sewell '27 (1970), Leslie L. Appelt '41 (1971), James R. Latimer, Jr., '44 (1972), Melvin Maltz '42 (1973), Joe H. Moore '38 (1974), John W. Caple '52 (1975), Mayo J. Thompson '41 (1976), John M. Knox '46 (1977), Harvey Cash '33 (1978), and Robert Smith III

San Antonio A&M Club Past Presidents' Dinner, May 10, 1978. *Left to right, seated:* Willson Davis '27, Russell White '26, Louis Hartung '29, C. J. Stromberger '26, Chester Slimp '38, Tom Murrah '38, Sterling Evans '21, Harvey Cash '33, Tom Harrington '22, Jennings Anderson '45, Bob Gulley '42, Bubba Reeves '41, John Kenagy '41, Jack Hollimon '42, Richard ("Buck") Weirus '42, and Cosmo Guido '44. *Second row:* Richard Jochimsen '27, Ivan Moser '50, Will Ed Jauer '39, Jim Uptmore '53, Charles Smith '53, A. J. Specia '43, David Wolf '52, J. D. Strickel '49, Charles Eckert '49, Dick Alterman '49, Wallace Larson '54, Melvin Mitchell '52, Forrest Jordan '39, Jim Page '49, Raul Fernandez '59, Lad Herold '54, Wayne Freiling '62, Sam Stracke '44, and Damon Tassos '45. *Top row:* T. B. ("Gype") Sebastian '33, William A. Wurzbach '25, Jim Singleton '42, George S. Harris '41, John Caple '52, Woody Bell '38, L. S. ("Tiny") Keen '22, Bob Latimer '44, C. D. Long '34, Charles Wiseman '57, assistant football coach Tom Wilson (special guest), Dick Kistner '65, Charles Milstead '60, Barlow ("Bones") Irvin '26, and Tom F. Murrah '66.

Renowned Texas artist and former A&M artist-in-residence Buck Schiwetz '21 being honored by the Legislature of Texas. He is flanked by Lieutenant Governor Bill Hobby *(left)* and State Senator Bill Moore '40 of Bryan.

A Partnership in Higher Education

The Centennial

'61 (1979), have helped establish the Texas A&M Association of Former Students as something of a legend in its own time.

As the centennial celebration of the university neared, an old dream became a reality. After more than ninety-five years and seven moves to various temporary locations, the association staff occupied the James ("Scotty") Forsyth Alumni Center, built specifically for association needs in the Memorial Student Center. Over the years, the association offices had always been on something of a temporary basis.

During the planning of the new MSC addition, and after a sizable donation by J. M. ("Cop") Forsyth '12 in honor of his father, Ford Albritton led a drive before the university Board of Directors to locate the alumni quarters in the heart of the campus. Albritton's efforts proved successful, and the Forsyth Alumni Center, located in the southwest wing of the MSC, was opened in early 1973, providing spacious and comfortable quarters for the association offices.

In late 1975 the association, the administration, and the student body made plans for the Texas A&M centennial celebrations to culminate with a convocation of the university's one-hundredth anniversary on October 4, 1976. The centennial celebrations were launched with the publication of a two-volume *Centennial History of Texas A&M University, 1876–1976*, and a separate *Pictorial History of Texas A&M University, 1876–1976*, both written by A&M Professor of History Henry C. Dethloff. The 120-page centennial issue of *The Texas Aggie*, published in November, 1975, also contained a special "Journal of Texas A&M History." The Association of Former Students provided the money for the writing and publication of Dethloff's histories and then dedicated the proceeds from the sale of the books to a revolving fund of the newly established Texas A&M University Press. The press, directed first by Frank H. Wardlaw and then by Lloyd Lyman, has received the active support of the Association of Former Students and provides a bright new dimension in the educational services of Texas A&M University. Later in the centennial year the association sponsored the publication by the press of a series of eight prints depicting campus scenes by the inimitable artist Edward M. ("Buck") Schiwetz '21. Finally, in October, 1976, as alumni, students, staff friends, and academic representatives from universities throughout the world gathered to hear the keynote speech of former Texas Governor and U.S. Secretary of the Treasury John Connally, former students could look with just and lasting pride on the diversified university assistance programs which had helped Texas A&M University become one of the truly great institutions of higher education in Texas and in the nation.

On August 1, 1977, Jarvis E. Miller '50 became the eighteenth president of Texas A&M University when Jack K. Williams was named chancellor of the Texas A&M University System. Miller, who had served the university as professor of agricultural economics and director of the Agricultural Experiment Station since his return to the campus as a member of the faculty in 1958, pledged his administration to the continuing pursuit of excellence in teaching, research, and public service (both foreign and domestic), to the preparation of military leaders, and to the development of a scholarly environment.

To the former students Miller pledged "to emphasize those strong, positive traditions of A&M which have made Texas Aggies unique and distinctive leaders while adapting to changing circumstances and needs. During this administration, this university will seek to enhance its reputation for excellence in all that it undertakes. And I pledge further my

The inauguration of Jarvis Miller '50 as president of Texas A&M University on October 4, 1977. (*Photograph by Kathy Young '75.*)

assistance to maintain and strengthen the Association of Former Students which has played such a vital role in making Texas A&M what it is today."

Proud, but never satisfied with the accomplishments of the past, the former students labor continuously to give that something extra to their alma mater. This love, loyalty, and unselfish devotion have been kindled out of a desire to perpetuate and build upon the opportunities that an education at Texas A&M has made available to each former student through the years. For A&M former students, the Texas A&M experience not only prepared them for earning a living, but provided a set of values, an incentive, and an invincible Aggie Spirit that sets the Aggie apart as a distinctive, indefinable person.

Gig' em!

Left, They're never satisfied. They complained when I didn't speak, and now they complain when I do! *Right*, Representatives of the National Capital Texas A&M Club Colonel Frank Gilchrist '38 *(center)* and Lieutenant Colonel Joe E. West '54 *(right)* place a wreath at the Tomb of the Unknown Soldier in Arlington National Cemetery during Aggie Muster, 1972. *(Photograph by Jim Latimer.)*

The Da Nang, Vietnam, 1970 Aggie Muster. Classes from 1943 to 1968 were represented. *(U.S. Army photograph.)*

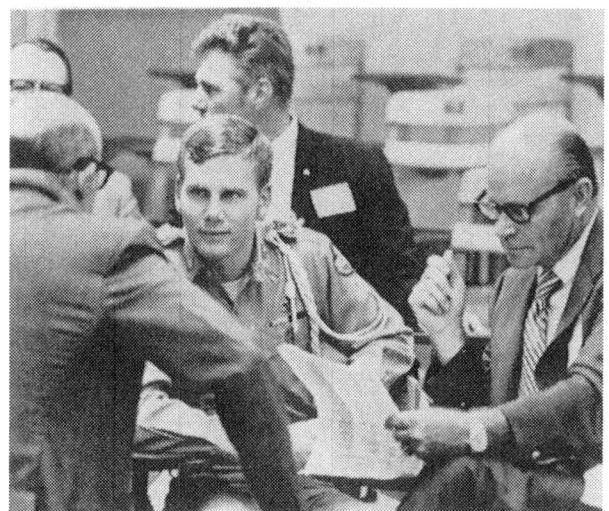 

Left, The Association of Former Students has always retained close contact with the students. *Left to right:* Gabe D. Anderson '41, Cadet Charles L. McGuine '72, and George A. Humble '48. *Right*, Military Day — 1973.

Joe Utay '08 with students *(left to right)* Jimmy Wright, Mark Shifrin, Tom Pardue, Henry Ostermann, and Paul Zinser of Utay Hall, Dorm 12.

A Partnership in Higher Education

Leslie Lyon '73 with Colonel Thomas R. Parsons '49 receiving the Fifth Army ROTC Award from Lieutenant General Patrick F. Cassidy in 1973. Aggies continue to excell in all aspects of military endeavor.

Left, Mrs. Marjorie E. Ramage, Hooks, named Aggie Mother of the Year in 1973. Her son Calvin '73 *(right)* and Ron Bento '73 present Mrs. Ramage with flowers. In addition to Calvin, Mrs. Ramage's husband, Jewel C. '42, and children Bart '75 and Ann also attended Texas A&M. *Right*, Harry J. Green, Jr., '52, the first association field director, 1969–1973.

Basketball Coach Shelby Metcalf surrounded by his team during the 1977–1978 season.

Lieutenant General Ormond Simpson '36 administering the oath at the August, 1976, summer commissioning and graduation.

A Partnership in Higher Education

The Visitors' Information Center has become the showcase of Texas A&M. *Left to right:* Buck Weirus '42, President Jack Williams, Melvin Maltz '47, Bob Latimer '44, Les Appelt '41, and the architect, Randy Waligura '67 at opening ceremonies in 1974.

The Houston A&M Club Past Presidents' Association third annual meeting, March 8, 1978. *Left to right, front row:* Brig. Gen. Vic Barraco '15; Charles Blumenthal '21; John C. Mayfield, Sr., '23; W. S. ("Nich") Nicholson, Sr., '24; V. P. Parr '26; Melvin Smith '28; Dr. Jack Williams (special guest); Edwin K. ("Lefty") Martin '30; Wilbur Godsey '31; Walter Swank '31; T. B. ("Gype") Sebastian '33; Dan R. Parker '37; and J. Doug Smith '37. *Middle row:* B. M. ("Mike") Hackedorn '39; J. E. ("Chubby") Nolen '40; Bernard C. Richardson '41; George G. Harris '41; Les Appelt '41; Raymond C. Loomis '42; Richard ("Buck") Weirus '42; C. J. ("Tex") Thornton '44; Eugene F. ("Gene") Howard '45; John M. Knox, M.D., '46; Robert S. ("Bob") Webb '46; Melvin Maltz '47; Maurice ("Rock") Robinowitz '48; and Harry D. Cain '50. *Back row:* Herschel Maltz '50; William D. ("Bill") Plagens '50; Ted W. Mohle, Jr., '52; T. K. Niland '53; Marvin Tate '55; Clifford L. Condit, Jr., DDS, '56; H. Eugene Holder '57; John C. Mayfield, Jr., '58; James W. ("Jim") Sebastian '65; Thomas F. ("Tom") Murrah '66; James R. ("Randy") Matson '67; Michael Casey '69; and Tom Murrah '38.

Left, Tom Nelson '63, field director of the association, 1973–1977. *Right*, Past Association President Melvin Maltz '47 and University President Jack K. Williams.

A check for one thousand dollars from the Association of Former Students provides "seed money" to the Class of '81 for planning class programs. Accepting the check from Associate Executive Director Randy Matson '67 are *(left to right)* class officers Patti Heaton, secretary-treasurer; Daniel Weinbaum, president; and Kay Whitcomb, social secretary. Traditionally, classes return many times more to Texas A&M in their class gift when they graduate. This was the second such grant made by the association to a beginning class.

A Partnership in Higher Education

Linda Cornelius Waltman '79 *(right)* ranks among the top female pentathletes in the nation.

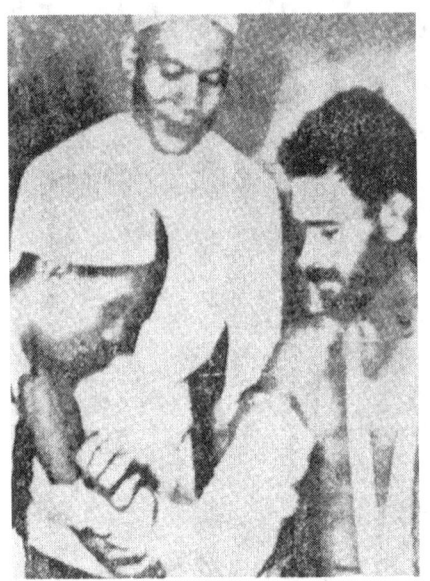 

Left, Major Robert N. Daughtrey '55 being treated for two broken arms while a POW in North Vietnam. *Right,* Mrs. Leonard F. Ray greeting her son, Captain James C. Ray '63, upon his return home after seven years of captivity as a POW in North Vietnam.

202 WE ARE THE AGGIES

Mike Mosley '81 moves outside against a Southern California defender at the 1978 Bluebonnet Bowl in Houston.

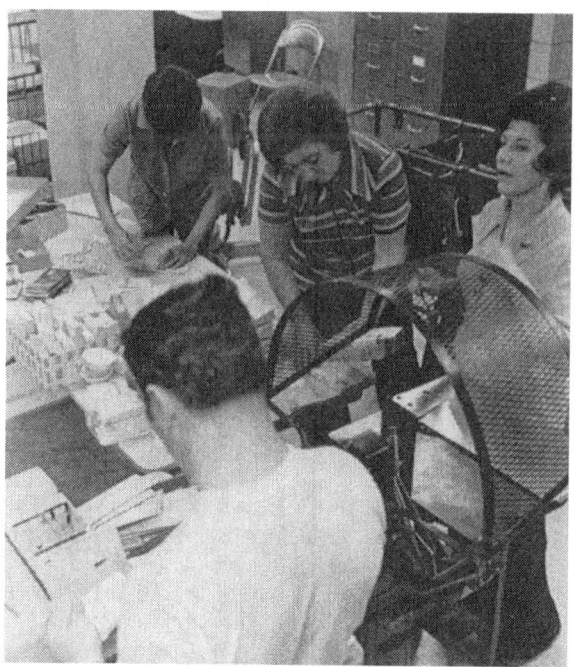

Left, The Association of Former Students Mail Room — pulse of the association's contact with alumni worldwide. *Right*, Kim Tomes '77 — Miss USA, 1977.

A Partnership in Higher Education

Left, Young Reveille IV with mascot handler Bob Vanderberry '78 at ceremonies honoring Reveille III. *(Photograph by Peter Leabo '78.) Top right,* Tony Franklin '79 signals his final field goal against Texas Tech in 1977. He booted field goals of 48, 51, 25, and 39 yards — all in the last quarter. *(Photograph by Kathy Young '75.) Bottom right,* Research is a key part of Texas A&M's far-reaching programs. This model of the Space Shuttle Enterprise underwent testing in the subsonic wind tunnel at Easterwood Airport at A&M.

The 1978 staff of the Association of Former Students. *Left to right, bottom row:* Connie Dodd, class programs assistant; Barbara Fite, computer recorder; Pat Morley, on-campus programs director; Olive DeLucia, class programs director; Juanita Murray '67, director of business affairs; June Robinson, assistant receptionist; and Susan Jauregui, word processing secretary. *Second row:* Wanda Cornforth, Annual Fund assistant; Mary B. Wilson '64, assistant editor; Jean Shearer, computer coordinator; Betty Cater, Annual Fund accountant; Pat Gersbach, A&M club coordinator; Charlotte Whitton, business affairs assistant; Peggy Cooper, word processing secretary; Pam Behling, receptionist; and Tommie Sorenson, associate executive director assistant and word processing center supervisor. *Top row:* Johnnie Taylor '32; Pete Garcia, mail room coordinator; Tom Rowell, graphics director; Dennis Parrish '68, off-campus programs director; Randy Matson '67, associate executive director; Richard ("Buck") Weirus '42, executive director; Sam Ford, machine operator; and Jerry Cooper '63, *The Texas Aggie* editor.

A Partnership in Higher Education 205

APPENDIX I
Past Presidents of the Former Student Organizations

Year of Presidency		Class
	Association of Ex-Cadets	
1879–1880	none elected	
1880–1881	William M. Sleeper	'79
1881–1882	William M. Sleeper	'79
1882–1883	Pinckney L. Downs	'79
1883–1884	Pinckney L. Downs	'79
1884–1885	Unknown	
1885–1886	Unknown	
	Alumni Association	
1886–1887	None	
1887–1888	None	
1888–1889	Andrew L. Shirley	'85
1889–1890	John W. Carson	'86
1890–1891	Walter Wipprecht	'84
1891–1892	Charles Pescay	'85
1892–1893	Edward W. Hutchinson	'89
1893–1894	John B. Hereford	'87
1894–1895	J. H. Forman	'87
1895–1896	Buell C. Pittuck	'94
1896–1897	E. J. Smith	'88
1897–1898	F. R. Ross	'94
1898–1899	E. W. Hutchinson	'89
	Alpha Phi Fraternity	
1896–1897	Edward B. Cushing	'80
1897–1898	Edward B. Cushing	'80
1898–1899	Unknown	
1899–1900	(merged with Alumni Association)	
	Alumni Association	
1899–1900	George W. McCormick	'91
1900–1901	Edward B. Cushing	'80
1901–1902	Phineas S. Tilson	'88
1902–1903	Lea E. Allen	'87
1903–1904	Frank A. Riechardt	'79

Year of Presidency		Class
1904–1905	Buell C. Pittuck	'94
1905–1906	L. D. Amsler	'89
1906–1907	Francis M. Law	'95
1907–1908	Francis M. Law	'95
1908–1909	R. C. Watkins	'96
1909–1910	James R. Cravens	'82
1910–1911	F. Kamp McGinnis	'00
1911–1912	Gen. Andrew C. Love	'99
1912–1913	Hal Moseley	'00
1913–1914	Pinckney L. Downs	'79
1914–1915	Pinckney L. Downs	'79
1915–1916	C. Otto Moser	'04
1916–1917	Robert J. Potts, Sr.	'06
1917–1918	Robert J. Potts, Sr.	'06
1918–1919	Charles Rogan	'79

Association of Former Students

1919–1920	Ervin H. Astin	'99
1920–1921	J. Webb Howell	'94
1921–1922	Charles A. DeWare	'09
1922–1923	Elton P. Hunter	'00
1923–1924	Marion S. Church	'05
1924–1925	Carl C. ("Polly") Krueger	'12
1925–1926	Luke L. Ballard	'05
1926–1927	Andrew P. Rollins	'06
1927–1928	Julius Schepps	'17
1928–1929	Owen W. Sherrill	'10
1929–1930	William W. Sterling	'10
1930–1931	Burt E. Hull	'04
1931–1932	Julian B. Thomas	'11
1932–1933	A. Kidd Short	'00
1933–1934	Thomas B. Warden	'03
1934–1935	Thomas B. Warden	'03
1935–1936	Irwin A. ("Bubba") Uhr	'17
1936–1937	Charles A. Thanheiser	'01
1937–1938	F. Dudley Perkins	'97
1938–1939	Charles L. Babcock	'20
1939–1940	Calvin P. Dodson	'11
1940–1941	Albert G. ("Bert") Pfaff	'25
1941–1942	Tyree L. Bell	'13
1942–1943	William J. Lawson	'24
1943–1944	Jake P. Hamblen	'27

Year of Presidency		Class
1944–1945	Rufus R. Peeples	'28
1945–1946	H. Dick Winters	'16
1946–1947	Carroll M. Gaines, Sr.	'12
1947–1948	A. E. ("Red") Hinman	'25
1948–1949	George G. Smith	'30
1949–1950	Louis A. Hartung	'29
1950–1951	A. Ed Caraway	'34
1951–1952	George B. Morgan	'18
1952–1953	Allin F. ("Smiley") Mitchell	'09
1953–1954	J. Harold Dunn	'25
1954–1955	Oscar T. Hotchkiss, Jr.	'24
1955–1956	W. Lambert Ballard	'22
1956–1957	Louis R. Bloodworth	'32
1957–1958	E. M. ("Jiggs") Freeman	'22
1958–1959	R. N. ("Dick") Conolly	'37
1959–1960	Tom A. Murrah	'38
1960–1961	Walter C. ("mAggie") McGee, Jr.	'31
1961	James W. Aston	'33
1962	Frank B. Harvey	'41
1963	Leland F. Peterson	'36
1964	John H. Lindsey	'44
1965	John F. Younger	'37
1966	Royce E. Wisenbaker	'39
1967	John A. Crichton	'37
1968	Jeff Montgomery	'41
1969	Ford D. Albritton, Jr.	'43
1970	James L. Sewell	'27
1971	Leslie L. Appelt	'41
1972	James R. Latimer, Jr.	'44
1973	Melvin Maltz	'42
1974	Joe H. Moore	'38
1975	John W. Caple	'52
1976	Mayo J. Thompson	'41
1977	John M. Knox	'46
1978	Harvey Cash	'33
1979	Robert Smith III	'61
1980	Raul B. Fernandez	'59

W. M. Sleeper
1880–1882

P. L. Downs
1882–1884, 1913–1915

J. W. Carson
1889–1890

W. Wipprecht
1890–1891

B. C. Pittuck
1895–1896, 1904–1905

G. McCormick
1899–1900

F. M. Law
1906–1908

J. R. Cravens
1909–1910

F. K. McGinnis
1910–1911

A. C. Love
1911–1912

H. Moseley
1912–1913

C. O. Moser
1915–1916

R. J. Potts, Sr.
1916–1918

C. Rogan
1918–1919

E. H. Astin
1919–1920

J. W. Howell
1920–1921

C. A. DeWare
1921–1922

E. P. Hunter
1922–1923

M. S. Church
1923–1924

C. C. Krueger
1924–1925

L. L. Ballard
1925–1926

A. P. Rollins
1926–1927

J. Schepps
1927–1928

O. W. Sherrill
1928–1929

W. W. Sterling
1929–1930

B. E. Hull
1930–1931

J. B. Thomas
1931–1932

A. K. Short
1932–1933

T. B. Warden
1933–1935

I. A. Uhr
1935–1936

C. A. Thanheiser
1936–1937

F. D. Perkins
1937–1938

C. L. Babcock
1938–1939

C. P. Dodson
1939–1940

A. G. Pfaff
1940–1941

T. L. Bell
1941–1942

W. J. Lawson
1942–1943

J. P. Hamblen
1943–1944

R. R. Peeples
1944–1945

H. D. Winters
1945–1946

Past Presidents of the Former Student Organizations

C. M. Gaines, Sr.
1946–1947

A. E. Hinman
1947–1948

G. G. Smith
1948–1949

L. A. Hartung
1949–1950

A. E. Caraway
1950–1951

G. B. Morgan
1951–1952

A. F. Mitchell
1952–1953

J. H. Dunn
1953–1954

O. T. Hotchkiss, Jr.
1954–1955

W. L. Ballard
1955–1956

L. R. Bloodworth
1956–1957

E. M. Freeman
1957–1958

R. N. Conolly
1958–1959

Tom A. Murrah
1959–1960

W. C. McGee, Jr.
1960–1961

J. W. Aston
1961

F. B. Harvey
1962

L. F. Peterson
1963

J. H. Lindsey
1964

J. F. Younger
1965

R. E. Wisenbaker
1966

J. A. Crichton
1967

J. Montgomery
1968

F. D. Albritton, Jr.
1969

J. L. Sewell
1970

L. L. Appelt
1971

J. R. Latimer, Jr.
1972

M. Maltz
1973

J. H. Moore
1974

J. W. Caple
1975

M. J. Thompson
1976

J. M. Knox
1977

H. Cash
1978

R. Smith III
1979

R. B. Fernandez
1980

Past Presidents of the Former Student Organizations

APPENDIX II

Executive Secretaries of the Former Student Organizations

1879–1884	Edward B. Cushing '80
1884–1886	None
1886–1889	Frederick E. Giesecke '86
1889–1891	Walter Wipprecht
1891–1894	Frederick E. Giesecke '86
1894–1895	E. W. Hutchinson '89
1895–1897	Frederick E. Giesecke '86
1897–1901	Phineas S. Tilson '88
1901–1902	W. C. Martin '98
1902–1904	Eugene W. Kerr '96
1904–1905	W. C. Martin '98
1905–1906	Edwin J. Kyle '99
1906–1914	Alva Mitchell '94
1914–1915	Dillon T. Stevens '13
1915–1918	Frank J. Skeeler '10
1916–1920	Nester M. McGinnis '08*
1918–1920	William L. Stangel '15
1920–1923	William B. Cook '20
1923–1926	Ike Ashburn†
1926–1947	Everett E. McQuillen '20
1947–1963	James B. Hervey '42
1963–present	Richard ("Buck") Weirus '42

*College alumni secretary hired by President William B. Bizzell to edit *The Alumni Quarterly* and to keep records. This was not an association position.
†First full-time salaried association executive secretary.

APPENDIX III
Distinguished Alumni Award Recipients

Dr. Edward F. Knipling '30, USDA Entomologist (1962)

W. W. Lynch '22, Chairman, Edison Electric Institute (1962)

John W. Newton '12, Vice-President, Mobil Chemical Corporation (1962)

General Bernard A. Schriever '31 (USAF), Air Force Systems Commander (1962)

Tyree L. Bell '13, President, Austin Bridge & Road Company (1964)

R. Wofford Cain '13, Chairman, Aztec Oil & Gas Company (1964)

J. Harold Dunn '25, Chairman, Shamrock Oil Corporation (1964)

H. B. Zachry '22, Chairman, Zachry Company, Contractors (1964)

W. T. Doherty '22, President, The Mound Oil Corporation (1966)

Richard A. Goodson '27, Chairman, Southwestern Bell Telephone Company (1966)

Dewitt C. Greer '23, Comm., Texas Dept. of Highways and Public Transportation (1966)

Olin E. ("Tiger") Teague '32, Congressman (1966)

James W. Aston '33, Chairman, Republic National Bank (1967)

Ernest D. Brockett '34, Chairman, Gulf Oil Corporation (1967)

Major General Alvin R. Luedecke '32 (USAF), Gen. Mgr., Atomic Energy Commission (1967)

Horace A. Sawyer '16, Chairman, Lone Star Cement Corporation (1967)

Lieutenant General A. D. Bruce '16 (USA), Chancellor, University of Houston (1968)

Roy B. Davis '27, Chairman, World Cotton Congress (1968)

Carl C. ("Polly") Krueger '12, Chairman, SAMSCO Machine & Supply Company (1968)

Michel T. Halbouty '30, Consulting Geologist, Petroleum Engineer, Independent Producer (1968)

W. C. ("mAggie") McGee '31, President, Tennessee Gas Pipeline Co. (1969)

Dr. William E. Morgan '30, President, Colorado State University (1969)

Edward J. Mosher '28, Chairman, Mosher Steel Corporation (1969)

Francis C. Turner '29, Federal Highway Administrator (1969)

J. H. Galloway '29, Vice-President and Director, Exxon Oil Corporation (1970)

M. J. Neeley '22, President, Hobbs Trailer Corporation (1970)

Sam H. Sanders, M.D., '22, Head, Dept. of Otolaryngology, Univ. of Tenn. Medical School (1970)

Major General J. Earl Rudder '32 (USAR), President, Texas A&M University System (1970)

William C. Tinus '28, Head, Bell Laboratories (1970)

Lt. General Robert W. Colglazier '25 (USAR), Commander, Fourth U.S. Army (1971)

Rex B. Grey '41, President, ITT Africa and Middle East (1971)

John M. Knox, M.D., '46, Head, Department of Dermatology, Baylor College of Medicine (1971)

Norman N. Moser '37, Rancher and Chairman, National Livestock & Meat Board (1971)

Dr. M. T. Harrington '22, Chancellor, Texas A&M University System (1971)

Hal N. Carr '43, Chairman, North Central Air Lines (1972)

Harold J. Haynes '46, Chairman, Standard Oil of California (1972)

Edward M. ("Buck") Schiwetz '21, Artist (1972)

Dr. Durward B. Varner '40, President, University of Nebraska (1972)

Frank J. Malina '34, Rocket Scientist and Kinetic Artist (1972)

M. ("Buddy") Benz '32, Floriculturist and World Floral Designer (1973)

Sterling C. Evans '21, President, Houston Federal Land Bank (1973)

James M. ("Cop") Forsyth '12, President, Forsyth Engineering Company (1973)

Royce E. Wisenbaker '39, President, Wisenbaker, Fix & Associates — Engineering (1973)

Robert R. Herring '41, Chairman, Houston Natural Gas Corporation (1974)

Bernard G. Johnson '37, Chairman, Johnson Engineering Corporation (1974)

Owen W. Sherrill '10, Texas All-Time Farm and Land Broker (1974)

J. B. Thomas '11, Chairman, Texas Electric Service (1974)

Robert W. Baker '44, Attorney, Banker, and State Senator (1975)

Dr. Lawrence E. Fouraker '44, Dean, Harvard Graduate School of Business (1975)

George D. Comnas '35, Executive, International Shipping Industry (1976)

Fred Hale '22, Animal Scientist (1976)

William T. Moore '40, Attorney and State Senator (1976)

L. F. Peterson '36, Petroleum Engineer, Operator, and Consultant (1976)

Ernest Lee Wehner '41, Vice-President, Arthur Andersen Company, CPA's (1976)

General Otto P. Weyland '23 (USAF), Commander, Tactical Air Command (1976)

Distinguished Alumni Award Recipients

Ford D. Albritton, Jr., '43, Chairman, Tipperary Corporation (1977)

Leslie L. Appelt '41, Engineer and Industrial Realtor (1977)

George P. Mitchell '40, Oil Producer and Real Estate Developer (1977)

J. Roy Quinby '24, Agronomist and Sorghums Researcher (1977)

Searcy Bracewell '38, Attorney and State Senator (1978)

John H. Lindsey '44, Insurance Broker and Fine Arts Patron (1978)

Joe Hiram Moore '38, Petroleum Engineer; Independent Producer and Operator (1978)

James L. Sewell '27, Chairman, Delhi Taylor Oil Corporation (1978)

APPENDIX IV

Campus Muster Speakers, 1945–1978

1945	Lieutenant Clifton H. Chamberlain '40, returned POW from among the twenty-five who attended 1942 Corregidor muster
1946	General Dwight D. Eisenhower, Chief of Staff, U.S. Army
1947	Texas State Senator W. T. ("Bill") Moore '40 Colonel Willard Chevallier, Corregidor defender
1948	A. E. ("Red") Hinman '25*
1949	James W. Aston '33, President, Republic National Bank, Dallas
1950	General Louis Henturvey '29*
1951	James H. Pipkin '29
1952	State Senator Searcy Bracewell '38
1953	Governor Dan Thornton of Colorado
1954	Governor Allan Shivers of Texas
1955	General Otto P. Weyland '23
1956	Texas Land Commissioner James E. Rudder '32
1957	(no muster due to Easter recess)
1958	Major General Bernard A. Schriever '31, USAF
1959	Congressman Olin E. ("Tiger") Teague '32
1960	General A. D. Bruce '16, Chancellor, University of Houston
1961	James W. Aston '33, President, Republic National Bank, Dallas
1962	Eli L. Whiteley '41, Medal of Honor winner in World War II in the Battle of the Bulge, 1944
1963	L. F. Peterson '36, President, Association of Former Students
1964	Dr. E. King Gill '24, the first "12th Man"
1965	C. Darrow Hooper '53, Texas A&M Athletic Hall of Fame
1966	Penrose B. Metcalf '16, former Texas state representative and senator
1967	Major General Raymond L. Murray '35, Inspector General, USMC

*Broadcast statewide via the student radio station, WTAW.

1968	Major General Wood B. Kyle '36, Commander, Fifth Marine Division, Camp Pendleton, California
1969	Mayo J. Thompson '41, Houston attorney
1970	Yale B. Griffis '30, Dallas attorney
1971	Jack K. Williams, President, Texas A&M University
1972	Larry Kirk '66, Vietnam War veteran, White House Fellow
1973	Captain James Edwin Ray '63, prisoner of war in Vietnam for six years
1974	Sheldon J. Best '63, Vice-President, United Air Lines
1975	Reagan Brown '43, Special Assistant to Governor Dolph Briscoe
1976	Charles G. Scruggs '47, Vice-President and Editorial Director, *Progressive Farmer*
1977	Major James Edwin Ray '63
1978	Thomas Dooley '35, Corregidor defender, present at the April, 1942, muster on "The Rock"

APPENDIX V
Flag Officers by Texas A&M Class

Class	Rank	Name	Service
1906	MG	Bennett Puryear, Jr.	USMC
1908	MG	George F. Moore	USA
	BG	D. B. Netherwood	USA
	BG	John A. Warden	USA
1910	BG	William C. Crane	USA
1911	MG	Howard C. Davidson	USAF
	BG	John F. Davis	USA
1913	MG	Oscar B. Abbott	USA
	BG	Eugene A. Eversberg	USA
	GEN	Jerome J. Waters	USA
1914	BG	William E. Farthing	USA
	BG	Robert R. Neyland	USA
1915	MG	Roderick R. Allen	USA
	BG	Victor A. Barraco	USMC
	MG	Percy W. Clarkson	USA
	MG	Edmond H. Leavey	USA
1916	LTG	A. D. Bruce	USA
	BG	Claudius M. Easley	USA
	MG	Ralph H. Wooten	USAF
1917	RA	Albert M. Bledsoe	USN
	BG	Durant S. Buchanan	USMC
	BG	W. J. H. Galliford	USMC
	MG	Harry H. Johnson	ARNG
	BG	Nat S. Perrine	USA
	LTG	John T. Walker	USMC
1919	MG	H. M. Ainsworth	USA
	BG	George H. Beverley	USA
	BG	Paul L. Neal	USA
	BG	John L. Pierce	USA
1921	MG	J. D. Hill	USMC
	BG	A. B. Knickerbocker	USA
	BG	C. C. B. Warden	USA

Class	Rank	Name	Service
1923	RA	Gerald Bogle	USN
	BG	Aubrey L. Moore	USAF
	GEN	Otto P. Weyland	USAF
	MG	Robert B. Williams	USAF
1924	MG	William D. Old	USAF
1925	MG	Ion M. Bethel	USMC
	BG	Spencer J. Buchanan	USA
	LTG	R. W. Colglazier, Jr.	USA
	BG	Richard J. Werner	USA
	BG	William R. Frederick	USA
1926	MG	Manning E. Tillery	USAF
1927	BG	William L. Lee	USAF
1928	MG	George P. Munson	USA
1929	MG	B. H. Pochyla	USA
	MG	H. F. Weston	TXNG
	MG	Stuart S. Hoff	USA
1931	GEN	B. A. Schreiver	USAF
1932	BG	Charles S. Hays	USA
	BG	T. M. Hetherington	USAF
	BG	John A. Hilger	USAF
	BG	Graber Kidwell	USA
	MG	Alvin R. Luedecke	USAF
	MG	John W. White	USAF
	MG	J. Earl Rudder	USA
1933	MG	Robert F. Worden	USAF
1934	LTG	Harry H. Critz	USA
	BG	John M. Kenderine	USA
1935	BG	Odell M. Conoley	USMC
	BG	Kay Halsell, II	ARNG
	MG	Bruno A. Hochmuth	USMC
	RA	Raymond A. Moore	USN
	MG	Raymond L. Murray	USMC
1936	MG	Wood Kyle	USMC
	BG	C. M. Simmang	USA
	LTG	Ormond R. Simpson	USMC
	BG	Carter S. Speed	USA
1937	BG	Jack T. Brown	ARNG
	MG	Robert L. Pou	ARNG
	BG	Kyle L. Riddle	USAF
	BG	Clarence A. Wilson	

Class	Rank	Name	Service
1938	BG	Theodore H. Andrews	USA
	BG	Robert M. Williams	USA
1939	BG	O. D. Butler	USAR
	BG	Andrew W. Rogers	USA
	MG	Andrew P. Rollins	USA
	MG	Woodrow Vaughan	USAF
1940	LTG	Jay T. Robbins	USAF
	MG	John H. Buckner	USAF
	BG	Joe G. Hanover	USA
	LTG	J. F. Hollingsworth	USA
	MG	Homer S. Hill	
1941	MG	William R. Becker	USA
	BG	George P. Cole	USAF
	BG	H. D. Johnson	USAF
	BG	H. O. Johnson	USAF
	BG	Thomas F. McCord	USA
1942	BG	Seaborn J. Buckalew	USA
	BG	Charles M. Taylor	USA
	MG	Harold C. Teubner	USAF
	BG	Otto E. Scherz	ARNG
1943	BG	Mike P. Cokinos	USAR
	BG	Charles Van L. Ella	USA
	MG	Harold B. Gibson	USA
	BG	Jack N. Karas	USA
	MG	T. E. Marchbanks	USAF
	BG	Guy M. Townsend	USAF
1945	BG	Irby B. Jarvis, Jr.	USAF
	BG	Joseph E. Wesp	USAF
1946	BG	Wesley Peel	USA
	BG	John H. Miller	USMC
1947	MG	Guy H. Goddard	USAF
	BG	Thomas G. Murnane	USN
1948	BG	Robert M. Mullens	USA
	BG	Carl G. McIntosh	USAF
1949	MG	Charles R. Bond	USAF
	BG	Charles I. McGinnis	USA
	BG	Billy M. Vaughn	USA
1950	BG	Walter Bachus	USA
	BG	James L. Brown	USA
	MG	E. M. Johansen	USA

Class	Rank	Name	Service
1951	BG	Waymond C. Nutt	USAF
	BG	Wilman D. Barnes	USA
	BG	Hermon O. Thomson	USAF
1952	BG	James W. Taylor	USA
1953	BG	George R. Harper	USAR
	BG	Harry B. Steel	ARNG

APPENDIX VI

Presidents and Annual Giving of the Aggie Club

Year	President	Annual Giving
1950	A. E. Foerster '24	$ 16,182.00
1951	Jimmy W. Williams '18	30,190.00
1952	C. L. Babcock '20	23,657.00
1953	C. L. Babcock '20	18,409.00
1954	H. C. Heldenfels '35	35,778.00
1955	John C. Mayfield, Sr., '23	34,805.00
1956	John C. Mayfield, Sr., '23	33,113.00
1957	Pat Stanford '44	34,442.00
1958	Jake Hamblen '27	29,146.00
1959	Wes McKemie '37	40,307.00
1960	Bruno Schroeder '39	31,723.00
1961	Bruno Schroeder '39	31,657.00
1962	J. Ben Templeton, Jr., '50	46,672.00
1963	J. Ben Templeton, Jr., '50	37,729.00
1964	Guy King, Jr., '52	55,969.00
1965	Herschel G. Maltz '50	63,627.00
1966	Herschel G. Maltz '50	108,902.00
1967	Jim Uptmore '53	160,167.00
1968	Jim Uptmore '53	200,043.00
1969	Tom O'Dwyer '47	225,253.00
1970	Royce Wisenbaker '39	219,064.00
1971	J. L. Huffines '44	219,320.00
1972	Joe Richardson '49	290,067.00
1973	Bob Bernath	312,708.00
1974	Bob Bernath	358,773.00
1975	Cyrus Johnston '56	464,105.00
1976	Charles Wiseman '57	628,355.13
1977	Gus S. Majalis '56	1,049,989.00
1978	Robert B. Little '41	—
1979	William Lewie, Jr., '50	—

Comments on Sources

During the initial research for this project there was some question whether adequate factual documentation was at hand for such an undertaking. In time I determined that there were numerous sources; the only question that remained was to ascertain if these items could be trusted as "factual," reliable material. In order to separate fact from fiction I found that a careful cross-examination of the material would prove to uphold or refute items of association and Texas A&M heritage that more often than not had evolved in the minds of many from a collection of myths which have been passed down and printed as legends. Much to my pleasant surprise, the legends did have solid background.

There were four primary channels of source material employed: (1) documents and official minutes of the Association of Former Students, (2) oral interviews with key alumni and other individuals closely connected with Texas A&M, (3) specialty documents and personnel papers from the Texas A&M Archives, and (4) various books, newspapers, and magazines which provided background information.

The volume and availability of material proved invaluable in reconstructing the events during the early years. Association records were unusually complete and detailed. When reviewed in conjunction with the more-often-than-not vocal press of the period, an accurate chronicle of events was established. Additional specialty books and magazine selections, along with A&M school records, added a clue to both the evolution of and trends within the association. The available material doubled in amount each decade after 1890.

The most intriguing source of information and reference proved to be the hundreds of individuals I interviewed throughout the Southwest. Most important were the former students, most of whom had had some actual involvement with and concern for the association and the university. During the early part of my research in 1975, A. J. ("Niley") Smith '08 of Cameron, Texas, offered a most interesting aside at the conclusion of our conversation about his days as a student after the turn of the century; when I pointedly asked how he could be so sure of events and facts that occurred some seventy years before, he replied, "I know it's right 'cause I was there." Of course being "there" is not always the final judgement, yet in this case it proved invaluable to placing the proper perspective on the dynamic history of the Texas A&M former students and their interaction with A&M.

Index

A&M Clubs, 59; involvement of with placement, 32; involvement of with Strike of 1908, 56–58
A. and M. College Regiment, 107–108
A&M Distinguished Alumni Award, 41
A&M Mothers' Clubs, 191–192
A&M World War I Service Flag, 104
ABC Corporation, 167
Academic Building, 81–82. *See also* Old Main
Adams, A. Semones, 56–57
Adriance, Guy W., 167
Aggie Band Association, 192
Aggie Ring, 74–76
"Aggies", 6, 28; description of, 3–5, 183; traditions of, 4, 6, 13; in Spanish American War, 46; in World War I, 101–111; in World War II, 149–163; jokes about, 4
Aggie Spirit, 13
Aggie traditions, 4, 6, 13. *See also* Muster; Twelfth man; *Aggie War Hymn*
Aggie War Hymn, 4, 118–120
Albritton, Ford D., 188, 194
Alexander, David E., 9
Allen, R. F., 167
All Faiths Chapel, 166, 168, 177
Alpha Phi Association, 22, 39–50; organization of, 39; fraternity directory of, 39; local chapters of, 42; and Alpha Phi Hall, 39–40
Alumni Association: creation and organization of, 15–17; first constitution of, 17; constitution of revised, 29; involvement of, with 1908 strike, 56; unification of, 62; chapters of, 73–74
Alumni Building, 39–42. *See also* Memorial Student Center; Forsyth Alumni Center
Alumni Bureau, 32
Alumni Council, 179
Alumni Hall. *See* Alumni Building
Alumni Quarterly, 32, 51, 91–94, 103, 122
Amsler, W. H., 83, 88
Annual Fund Drive, 163–166
Appelt, Leslie C., 192
Ashburn, Ike, 32–33, 98, 131–133, 135–136, 139
Ashby, Lynn, 4
Ashton, John, 153
Association Executive Committee, 30
Association of Ex-Cadets, 8–12, 15
Astin, Erwin H., 83, 85, 96, 113
Aston, James W., 167, 177, 179, 188
Athletic Council, 53
Austin, J. R., 82
Austin Daily Statesman, 50
Austin Literary Society, 41
Avery, Hank, 154

Babcock, C. L., 146
Baker, Newton D., 109
Ballard, Luke L., 130, 135–138
Ballard, W. Lambert, 177
Banks, Andrew L., 35, 38–39, 42, 44
Banks, W. A., 7
Barraco, Victor A., 101
Barton, Thomas H., 107
Battalion, The, 22, 26, 39
Beasley, T. J., 83
Beaumont A&M Club, 61, 143
Bee, Hamilton P., 7
Bell, Tyree, 87, 97, 101, 125, 146, 167, 184, 186
Bell County A&M Club, 61
Bennett, Val, 97
Bevo, 90–91
Bible, Dana X., 117, 136, 153
Bizzell, William B., 92, 94–95, 101, 104, 109, 113, 117, 135, 138
Blake, Thomas W., 115, 130, 135
Board of Directors, Texas A&M, 8, 29, 35–38, 51, 53, 59–65, 70, 77, 82, 96, 109, 135
Bockhorn, Harold, 184
Bolton, Frank, 167
Bothma, Jacobus D., 4
Bowers, Reuben D., 138
Bradley, Omar, 161
Brannin, Carl P., 55
Brazos County A&M Club, 44, 85, 92, 110, 171
Brogdon, Daisy, 141
Brown, William H., 9, 11
Bruce, A. D., 101
Bryan, W. J., 113
Bryant, Irving H., 138
Bryant, Paul ("Bear"), 175
Burghard, C. L., 17
Burgoon, Charles E., 46
Buser, Joe J., 184

Cain, R. Wofford, 166
Caldwell, Roy, 184
Calliopean Literary Society, 41
Campbell, Thomas M., 55
Caple, John W., 192
Carson, J. M., 17
Carson, J. W., 17, 19
Carswell, Horace S., Jr., 158–159
CASE. *See* U.S. Steel Foundation Award
Casey, Paul A., 59
Cash, Harvey, 192
Centennial Directory of Former Students of Texas A&M University, 4
Centennial Endowed Scholarships, 171

Centennial History of Texas A&M University, 149, 194
Century Club, 189–190
Century Council, 186–187
Century Study, 187
Chamberlain, Clifton, 154
Chatham, Robert C., 9
Church, Marion S., 4, 83, 99, 101, 108–109, 115, 122, 129–130, 133, 135–137
class agents, 26–27, 30
class reunions, 125–127
coeducation at Texas A&M, 173–175
Cofer, David Brooks, 17
Coke, Richard, 6
College Journal, 21–22, 26
Colorado A&M Club, 61
Colquitt, Oscar Branch, 81–82, 85
Commission on Higher Education in Texas. *See* Coordinating Board
Congressional Medal of Honor, 106, 154, 158–160
Connally, John, 194
Connally, Tom, 153
Connolly, R. N. ("Dick"), 177
Cook, William B., 96, 122–124, 126–128
Cooper, Jerry C., 184
Coordinating Board, Texas College and University System, 179
Corps trips, 47, 55, 89
Corregidor, 149, 153–154
Cottingham, I. A., 17
Cotton Bowl, 117–118. *See also* football
Craig, Brad, 161
Cravens, James, 57–58, 60, 67, 83, 88
Crawford, C. W., 167
Crawford, Mary E., 117
Crichton, John A., 167, 188
Crisp, John C., 8
Crockett, James B., 81
Culberson, Charles A., 35–36
Cushing, Edward B., 9, 11, 36, 39, 50, 62, 67–69, 72, 80–81, 83, 85, 88, 95, 97, 101

Dal-Aggie, 137
Dallas A&M Club, 56–57, 107–108, 137
Dallas A&M Mothers' Club, 97–98
Danklefs, James T., 151
Davis, J. N., 17
Davis, Jefferson, 6
Dazey, William L., 62
Dethloff, Henry C., 194
Development Foundation, 186
DeWare, Charles A., 96, 117, 124, 125
Dinwiddie, Hardaway Hunt, 17–18
Diplomas, miniature laminated, 146
Directory of Former Students, 9, 168–169

Index 229

Distinguished Alumni Award, 184
Dixie Classic. *See* Cotton Bowl
Dodson, Calvin P., 146
Doherty, W. T. ("Doc"), 166, 177
Doolittle, James, 158
Downs, Fred L., Jr., 98
Downs, Pinckney Lovick ('79), 9–10, 35–36, 83, 88, 138
Downs, Pinckney Lovick ("Pinkie"; '06), 129, 135
Drisdale, John V., 98
Dunn, J. Harold, 167, 184, 187

Eckard, R. C. ("Connie"), 84
Edwards, Daniel R., 106
Eisenhower, Dwight D., 154
Ekfelt, Fred E., 176
Elmquist, Karl, 184
Evans, Charles O., 81
Evans, Claude M., 92
Evans, Sterling C., 167
Ex-Cadets Association. *See* Association of Ex-Cadets
Ex-Students Association of the University of Texas, 112

Faculty Distinguished Achievement Award, 175–176
Fairleigh, George, 119
"Farmers," 6, 28. *See also* "Aggies"
Farmers' Congress, 58–59
Fearhake, John D., 19, 36
Ferguson, Alex M., 28, 32, 46–50
Fitzhugh, Edward E., 9
football, 22, 28, 48–49, 51–53, 72, 91, 117, 144, 169, 175. *See also* Cotton Bowl
Ford, Gerald R., 3
Forman, J. H., 29
Former Fish Drill Team Association, 192
Forsyth, James M. ("Cop"), 194
Forsyth Alumni Center, 194
Founders' Day, 143. *See also* muster
Fowler, Thomas W., 158–159
Francis, Mark, 18, 92–93
Franklin, T. Hadley, 42
Freeman, J. H., 42
Freeman, W. C., 167
Friley, Charles E., 115, 122
Fuller, Thomas A., 9, 11
Furneaux, William, 56–57

Gaines, Carroll M., 166
Galveston Daily News, 15
Gathright, Thomas Sanford, 6, 8, 44
General Athletic Association. *See* Athletic Council
Giddings (member of "Houston Committee"), 88
Giesecke, Frederick E., 15, 17, 26, 29–30, 67, 69–70
Gifts and Bequests Office, 166, 168. *See also* Development Foundation
Gilbert, Joe, 56
Gilchrist, Gibb, 154, 167
Gill, E. King, 118
Gold Star Fund, 168
Green, Harry J., 188
Griffin, Gerald, 4
Griffiths, T. W., 83
Gross, Abe, 108

Guion, John I., 95, 103–104
Gulley, Frank Arthur, 18

Hall, Wayne C., 176
Haq, Mohammed, 4
Hardesty, Walton D., 176
Hardy, George W., 9, 138
Harrell, William G., 107, 158–159
Harrington, Henry Hill, 18, 54–56, 58, 60–63, 65, 138
Harrington, Marion T., 167, 173, 177, 179
Harris County A&M Club, 57–58
Harrison, Guy F., 184
Hart, L. J., 96, 109
Hartung, Louis A., 166, 168
Harvey, Frank B., 188
Hatch Act of 1887, 18
Heep, Herman F., 166–167, 179
Heldenfels, H. C., 167
Hervey, J. B. ("Dick"), 165–166, 179, 181, 184, 187
Hervey, Stewart C., 92
High School Day, 169, 171
Hilger, John S., 158
Hinman, Adolph E., 166
Hobby, William P., 107
Hogg, William C., 96
Hohn, Caesar ("Dutch"), 87, 125, 136
Holloway, Louis E., 122–124
Hollywood Shacks, 117, 131
Hopkins, Edward D., 97
Horseley, Wendell R., 34
Hotchkiss, Oscar T., 169, 177, 184
House Joint Resolution No. 29, 110, 112
Houston, David Franklin, 53, 70, 152
Houston, Sam, 152
Houston A&M Club, 61, 85
Houston Aggie, 137
"Houston Committee," 88
Houston Rifles. *See* Ross Volunteers
Howard, Gene, 184
Howell, J. Webb, 62, 83, 96, 117
Hughes, Lloyd D., 158–159
Hunt, Asa, 137
Hunter, Elton P., 127–128, 135
Hutchinson, E. W., 26, 35–36, 38, 83
Hutson, Charles W., 55, 65
Hutson, Miles, 56

intercollegiate athletics, SWC beginnings of, 22
interurban trolley, 53, 70

James, John Garland, 8, 138
Jonas, Edward C., 74
Jones, Jesse H., 153
Jordan, H. P., 42, 53
Jouine, G. P. F., 101

Keathley, George Dennis, 158–159
Kennedy, A. J., 83
Kernodle, Ida Wipprecht, 70
KK's (secret society), 125
Knox, John M., 192
Kopke, Louis J., 9, 83
Krueger, C. C. ("Polly"), 101, 122, 130, 135–137
Kuanyin, Emmanuel B., 4
Kunze, George W., 191
Kyle, Edwin J., 77, 103

Kyle, H. C., 62
Kyle, J. A., 83, 115
Kyle Field, 89

Lacy, Walter G., 96, 135
Langford, Ernest, 79, 103
Lanham, Samuel W. T., 67
Larson, L. L., 56
Latimer, J. R. ("Bob"), 171, 188, 192
Law, Francis Marion, 58–60, 83, 96, 135
Lawson, W. J., 163
Leipper, Dale F., 167
Leonard, Turney W., 158–159
Leon Springs, 131
Lettermen's Association, 192
Lindsey, John H., 188
Livingston, William E., 109
Locke, Lonnie, 141–143, 166
Longhorn, 59, 121
Long Range Planning Committee, 186
Love, Andrew C., 72, 97, 130, 135
Luedecke, Alvin R., 192

MacArthur, Douglas, 149, 154
McCall, John D., 108
McCrory, Dorsey E., 167
McGee, Frank S., 98
McGee, L. E., 108
McGee, W. C. ("mAggie"), 177, 179
McGinnis, Francis Kamp, 72, 83, 107, 109
McGinnis, Nester M., 92, 94, 103–104, 122
McGuire, J. G. ("Mickey"), 34
Machemehl, W. P., 167
McInnis, Louis L., 8, 11, 17–18, 138
McQueen, J. B., 17
McQuillen, Everett E., 34, 99, 125, 135–137, 139, 141–143, 151–152, 163, 165–167, 171
Mallory, John S., 15
Maltz, Melvin, 192
March, Peyton C., 109
maroon and white, 120–121
Martin, Elmer L., 75, 115
Matson, Randy, 191
Memorial Student Center, 166, 168
Mess Hall, 79
Meredith, Carlton, 137
Miller, Jarvis E., 194
Milner, Robert T., 67, 81–82, 85
Mistrot, Gustave A., 125
Mitchell, Alva, 58, 67, 80, 83–84
Mitchell, E. F., 166
Monteith, E. E., 167
Montgomery, Jeff, 188
Moody College of Marine Sciences, 192
Moore, George, 148–149
Moore, Joe H., 192
Moore, William T., 141, 173
Moran, Charles B., 77–78, 87, 120
Morgan, David H., 166
Morris, W. H. H., 107
Moseley, Hal, 49–50, 77, 101
Moser, C. O., 88, 94
Moses, Andrew ("Bull"), 56, 59
Murrah, Tom A., 177, 184
Murray, W. A., 49
muster, 13, 127, 149–157, 169; of Aggies on Corregidor, 149–153; Roll Call origin of, 13; broadcast over radio station WTAW, 127; involvement of E. E. McQuillen with, 151–152

Neff, Asa J., 81
Newton, J. O., 113
New York City A&M Club, 61
Noton, James T., 113

oil, 140, 167
Olcese, Orland, 4
Old Main, 79–80
Opportunity Award Scholarships, 168, 171–172
Orth, W. A., 137

Paine, Herbert A., 138
Palestine A&M Club, 61
Parker, Travis J., 176
Pennington, R. E., 83
Perkins, F. Dudley, 143
Permanent Endowment Fund, 82–83
Perry, George S., 168
Pershing, John J., 100
Peteet, Walton, 81–82
Peterson, Leland F., 188
Pfaff, A. G., 146
Philpott, William B., 35, 49–50
Pictorial History of Texas A&M University, 194
Pittuck, Buell C., 29, 44, 58, 62
Placement Center, 34. *See also* Alumni Bureau
Platt, James Edward, 53
Porter, R. J., 75, 167
Potts, Arthur T., 103
Potts, Robert Joseph, 103–104
Powell, Nathan ("Stud Horse"), 55
President's Endowed Scholars, 99, 171, 188–189
project houses, 140
Puryear, Charles, 96

Ransom, Henry, 179
Reichardt, Frank A., 11, 38, 60
Ridgway, Matthew B., 175
Roberts, Oran M., 8
Rogan, Charles, 83, 88, 96, 103, 110, 113, 135
Roll Call. *See* Muster
Rose, Andrew J., 36
Ross, Lawrence Sullivan, 3, 22, 29, 35, 44, 109, 130
Ross Volunteers, 19, 98, 125, 168, 192
Rowell, T. D., 17, 88
Rudder, James Earl, 158, 177, 179, 183, 189, 192
Russell, Dan, 140

San Antonio A&M Club, 44, 46, 50, 61
San Antonio International Fair, 46–48
San Jacinto Day, 143, 149, 152. *See also* muster
Sargent, Herbert H., 54

Sbisa, Bernard, 36, 79, 82
Schiwetz, Edward M. ("Buck"), 194
Schuhmacher, H. C., 135
Scott Guards. *See* Ross Volunteers
Sea Grant Program, 192. *See also* Moody College of Marine Sciences
Sears-Roebuck Agricultural Foundation, 99. *See also* Student's Loan Fund
Senate Joint Resolution No. 18, 84–85, 87
Senior Ring Committee, 75. *See also* Aggie Ring
Sewell, James L., 188–189, 192
Sheppard, Willie Mae, 166, 169
Sherley, A. L., 17, 19
Short, A. Kidd, 99, 142
Shuffler, R. Henderson, 166
Skeeler, F. J., 94
Skrabanek, Robert L., 176
Sleeper, William M., 9–10
Small, William T., 9
Smith, E. J., 46, 59–61, 83, 88
Smith, George G., 166
Smith, Robert III, 192
Smith, Robert L., Jr., 169
Sneed, Glenn L., 109
Southerland, J. Malon, 34
Southwest Intercollegiate Athletic Conference (SWC), 89
Spanish American War, 46
Spann, E. W., 17
Standifer, Richard H., 108–109
Stangel, Wanzel L., 103, 113
Sterns, Josh B., 75
Story of Texas A&M, 168
Strike of 1908, 55–60, 63
student life, 5–7, 41, 46–49. *See also* Corps trips
Students' Loan Fund, 95–97, 99, 124, 128–129, 137, 141, 143, 165
Suarez-Arauz, Winston, 4
Sullivan, James, 121
Summers, Hatton W., 63
Swastikas (secret society), 125

Taber, John Q., 42, 59
tailor shop, 142
Taylor, C. W., 51
Teague, Olin E., 167
tent city, 54
Texas A&M Century Study, 184
Texas A&M Clubs, 138, 143, 153, 166, 171–172, 194
Texas A&M University Development Foundation, 165, 167–168
Texas A&M University Press, 194
Texas Aggie, The 26, 32, 92, 142, 146, 151, 166, 184, 194
Texas Agricultural Experiment Station, 18
Texas University Land Endowment, 140
Thanheiser, Charles A., 143

Thanksgiving Day football game, 50
Thomas, C. W., 126
Thomas, Julian B., 142
Thompson, Mayo J., 192
Tillotson, Leonard, 112
Tilson, M. D., 17
Tilson, Phineas S., 35, 72, 74, 83
Todd, Charles C., 44, 60–61, 83, 101
Trenckmann, Robert, 77
Trenckmann, W. A., 6, 9–10, 77, 83
True Texans (secret society), 125
Twelfth Man tradition, 118

Uhr, Irwin A., 143
University Data Processing Center, 169
University of Texas, 15, 32, 44
University of Texas alumni, 88
U.S. Steel Foundation Award, 191
Utay, Joe, 83, 85, 107–109, 113, 135

Valley Junction, 81, 84
Van Pelt, Louis, 34

Walden, W. J., 58
Walker, Robert L., 167
Walton, T. O., 75, 135–138
Wangomann, A., 83
Ward, A. C., 137
Warden, Thomas K., 142–143
Wardlaw, Frank H., 194
Watkins, R. C., 83
Weirus, Richard ("Buck"), 165, 168, 186–187, 189, 191
Wesson, J. M., 17
We've Never Been Licked, 161
Whiteley, Eli L., 158–160
Whitney, George S., 51
Williams, Jack K., 3, 192
Wilson, James Vernon, 118–120
Wilson, Woodrow, 100
Wipprecht, Walter, 15, 17, 21, 29, 83, 85, 103
Wisenbaker, Royce E., 188–189
Wood, Pat H., 184
Woodal, Howard, 56–57
Woodward, W. F., 17
World War I, Aggies in, 101–111
World War II, Aggies in, 149–163
Wright, H. L., 60
WTAW (radio station), 127, 152
Wurzback, Williams S., 113, 126, 129, 135

Yanger, Doug, 169
yell leaders, 119
YMCA, 67
Youngblood, Bonnie, 115
Youngblood, Charles, 96
Younger, John F., 188

Zachry, Pat, 179

Index 231

John A. Adams, Jr., '73 is a graduate of Texas A&M University with both bachelor's and master's degrees in history. He is presently completing studies for a Ph.D. in history while working as general manager of the Meiller Company in College Station, Texas.

As a member of the Corps of Cadets of Texas A&M, Adams served as commanding officer of cadet squadron Huslin' One and as administration officer of the Ross Volunteers. Adams lectures campus and former student groups on Aggie history and traditions and has written a series of newspaper articles on A&M history.